One in a
Million

One in a Million

by
Harry A. Cole
with
Martha M. Jablow

Little, Brown and Company
Boston   Toronto   London

FIRST EDITION

The authors are grateful to the Society for the Right to Die for permission to reprint their Living Will Declaration and to Concern for Dying for permission to reprint their Durable Power of Attorney form.

LIBRARY OF CONGRESS CATALOGING-IN-PUBLICATION DATA

Cole, Harry A.
  One in a million / by Harry A. Cole with Martha M. Jablow — 1st ed.
    p.   cm.
  ISBN 0-316-15117-3
    1. Cole, Jacqueline — Health.   2. Cerebrovascular disease — Patients — United States — Biography.   3. Right-to-die.   4. Cerebrovascular disease — Patients — Medical care — Moral and ethical aspects.
  I. Jablow, Martha Moraghan.   II. Title.
  RC388.5.C667 1990
  362.1'9681 — dc20
  [B]   89-13321
                                                               CIP

  10 9 8 7 6 5 4 3 2 1

  MV-PA

  Published simultaneously in Canada
  by Little, Brown & Company (Canada) Limited

  PRINTED IN THE UNITED STATES OF AMERICA

*For Jacqueline
and the children,
John, Christina, Thomas, Stephen, Beth,
and Vincent*

Contents

Acknowledgments

I owe a debt of gratitude and my sincere affection to many people who have played a part in our story and have made this book possible.

First to my family: my mother, my brother, Wayne, and Jackie's sister, Julie, who shared our suffering while standing by and supporting the children and me in the darkest hours of Jackie's illness.

To our friends: Bonnie and Paul Hoback, Ron and Mickey Bond, Maureen Ricker, Carol Parham, Adolphus Spain, and many others who kept the vigil with us and shared the celebration of Jackie's return.

To Dr. Thaddeus P. Pula, Jackie's attending physician and a source of great personal support, to Drs. Michael Hayes and William Anthony for their dedicated assistance, and to the superlative nurses of Maryland General Hospital, Vanessa Ajayi, Janice Budzynski, Elizabeth A. Conner, Brenda and Virginia Flentje, Nancy Hart, Carol Kienle, Glinna Michaels, and the countless other nurses, therapists, and staff members for their splendid care and devotion to Jackie both before and after she awoke.

To J. David Ash, Esquire, for his friendship and counsel.

To John Evans for being there at the kairotic moment.

To my friends in the clergy who visited Jackie and me and held us up in prayer.

To Professor Joseph Price and Chaplain Jon Moody, who invited me to lecture at Whittier College in Whittier, California, and to the members of the Honors Student Classes whose thoughtful comments and responses to my remarks helped to form the basis for the ethical reflections portion of this book.

To the congregation of Lochearn Presbyterian Church, who

suffered as we did and then rejoiced with us and encouraged me to tell our story across the country and in this book.

To Judge John Carroll Byrnes, to paramedics Bertha Butler and James MacFetrich, to Dr. Susan McCartney and nurse Pat Wiggins of Montebello Rehabilitation Hospital, to Dr. Robert Roby, Paul Johnson, Amy Tacy, and Roseanne Whittaker of Maryland General Hospital, and to Jackie's friends at the Maryland Department of Education, Evelyn DiTosto, Rosalie Lorenzet, Hilde Ramsey, Valerie Schwartz, Jean Sorrentino, Jodellano Statom, and Mary Washington, who all gave generously of their time and recollections to assist in the writing of this book. And to Society for the Right to Die, particularly its director, Alice V. Mehling, and to Concern for Dying for providing valuable information about the right-to-die issue.

To my agents, Sterling Lord and Elizabeth Kaplan, who heard our story and guided it to Little, Brown and Company, and to Fredrica S. Friedman, Little, Brown's executive editor, who enthusiastically piloted the story onto these pages.

And, finally, to the many friends across the country and overseas whose names I have forgotten or never knew, from the Jackie Cole in California to the Jackie Cole in Sussex, England, to all who were inspired by our story and wished us well — I again say, "Thank you, and God bless you all."

H. A. C.

One in a
Million

Prologue

"Oh, my God! I think I'm having a stroke!" Jackie pitched forward. She clutched her head with both hands, then felt her arm.

"I can move my hand, but I can't feel my arm! No! Oh, please, dear God, not a stroke!" Her terrified eyes shot her daughter a desperate plea. "Oh, Christina, I don't want to live this way."

MOMENTS earlier a violent headache had assaulted Jackie. "This isn't at all like one of my usual migraines," she told our teenagers. "It's far, far worse. So much more intense! I've never had a headache come on so fast — so fierce!"

Christina, Thomas, and John stared at their mother in silent, icy panic as she squeezed her left arm and said, "I can't feel anything. Oh, God! I can't feel my arm!"

Thomas grabbed the phone and dialed 911.

Within minutes, Christina heard the paramedics running up the stairs. Her brothers' voices were loud with fear as they led the way. "She's up here. Hurry! Please, hurry!" Christina pushed her mother's statement, "I don't want to live this way," to a distant corner of her mind.

The paramedics took Jackie's vital signs. Nothing irregular about her heartbeat. Her blood pressure was somewhat elevated. In taking her medical history, the paramedics learned that Jackie had frequent migraines, but, at age forty-three, she was otherwise healthy.

Within minutes, Jackie's voice faded, and she began to repeat herself: "I'm cold . . . get me a blanket . . . no . . . cold . . . I'm cold . . . no . . . no . . . blanket . . ."

Then she stopped talking.

3

"Mrs. Cole? Can you hear me?" a paramedic asked. A low moan was the only response.

"Mrs. Cole, how are you? Can you answer me?"

"Yes," Jackie said faintly. "Do you think I'm having a stroke?"

"Well, look, we don't know what's happening. That's why we're going to get you down to the hospital to see what's going on," the paramedic said.

"I'm cold . . . cold . . ." Her voice was barely audible. "Christina, I don't want to live this way. Remember, please." Jackie was slipping away while the children watched, fright frozen in their eyes.

As the paramedics carried Jackie downstairs and out to the ambulance, her body went rigid. One whispered to the other, so the children wouldn't become even more panicky, "This lady doesn't look good."

"Yeah, let's get her out of here fast."

Jackie's plunge from an alert and awake state to unconsciousness in just fifteen minutes signaled the paramedics to waste no time in getting her to the nearest emergency room. The driver switched on the beacon lights and hit the accelerator. The siren wailed, like a keen for the dead, uninterrupted for the three minutes it took to reach the hospital.

As the emergency room doctors and nurses fought to save Jackie, snatches of their conversation revealed the worst: ". . . a big bleed . . . worst kind of stroke . . . blood is percolating through her brain . . . not expected to survive . . ."

One

Jacqueline

Jackie was the best thing that ever happened to me. She brought joy, warmth — sparkle — into my life from the first day I saw her.

I was waiting for a job interview when I noticed her. Although I was pastor of a small Presbyterian church in downtown Baltimore, my position was only part-time. When I heard that the Maryland Department of Education had a job opening for someone to accredit veterans' college courses, I thought the job might blend well with my counseling training. Now the prospect looked even more attractive, with this woman in the same office. The skirt of Jackie's figure-hugging dress was mini even by 1973 fashion standards. The only conservative thing about it was the color: business gray. Her legs were long and shapely, her figure as slim and curvaceous as a model's. What a knockout, I thought, as I stared at her across the office. Her dark-green eyes caught mine and shot me a what's-it-to-you? look. Spunky, I thought, as I watched her strut back to her desk.

Everything in this building spoke of an impersonal bureaucracy: standard-issue metal desks, hard vinyl chairs, economically low ceiling, fluorescent lighting. But this woman had etched a personal stamp on her corner of the office. An old wooden Windsor chair, somewhat scratched, added a spot of warmth to the otherwise metallic surroundings. On her desk, a photo cube held snapshots of smiling children on a beach. I wondered if they were hers — yet she didn't wear a wedding ring. A huge picture of a pig lolling in a hammock hung on the wall next to her desk. She has quite the nonconformist streak, I thought. I'd love to meet her.

Within a month I had the job, and Jackie soon became a daily distraction. My new colleagues noticed that I had an eye on her, and some cautioned me that Jackie could be controversial. It was no secret that she was involved with another man from the office. Perhaps they saw me as a naive young minister, just a few years out of seminary, who needed a well-intentioned warning: "She is, you know, a twice-divorced mother of four children." I was surprised when I first learned that, but intrigued. I tried to picture her with a brood of little kids.

As I watched Jackie bounce around the office — cheering up a heartbroken secretary, helping a new colleague cut through a pile of paperwork, kidding a coworker about coming in late and looking exhausted ("Out till four A.M. again, eh?") — I wondered how she raised four children alone and still brought such vivacious good humor to her demanding job.

I had dated a number of women before I was hired by the Maryland Department of Education, but no one had ever attracted me quite as much as Jackie. From observing her at the office, I knew she was more than simply another good-looking woman. I wanted to know more about who she was, what made her tick. After a month or so, I thought, why not ask her to lunch?

Jackie usually skipped lunch to bargain-hunt. She was constantly watching her weight and preferred shopping to eating. Nothing seemed to delight her more than coming back to the office with a smashing, just-marked-down outfit. She scouted Baltimore on her lunch hours, and if she spotted handsome sweaters for her children or a silk blouse for herself, she'd check her impulse to buy. Instead, she would return several days later to see if there had been a further markdown. If something was reduced two or three times, she opened her wallet and returned to work with the latest treasure in tow. It was part of the office routine: Jackie's coworkers always expected her to swing in after lunch, shopping bag in hand, to unwrap her latest bargain.

So when I asked her to lunch, I was almost surprised that she accepted. As we sat down at William's Plum, a very English, baronial place in its own plastic way, Jackie began, "So you're a minister, Harry?"

"Yes, but only part-time right now. That's why I'm working at the education department, too. I also do some private counseling, and I'm about to start working on my doctorate."

"Why did you become a minister? Did you have a 'calling' or a revelation?"

"Oh, no, nothing like Paul on the road to Damascus or anything so dramatic," I answered, poking at my salad.

"Well, how did it happen?"

"You want my life story over lunch, eh?"

"If you'd like to tell me," she smiled. Her bright, broad smile was irresistible.

"Okay. In short, I'm the older of two sons in a fairly typical suburban family. I'm the fourth generation of our family to belong to Govans Presbyterian Church. The church was a big part of my life growing up. Every Sunday, we'd sit in the family pew, and I always sat next to my grandmother — she's been a big influence in my life. In fact, she probably planted the suggestion about becoming a pastor years ago. At least, that's the way my family enjoys telling the story, over and over again: I was such a talker as a boy, they tell me, that Grandmother used to say, 'I think we're going to have a preacher in the family.'

"Maybe her suggestion was there, subliminally, all those years. But as a teenager, I never thought much about 'what I was going to be when I grew up.' I was more interested in hanging out with my friends."

"What were you like as a boy?" Jackie asked.

"Average, I suppose. My oldest friend, Ron Bond, still kids me about being a straight-arrow, Boy Scout type. The school crossing guard. I never took any great risks, was never in trouble. Never caused my parents any concern until I flunked out of college."

"You did?" Jackie's eyes widened.

"Yes, and that's what probably turned me in the direction of the ministry. I started out at the University of Maryland. It was my first attempt at being on my own, and I just got blown away. I didn't like my studies. I thought I'd become a teacher, but the education courses seemed irrelevant. I did poorly and was put on academic probation. It was quite an anxious time. Everything seemed to be caving in, so I went to the college counseling center, where I met an extremely supportive counselor. Even though I flunked out after a year and a half, that counselor was very helpful to me. I think that may have been the moment, if there's ever a single moment when you decide these things, that the idea of becoming a counselor entered my thoughts. I really thought of counseling before I consciously thought of the ministry. But both have such similar goals and skills.

"Well, despite that counselor's support, I flunked out and that was my first real crisis — I had disappointed my parents, failed myself. It was very intense. But I suppose that's when I began to take life seriously for the first time. I looked around and suddenly realized that I would have to be on my own. I wasn't a boy living off Mother and Father any more. I got a job selling men's clothing in a department store. I was eventually promoted to assistant manager of the department."

"So, when did you return to college and become a minister?" Jackie asked, looking directly into my eyes. I sensed that she was genuinely interested in me and not simply making luncheon conversation.

"Well, I knew at some point that I would finish college. I didn't want to sell neckties all my life. When I returned to college, I had to foot the bill — my father made that quite clear. I enrolled full-time at the University of Baltimore and decided to make a serious attempt to learn something! I chose psychology as a major and the head of the department, Dr. Nell, happened to be a Lutheran minister. He was personally inspiring and his courses were excellent. He encouraged my interest in counseling, and, somewhere along the line, he broached the idea of my going to seminary after graduation. I'd also taken some speech courses and discovered I liked public speaking. So, with Dr. Nell's suggestion about seminary and my own interests in counseling and public speaking — call it preaching, if you like — seminary seemed to be the next logical step for me to take.

"You see, Jackie, I've always thought that the church can be immensely helpful to people and that the Christian faith is a good and decent way to live. God has always been a very real presence in my life, and I've always believed that sharing God's love is the answer to all of the suffering and pain in the world. So, when I was thinking about how I wanted to spend my life, the ministry seemed to be the best way to live out what I believed.

"When I graduated from college, I headed off to Vanderbilt Divinity School to study for my Master of Divinity degree, which I received three years ago, and I've been pastoring my church on a part-time basis since then."

"Well, how do you do that, Harry? I mean, I've only seen you working here in the education department in a jacket and tie. I have trouble picturing you wearing a minister's robe. When you're not in our office, what do you do as a minister?"

"On Sundays, of course, I preach. And since the congregation is mostly older, I do a lot of visiting parishioners in hospitals and making home visits to shut-ins. And I do a fair number of funerals. Occasionally I marry a couple or do a baptism — those are the real joys in my work."

Dessert and coffee were nearly finished when I realized that Jackie had made me compress my life into an hour, yet I'd discovered nothing about hers.

"I'm sorry, Jackie. I've rambled on about myself. Please tell me something about you."

"Don't apologize, Harry. I've enjoyed it thoroughly. But we hardly have time for my life story. Look at the time. Miss Rice will not be pleased when we return to the office so late."

On our way back to work, I learned only the sketchiest details about Jackie: She'd been born in New York City, had lived in the Baltimore area since she was eight, had a younger sister, and, as I already knew, had four children. She and I were nearly the same age. I told her I was thirty-one, and she said she was, too. A year later I learned that she was actually a year older than I.

I sensed that there was a great deal more to know about Jackie. I wanted to discover who was really beneath that attractive veneer, who was the real woman behind all the shopping bags, so I asked her to lunch again a few weeks later. What I discovered was how different our lives had been.

While I sailed through my first three decades fairly smoothly, Jackie's life had been turbulent. A bright, artistic child, she was frequently at odds with a strong-willed mother, an often absent father, and a sweet, quieter sister, Julie, eighteen months younger.

"From the earliest I can remember, I thought my mother misunderstood me. I never could seem to please her — I disagreed with her too much, I wasn't 'proper' enough, I was too temperamental for her," Jackie said.

Helen Lohsen loved Jackie but was highly critical of her. At one moment, Helen was proud of her precocious, pretty little girl, but the next moment she tried to mold Jackie into an image that matched her own wishes — an obedient, unassuming, unquestioning child.

"I grew up receiving mixed messages and craving attention and approval," Jackie told me.

Once, when she was only five, Jackie drew a landscape of hills and trees. A road wound through the scene and narrowed as it receded from the foreground. Helen was amazed that such a young child could sketch with perspective. She boasted of Jackie's talent to others, but she never praised Jackie for her creation.

"I did surprisingly well in school," Jackie said, "despite the fact that I was always gazing out the window, daydreaming, sketching, writing poems or little stories, making up plays."

Years later, when Jackie and Julie were adults, they looked back on their childhood and agreed on an analysis: their mother saw Jackie as her father's daughter and Julie as her own daughter, more like her side of the family. Even physically, Jackie resembled their father and Julie resembled their mother. Helen and John Lohsen's marriage was far from blissful, and Helen's frustrations with her husband were often transferred to Jackie. As John's daughter, Jackie was defined by her mother as a Lohsen: suspect, dishonest, headstrong — incredibly headstrong.

"She's been telling me for years how headstrong I am," Jackie laughed. "That's her favorite adjective for me. I suppose I am, and maybe it's not such a bad quality to have. Maybe I should thank her for helping me develop it! Oh, I love my mother, Harry. But she and I are just so dissimilar that our conflicts are inevitable.

"On the other hand, she defined my sister by the way she saw her own side of the family: Julie's tolerant, fair-minded, honest, sweet-tempered. And Julie really is, but my mother's constantly comparing me to her never helped me."

By adolescence, Jackie was reacting predictably — acting out in response to Helen's unacceptance of her. In high school, Jackie and a star athlete were the sweetheart couple, the cutest, handsomest pair in the school. She was pregnant at sixteen. At first she denied it even to the doctor — her period was just a little late, Jackie insisted. The anger, disappointment, and tension in the Lohsen home was palpable. Jackie and Jerry were married and set up housekeeping shortly before Stephen was born.

"It was 1959, and I was a seventeen-year-old mother," she said, shaking her head. "The marriage lasted about a year, and I moved back to my parents' home with Stephen. But I was determined to pull myself out of my dependency on my parents as soon as I could."

I couldn't help but admire her strength as she told me how she finished high school and then enrolled at Loyola College at night. Her parents adored Stephen and helped Jackie both with his care in the evenings, when Jackie would hop on a crosstown bus for classes, and with her financial needs. Though she appreciated their support and couldn't do without it, she chafed at the tether that bound her to her parents. In many ways they still treated her like a little girl, she felt. Yet, at the same time, those were happy years for Jackie and her parents, largely because little Stephen drew the three adults closer together than they'd ever been.

Then Jackie married again, at age twenty-one. She met the son of a wealthy banking family at a night course at Loyola.

"He drove a sports car," she told me with a wry laugh, "and wooed me with such pretentious touches as peeling the label off a bottle of fine wine and presenting it to me with a single rose. It may sound simplistic, Harry, but I was so young and vulnerable. Here was a handsome, well-heeled prince come to rescue me from living at home with my parents. He seemed to adore me, and Stephen, too. At the time it appeared so perfect. A fairy-tale ending to my adolescent misadventures."

Three children were born, one right after the other: Thomas in 1965, Christina in 1967, John in 1968. The marriage was rocky from the start. By the time Jackie was pregnant with John, the marriage was over in all but the legalities. John would grow up never seeing the man.

After her second divorce, Jackie worked full-time as a teacher certification specialist for the state education department. And she began courses at night toward her master's degree at Johns Hopkins University. Her parents helped out with the children's private-school tuition through the years because they, like Jackie, wanted to give the children the best education money could buy. On her modest salary, Jackie was always struggling to give her children extra advantages. I learned later that the excuse she gave her co-workers for not joining them for a $5 or $10 lunch — "I'm dieting" — was not the true reason. She was saving money for her kids, to buy a piano, to give them art, ballet, or music lessons.

OVER our first few lunches, Jackie and I talked and laughed easily. I think each realized that a relationship could grow if either one of us encouraged it. A few weeks later, I asked her for our first real date. Would she like to join me for "Paint and Powder," a variety show staged annually by Baltimore's rising young businessmen to raise money for charity? She certainly would.

Not a simple date to arrange, though. Jackie was still involved with "the other man in the office," who knew by now that something was afoot between Jackie and me. That evening Jackie took her children to her parents' house and then — in case the other fellow should drop by and find her preparing for an elegant evening out with someone else — carted her makeup and full-length gown across town to a friend's house, where I would pick her up.

I, too, had some cloak-and-dagger logistics to arrange. I was living on the top floor of a Bolton Hill town house. Bonnie and Paul Hoback, who owned the house and lived on the first and second floors, were tossing a party before "Paint and Powder." I had been dating a woman who lived right across the street, so, not wanting to hurt her by parading up the street with Jackie, and with a pang of guilt, I drove through the back alley and parked behind the Hobacks' house. From there we proceeded to the performance and a formal dance that followed. That evening was the first time Jackie met several of my friends. And she charmed them.

Slender and lithe in her lovely peach gown, she danced all night. At one point everyone on the dance floor backed away and watched Jackie and a friend of mine dance to a fast disco number. I just watched, mesmerized. After the dance, we went back to my apartment. Our first date ended when I took her home at 5:00 A.M.

A few weeks later, we attended a retirement party for Miss Eleanor Rice, who had headed our office for years. Even before starting work at the education department, I had known of Miss Rice through her activities in another Presbyterian church. At work she ran a properly professional office, but she never could conceal her fondness for Jackie, whom she had hired several years earlier. Like a stern schoolmarm who couldn't quite punish her teacher's pet, Miss Rice didn't reprimand Jackie and me when we returned late from those lunches, but we knew she was having trouble finding a place to deposit her irritation.

After Miss Rice's retirement party, which Jackie had largely planned and executed, Jackie and I headed into the balmy night air and across the parking lot, in our formal attire, toward my Jeep. Before I started the engine, we sat and began to talk. Suddenly Jackie unwrapped her innermost life before me. All I had learned about Jackie during our lunches, those hard facts of her childhood and earlier marriages, now took on layer upon layer of emotion. At first I'd been attracted to a beautiful woman, I realized. Then I'd begun to know a strong, determined mother, who was raising four youngsters and managing a demanding job. But that night in the Jeep, Jackie revealed even more of her substance as she talked about how wounded she had been by men in her life.

"I don't know why, Harry, I get myself into situations where I'm going to be disappointed and hurt. It seems it's been that way all my life."

"Oh, Jackie, I see you as smart and resilient, determined to get what you want for yourself and your kids."

"Yes, for my kids. I would do anything for them. But I have a knack for letting myself get hurt."

Until one o'clock in the morning, we sat in the Jeep, and Jackie talked about how she had adored her father and craved his attention when she was young and how disappointed she was when she didn't win his approval. He wasn't at home when she needed him on her side, especially when she felt under attack by her mother. And she talked about her husbands — how the first was just a teenager, as immature as she when they got married. Jackie voiced no bitterness toward him, but the hurt in her voice was thick. When she spoke of her second husband, her pain took on a decidedly bitter tone. "He didn't hurt only me. Look at his total disregard for the children. He has just never been a father to them!"

I saw for the first time how vulnerable and damaged Jackie was. My heart ached to rescue her. I wanted to do more than just put my arm around her shoulder and dry her tears. I wanted to help her heal her deepest wounds. I wanted her to be able to trust a man again. I wasn't certain if I would be that man, but I wanted her never to suffer even a fraction of the pain that had already scarred her life. I thought of telling her how God could give her the solace she needed in her life. But that moment was not the appropriate time. We had only begun to know each other. I didn't want to put her off by putting on my clerical collar.

I've met ministers who always wear their collars. Even in the most informal situations — on a tennis court or at a restaurant — they are always onstage. I have never been comfortable with that style of ministry. I enjoy fulfilling my professional role within the church, but beyond its walls I want people to see me as they see themselves — not just because I am like them with my own needs and weaknesses, triumphs and joys, but because I want them to know me for who I am.

That evening, as I listened to Jackie unmask her pain, I offered her my shoulder to cry on, but I didn't talk about God. Give me time, Lord, I thought. Give us time to know each other better.

And over time, Jackie and I had many long spiritual discussions.

"You're not a stereotypical minister, are you, Harry?" she once commented.

"I really don't know, but I've never felt I had to demonstrate my professional competence by preaching outside the pulpit. I'd rather live my life as an example of how God wants us all to live together in harmony and love. That means, for me, helping people find viable solutions to their very real problems: locating a drug clinic for an addicted son, marital counseling for a distraught couple, or nursing care for a bedridden parent. And as we search together in their dark hours for solutions, I want to help people experience God's love and mercy."

"You know, Harry, when I was growing up, my parents sent Julie and me to church. They didn't take us. My mother's family had been Roman Catholics, but she wasn't a practicing Catholic, and my father was raised as an Episcopalian. That's where they sent Julie and me, to the Episcopal Church. But when I was in eighth grade, they sent me to a Catholic school. That was one of the best gifts they ever gave me, because the teacher I had that year, Sister Helen Lawrence, was the kindest, best teacher I ever had. She was probably the first person to give me a sense of my own worth. She didn't criticize me for every shortcoming. She praised me, accepted me for who I was."

Despite her lack of religious training as a child, I discovered that Jackie had deep feelings and a profound interest in spiritual questions. We often talked for hours about the meaning of life.

"How can a good God allow so much evil in the world, Harry?" she'd ask. Jackie was well read and she'd point out in graphic detail some current injustice, famine, or war.

"I don't believe God throws evil into our lives, Jackie. I think he is a God of love, of mercy, of redemption. I do believe there is some evil power in the world, though, and that our job is to withstand it with the grace and power of God. I think God is present in our lives, if we allow him to be, if we respond to his love. And he gives us his love to sustain us through the evil."

"Maybe I should come to your church and hear you preach," Jackie said with a smile.

"Anytime you'd like! But it's not just words, Jackie. It's not just listening to a sermon. You know, the other day I visited a parishioner whose life is falling apart. She's a widow, living on a small pension. Her children have grown up, left home, and they ignore her. She just learned that she has cancer. As she was telling me this, she was struggling to be brave, to contain her fear. I listened and took her hands and told her, 'It's all right to cry; you have every reason to feel frightened. But we'll pray, and we'll know that God relieves suffering, that his love is all-encompassing, even in the darkest time.' And we did pray together, and I told her that God loves her, that he'll always be with her. Now, I can't cure her cancer, Jackie, but I can ask God to help her to cope with the present and future. And I believe he will."

"Yes, Harry, I can see that you do. You really have a gift. I don't have your kind of faith, but sometimes I wish I did."

As I began to glimpse the profound side of Jackie, as she gradually revealed her deepest feelings, I sensed that she had great spiritual potential. I wanted to share that with her. I wanted to see her shut her eyes and take a grand leap of faith. But she'd been hurt and disappointed throughout her life, and she knew that if you leap, you may fall and break. Jackie wasn't yet ready to take that risk.

AS attracted as I was to Jackie, it would take me three years to propose to her. During those years, we each dated other people on and off. I still relished my bachelor's freedom and was not yet ready for the responsibility of a permanent relationship. I joked with Jackie and other women that, as an almost nonstop student from kindergarten through seminary, I'd been adolescing until I was twenty-seven, when my serious socializing began after seminary.

I left the state education office during those three years and worked as a college counselor, at a family counseling center, and in a private counseling practice. I continued my part-time ministry at the First and Franklin Presbyterian Church and began my doctoral work. I didn't see these as a patchwork of jobs I'd put together to form a "career" or simply to earn a living. I saw each facet as a part of my total ministry. I enjoyed counseling bewildered, distraught college students such as I had been, families in trouble, individuals with spiritual and practical needs. In seminary, I'd concentrated my courses on pastoral counseling because I wanted to help people on a one-to-one basis. I wanted to sit down with them, hold their hands when appropriate, advise them, comfort them in their sorrow, pray with them in faith and love of God. After seminary, I wanted to do pastoral counseling as much or more than preaching, though I have always loved to write and deliver a sermon.

But as Jackie and I dated more seriously, I started thinking about a steady job with a more predictable income than counseling fees. I had no desire for a large church with numerous administrative duties removed from people, but a full-time parish would be an economic necessity if I were to ask Jackie to marry me.

I've always thought that there are seasons for everything. I've often mentioned in sermons that Providence works its way in seasons — a time to reap, a time to sow. Throughout my life, I tended to intuit, to sense, time. And after three years of dating Jackie, I sensed that the time had come to make our relationship permanent. We had grown to know and love each other deeply. I felt blessed to find such an intelligent, talented woman with such fine mothering abilities. Yet Jackie had a tremendous vulnerability, a great need to be loved, and I had a need and desire to love. She and her children gave me that glorious chance.

I always knew I wanted a family, but I never went looking for a ready-made one. When I fell in love with Jackie, I fell in love with her children as well. When we began dating, Jackie talked about her children, but she kept them at a distance. This seemed to be her way of protecting them.

"You're like the other Jackie, Jackie Onassis, keeping photographers away from her children. You keep yours away from your dates," I teased her. They'd always be at her parents' house when I picked her up for a date. It wasn't until we'd dated several times that I was invited to meet them.

And when I did meet them, I was captivated immediately. John, the youngest at six, bounced into the room, his platinum hair flying, his huge blue eyes shining, and tossed me a spongy softball. Christina pirouetted through the house in a pink leotard and tights. Thomas was practicing lines for a school play, and he made me his tryout audience. Fifteen-year-old Stephen breezed in, shifted his basketball to his left hip, and shook my hand firmly. "Nice to meet you, sir. Bye, Mom." He was off to shoot baskets with his friends.

I had seen the glamorous Jackie at work and on the dance floor.

I'd begun to know the emotionally damaged side of Jackie with her hurts and spiritual needs. But now, in her home for the first time, I saw another dimension, the maternal one.

When she spoke to the children, her voice was firm when she said, "I expect you to brush your teeth and be in bed at nine o'clock." Her tone was loving and not authoritarian.

"We will be, Mom," Thomas promised, as solemnly as any nine-year-old could. Christina and John, their guileless faces framed, halo-like, by their blond hair, nodded and threw their arms around Jackie's shoulders to kiss her good-night.

There was warmth and love and comfort in this home, I sensed, and Jackie was the hearth. The more time I spent with Jackie and her children, the more I admired her mothering skills. If the youngsters grew rambunctious, she didn't scream and yell. She captured their attention by holding their chins in her hands, squatting down to their height, looking them in the eye, almost nose to nose, and saying, "I expect you to . . ." whatever the appropriate behavior was in that situation. Then she kissed them on the forehead or patted them on the head. They obeyed her, not because she was threatening or stern but because they loved her and wanted to please her.

One evening I walked into their house and was greeted with the sweet aroma of chocolate chip cookies. Christina, bearing a plate of them with outstretched arms, said, "Would you like some, Harry? Mom made them with me to cheer me up."

"What's the cookie therapy?" I asked Jackie later.

"Oh, Christina's feelings were trampled by some little girl in her class. When kids are upset, a good cure is to do something with them like baking bread or cookies or making homemade play-dough. They get their hands warm and gooey and the dough or batter pulls out the hurt."

"Sounds effective. I wonder if I could work that into a sermon," I deadpanned. "Maybe draw a theological analogy about the relief of suffering . . ."

"Oh, Harry, you smart aleck!" Jackie laughed, snapping a dish towel at me.

But over the years, whenever I walked into the kitchen and saw

Jackie and one of the children dusted with flour and kneading dough, I knew someone's feelings were being soothed. And I loved Jackie all the more for it.

Over those three years before we were married, I found myself being pulled, almost magnetically, into this fatherless family. Once when I had to visit Vanderbilt for consultation on my doctorate, I found myself wondering about Field Day at John and Christina's school. They were swift runners and had told me how much they hoped to win each of their races. I felt sad that I couldn't be there to cheer them. I broke away from my doctoral business and found the nearest pay phone.

"How many blue ribbons did we win?" I asked Jackie as soon as she answered.

"Six, total! Want to talk to the speediest two kids in Baltimore?"

I congratulated John and Christina and found myself gushing with pride in them.

I also found myself at school plays, bazaars, and basketball games. Stephen was turning into an outstanding basketball player who would captain his team and hit six feet four. There I was in the stands, among the moms and dads of his teammates, cheering loudly.

I joined Jackie at Thomas's school plays and we applauded proudly from the orchestra seats. When I discovered that Thomas also shared my childhood love of electric trains, I spent hours with him on the floor, setting up tracks and switches. And when I saw him intently carving a piece of wood with a dull kitchen knife, I went out and bought him a carving set.

I clearly knew what was happening. I was becoming more and more enveloped in their lives — and I loved every moment I spent with them. Not just because they were sweet, bright, polite children, but because they were Jackie's. They complemented her. They were such an integral part of her life — these four terrific kids whom she cherished and nurtured and raised practically alone — that I couldn't imagine her without them or them without her.

If I'd been asked years earlier whether I wanted a wife and children, I surely would have said, "Yes, I'd someday like to get married and then have children." That was the usual order of things. But Jackie came with kids. When I knew I wanted her, I knew I wanted the whole, wonderful, five-member package.

If I'd never met Jackie, she and her children might have gone on just as they had been for years: four children and mother. The children never felt the need for a father. Stephen, who spent a good part of his youth with Jackie's parents, had Jackie's father as a father figure. The younger three had never really known a father, and someone they didn't know, they didn't miss.

"When an elementary school counselor spoke to the kids from 'broken homes,'" John once said, "I didn't think it concerned me. We had Mom and she was all we ever needed."

Though the children felt no need for a father, Jackie and I both realized, as they grew older, that her picture-perfect family was missing a crucial member — Dad — who could share the parenting load with her. Me! I began to imagine them calling me "Dad" instead of "Harry." If Jackie and I married, I would get a ready-made family, and they would get a husband-father. The camera was loaded on the tripod. Jackie and the children were poised. All I had to do was step into the frame, and the portrait would be whole.

So after three years of getting to know Jackie and her children, the right season had arrived. I knew I loved them and wanted to be a part of their — no, our — complete family. When I decided to ask Jackie to marry me, I traded in my bachelorhood for matrimony at an automobile dealer's lot. I sold my little sports car (the Jeep was long gone) and bought a roomy, reliable station wagon for Jackie as an engagement present.

Jackie was vacationing with the children and her mother at the ocean, and I was to join them on the weekend. As I drove up to the rented beach house, Jackie and the kids were strolling toward me. Jackie's white bikini accentuated her deep tan. I jammed on the brakes and hopped out. Her smile gave away her instant recognition of the reason for the new car. A ring might not have surprised her, but a station wagon did. She soon began calling it "my engagement station wagon."

I was unaware of it at the time, but Jackie's friends had seen us as a potential mismatch. They saw me as staid Presbyterian minister, probably rather conservative and dull, and Jackie as something of an outspoken nonconformist. Jackie's friends always counted on her to be a truthful friend, and they, in turn, were direct with her: "Harry's a minister, Jackie. Do you see yourself in the role of minister's wife, pouring tea for the Ladies' Association?" Or, "Harry has been a bachelor for a long time, and you've been married twice and have four kids. How's that going to work?" Or, "You've been through two bad marriages, Jackie. You'd better be sure about this one." But Jackie knew her own mind. She wasn't sixteen or twenty-one this time. She was a month shy of thirty-five.

The day after I arrived at the beach, Jackie and I left the children with her parents and drove through the Chesapeake Bay Bridge–Tunnel to Williamsburg, Virginia. At the elegant Williamsburg Inn, I wanted every detail to be perfect. I arranged for a special table in the Regency Room, by a window overlooking the golf course. After a delicious, romantic dinner, Jackie excused herself for the ladies' room. I called over the waiter and busboy.

"I'm going to propose to this woman, and I'd like everything cleaned off the table, please. I'd like fresh coffee. New napkins. Your best brandy. And — please — bring it here in two minutes." They did.

Jackie always carried a tiny notebook everywhere to scribble an address or a thought or to remind herself to call or write someone. While she was in the ladies' room, I wrote on the last page of her notebook, "Will you marry me?" I propped the notebook open on a clean plate at her place. When she returned, Jackie looked at the note, smiled her widest, and reached for the pen.

"Yes," she wrote, and handed the notebook back to me.

THE next evening, as we strolled along the cobbled walks, horse-drawn carriages slowly clack-clacked past us. The sun at our backs cast our elongated shadows before us.

"Look, Jackie, we're walking into our shadows just as we're walking into our future together, hand in hand."

"Harry, I love you in so many ways. You're solid. So good and decent. You're totally different from anyone else I've known. You'll never disappoint or hurt me, I know. I never imagined I'd be so fortunate as to find a man willing to love me with all my faults and take on my four kids, too!"

"Oh, don't make me a saint, Jacqueline."

"No, I know you're not perfect," she teased. "I know you're something of a perfectionist, in fact, who can be impatient at times. But you are generous and good to my kids. You're going to make a great father. And I'm going to make you the best wife, by God!"

"Oh, yes, do I know that!"

THE wedding was set for November 25, 1977. To economize, we decided not to hire a caterer but to buy and prepare the food ourselves. Jackie loved to cook and entertain. Whether it was a small dinner party for our mutual friends or a grand office party buffet, Jackie's chocolate mousse was legendary for its rich density, her shrimp salads notable for the biggest, pinkest, most luscious shrimp.

For weeks before the wedding, she clipped recipes from *Bon Appetit* magazine. We went downtown to the Lexington Market and bought veal, chickens, shrimp, and all kinds of vegetables, which Jackie prepared, froze, and then stashed with every friend who owned a freezer.

Two hundred people were invited to the wedding at First and Franklin Presbyterian Church. It was a perfect setting for a wedding — a beautiful Gothic brownstone structure that could seat one thousand people, the oldest Presbyterian church in Baltimore, with the tallest steeple on the eastern seaboard. With a huge organ at the back and sparkling stained glass windows on both sides, the sanctuary was filled with dark wood pews, towering pillars, and a high center pulpit. A simple Communion table stood in front of the pulpit. On the table were bouquets of flowers and silver candelabra loaned to us by friends for the 6:00 P.M. candlelight ceremony.

In an icy drizzle, I drove around town that afternoon to collect our frozen casseroles. One of my other duties was to borrow extra china and silverware for the reception from another church. When Ron Bond, my best man, and I walked into the church kitchen about 5:00 P.M., the place was empty. I had known that the church was about to be closed and its contents sold, but I hadn't expected to find the cupboard as bare as Mother Hubbard's on my wedding day. Ron — in his tuxedo — raced to the supermarket to buy paper plates, plastic knives, forks, and spoons, while I went home to shower and dress.

When I arrived at First and Franklin a half-hour late, Jackie was fussing with the boys' ties in my office. I saw her through the window as I crossed the courtyard. She looked up and glared. Being late was not the way to please one's bride, I realized.

Though it started late, the wedding service was perfect. A trumpeter from the Baltimore Symphony and an organist played Bach. At eighteen, now at his full height of six four, and darkly handsome in his blue suit, Stephen gave away his mother, the bride.

Jackie wore a floor-length mauve dress with an off-the-shoulder flounce and tiny pleats in the skirt. A light shawl, shot through with satin ribbons, covered her soft shoulders. I'd performed a lot of weddings, but I had never seen a more radiant bride than my own.

After the service, guests sloshed through a downpour and across the courtyard to the parish house. But the reception couldn't begin immediately because all the carefully prepared food hadn't fully defrosted. And if that weren't enough, the church ovens would barely heat.

Jackie's sister tried to speed things up in the kitchen and gashed her finger while slicing bread. Julie spent the rest of the reception holding a napkin tightly wound around her finger.

And the bartender failed to show.

So, with damp, hungry, thirsty guests waiting, including my eighty-one-year-old grandmother and eighty-eight-year-old grandfather, we said, "Break out the champagne." An hour and a half later, the food was finally hot enough for our guests to attack with their plastic cutlery.

Julie, holding her napkin-bandaged finger, just shook her head and smiled. Our wedding day was typical of us, she said: helter-skelter, disorganized, what-else-can-go-awry? But it ended far more happily than it began, as we left on an overnight train for a honeymoon at Kiawah Island, South Carolina. We had the railway car all to ourselves. We snuggled together as we watched lights whiz past, streaking the darkness of our first night as husband and wife. I loved Jackie more than I could have ever imagined loving anyone. As we walked the deserted November beach the next several days, Jackie's eyes kept returning to her new diamond wedding band. She wiggled her finger to catch the sunbeams and the diamond shot back gleaming rays. How I loved watching her do that. The reciprocity of her wiggling finger and the sun's response symbolized our love, I thought. We would each give to the other and be blessed with love in return.

THE first years of our marriage were the building years, a time to build our nest. Nearly perfect years.

Very soon after Jackie and I were married, I adopted the children and they became Coles. I was proud that they would bear my name. John even took my middle name, Alexander, as his. "Now you can call me 'Dad,'" I told them. And they did, with apparent ease because I had been a part of their lives for nearly three years. Adopting them was a validation, I felt, of a relationship already forged. When the formal adoption papers arrived in the mail, we celebrated with a big dinner, and I wrote a poem for the occasion:

> You are my children — my handsome sons, my beautiful
>   daughter.
> The law says now you belong to me. But I came to know
>   long before this that you already belonged to me.
> There is a hymn you may learn, called, "God Is Working His
>   Purpose Out." I believe that and I believe that he fixed
>   things so that we would be a family together, and I believe
>   that he did that on purpose.
> He could have done it better, sooner, faster, easier, happier,
> But he didn't.
> I believe he is leaving all of that up to us.
> There is a saying you may learn some day, "Consistency is
>   the mark of a small mind."
> Well, no one can ever accuse God of that as far as we are
>   concerned.
> We have all worked very hard and come a long way to meet

and be here today to begin our new work together and our new lives together.

It takes lots of work still to be a family, and even more love.

I work hard, and I am going to love each of you even harder and even more than I have before.

Because every day we are older, and closer and more trusting of each other.

And every day we have more to share and more to love.

Thomas, you have your trumpet! When I look at you, I see myself — summoning forth all the tight-lipped, compressed energy my adolescent body could muster to make a pleasing, if not joyful, noise. When I look at you, Thomas, I see myself: serious, intent on doing life right, with your emerging sense of humor that may soon come to see your world as less serious and more absurd than it seems to be. You are on your way, Thomas, more than you know. You will take pains to grow, my son, and I will take time to care for you.

Christina, my pretty ballerina! When I look at you I see your mother — together I have two of you! But you are altogether unique, and altogether too quickly changing.

You are my favorite little girl, but you are at the same time a young lady and all too soon a grown-up one.

Sometimes I am pleased with all that — as I begin to think about what you will be like when you are a woman. I can see some of it now when you toss your hair back from your face, when you smile at me in a way that assures me that you will love me when I am old, when you make more sense out of your brothers' silliness than I can. But still, like any father, I will always want you to be my little girl. Please promise that to me as you dance and grow and love in the years we have ahead of us.

John — John Alexander! When I look at you, I see your mother and myself. But I see you most of all.

You are unique — from your white hair down to your broad shoulders, down to your tenth pair of tennis shoes.

You are my fair-haired boy — growing more quickly than all of us can keep up with. I see just how big and wise and

good you are. When you and I have a "special day"
together, or a special time romping on the living room rug,
and when I carry you upstairs and tuck you into bed, I
like to see you as my own little guy, who needs me very
much — a guy who needs his dad. I came to you late,
John, but I have given you my name. Be proud of that for
me and live to become all the things that you are.
Remember I will always love you.
I WILL ALWAYS LOVE YOU ALL.
YOU ARE MY CHILDREN!

Dad

ABOUT eighteen months after our wedding, I was called to be the minister of the Lochearn Presbyterian Church, on the edge of Baltimore's northwestern suburbs. Unlike First and Franklin, it offered a full-time job. Built after World War II to serve the postwar burgeoning suburbs, Lochearn is a red brick colonial-style church with a tall white steeple in a quiet neighborhood of mostly brick modest single-family homes. Dick, Jane, Sally, and Spot could have lived on these streets.

I saw Lochearn as a great challenge. Its congregation had changed and dwindled to about two hundred members in the quarter century from its beginning to my arrival. The neighborhood had become integrated, many of its early members had moved farther out into the suburbs, and the remaining ones were aging, their children long since moved away. My challenge was to build up the congregation and minister to its changing needs. I plunged in. I started a counseling center, an endowment program, and turned the chapel at the rear of the church building into a daycare center. Because this was an integrated neighborhood, I began to work toward hiring a black co-pastor. I wrote letter after letter, proposal after proposal, justifying that need to the Presbytery and the General Assembly. It would take years, but we eventually succeeded.

About a year after I took the Lochearn post, Jackie, the kids, and I were able to move out of the small house she had bought several years before our marriage and into a larger place.

The white brick house on Kensington Road was near Jackie's

parents' home. After Easter dinners there, walking by and admiring 409 Kensington Road had become almost as much a ritual as the children's Easter-egg hunts. A picture-book house, the kind that could illustrate a child's fairy tale, it was the sort of house a television producer would shoot as the opening scene of a family show.

"An English country cottage" was the realtor's description. There were gables, casement windows, and a slate roof that appeared almost thatched because each slate had been hand-cut with a jagged edge. Even the setting looked as if a landscape painter's brush had created it. Woods curtained the sides and back of the house like a stage backdrop. The rest of the property's full acre was dotted with eight flower beds.

Built in 1932 for the president of the city gas and electric company, the house reflected a grand style suitable for his status. When the utility magnate's widow put it on the market in 1979, we realized how little had been done to maintain it over the years, but we loved the house and its grounds all the same and wanted to make it our own. The "needs-work" condition of the house dropped its price into the affordable range, and, now that I had a full-time position at Lochearn, we were able to buy it.

I built a deck off the kitchen, laid a flagstone patio, and hung new chandeliers. Jackie painted, wallpapered, made curtains, and tiled the kitchen and powder-room floors. Thomas became a young Homer Formsby, stripping, sanding, staining, and polishing pine floorboards, banisters, and railings. The work seemed endless. But at this point in our lives, it seemed we could have it all, even if that meant doing it all ourselves.

As we feathered our English-country-cottage nest, we also built new relationships as a family. As Jackie's oldest, Stephen spent much of his childhood with Jackie's parents while she worked and went to college. From the time he was a year old, into Jackie's second marriage and beyond, Stephen looked to his grandparents as almost coparents with Jackie. While she and I were dating, I never saw as much of Stephen as I did of Thomas, Christina, and John. Stephen was always friendly, but he and I simply didn't have as close a relationship as I had with the younger three. He was a teenager, off with his friends and frequently at his grandparents' home. Stephen was about to begin college when Jackie and I were married. Yet, from his outer orbit of our immediate family, Stephen asked if he could be included in the adoption proceedings, which surprised and touched me greatly. He wanted to share the same last name with the rest of us.

Thomas, Christina, and John were a tight knot, extremely close to each other and to Jackie. When she married me, they were twelve, ten, and nine. In the early years of our marriage, I thought that being a father was a piece of cake. Fathers set the rules and children kept them. Thomas, Christina, and John were good kids, and we had only normal, minor skirmishes. But as they approached their teens, strains between us inevitably developed, as they do in many families. I know they were fond of me, and they often showed their affection, but I suppose I was more rigid with them than Jackie. My only role model was my own father, a somewhat stern man whom I had always obeyed and whose authority I'd never questioned. When the children left clothes, books, toys around the house, I bristled. My reminders to pick up their things were ignored. Reprimands about their messy rooms sometimes brought more confrontation than compliance. When Thomas was sloppy about his woodwork refinishing, I grew impatient. I admit I'm something of a perfectionist — I'd launch into a lecture on the importance of doing the job "right!" Though I was a trained counselor, I couldn't always apply my problem-solving skills in my own family.

The sweet children who charmed me when I first met them at ages nine, seven, and six were becoming challenging teenagers. When I was dating Jackie and taking them on outings, we were great pals. But when we all moved under the same roof and had to learn to live together, our relationships gradually shifted. They had been accustomed to Jackie's more gentle style. She let them know what she expected of them: serious schoolwork, coming home on time, letting her know where they were going and who would be with them. But she was not a lecturer or a fumer. As a last resort, she'd take a wooden spoon and give the boys an occasional whack on the backside — she had long ago switched to a wooden spoon because she found that a quick swat with her hand could hurt her more than them, as they'd quickly turn and her hand would fall on a belt buckle or wallet-stuffed pocket. After a disciplinary session like that, though, Jackie let go of it. She would offer them a hug, a smile, a joke, and peace was restored. I don't think they ever doubted her love and support for them, even when she had to pull them into line.

My style was different. I decided at some point that the kids needed to do regular household chores. I made a list and assigned chores to each child. Jackie went along with the idea without much enthusiasm. When the chores weren't done, Jackie and I would fall into a power scuffle: her philosophy versus mine.

"Oh, Harry, they're just children. Sometimes they simply forget. You can't expect them to perform perfectly all the time," she'd say.

"But we can't live without some organization around here, Jackie. They have to learn that everyone has to do his or her part."

"You're being dogmatic, Harry."

"No, I'm being misunderstood . . ."

We would go round and round like that without resolution. I had more trouble letting go of my frustration than Jackie did. I'd sputter or lecture, sometimes for several days. Or I would sink into silence and then feel angry and guilty. And Jackie would feel wounded, she'd tell me later, after time had swept aside the arguments like so many dustballs under the furniture.

As tiny fissures opened up in the children's relationship with me, I realized that they sought Jackie as their ally. In the beginning, she found herself in the middle, trying to make peace between us. But her children had always been the heart of her life. Through all her up-and-down years, they had been top priority, no matter how little money she had in her checking account, no matter what the car repair bills were, no matter who the man in her life was. The children were her anchor, and she was theirs, however momentarily choppy their seas. That wouldn't change. Over the next several years, as conflicts arose, the balance slowly tilted — though I'm not certain how conscious we were of it at the time — in our newly forged family.

"John, you're grounded for the weekend," I'd insist when he came home later than his designated time.

"Oh, Dad, I was only a half-hour late. I couldn't get a ride sooner."

"You know the rules."

"But, Dad . . . ," he'd drift off. Days later I would learn that he had prevailed on Jackie to un-ground him.

Over time we gradually fell into a line-up: Jackie-and-the-children on one side and me, alone, on the other.

THE English country cottage was revitalized, thanks to our sweat equity. But it took more than our talents and hard work. It was becoming incredibly costly. We put in a new kitchen, new electrical wiring, a new bedroom, and we refinished the basement. For all its English charm, the house came with an English climate as well. What a monster to heat! In the kitchen, we hooked up a coal stove, which did a splendid job of heating that room, but the rest of the house was chilly all winter.

In addition to our two full-time salaries, I did some work for a private counseling practice, and Jackie had a job one night a week at Johns Hopkins, advising teachers on how to meet certification requirements. But there never seemed to be enough money to heat the house, refurbish it, pay the kids' tuition, run the cars, entertain family and friends. And we did love to entertain, especially on holidays. Dinner for twenty at Christmas, hundreds of lights on the tree, piles of gifts. Jackie baked for hours at night, while I stayed up until dawn to set up model train sets under the Christmas tree. Even though these things grew costly, we thought they were worth the extra work and money because family celebrations were important to us. They welded us as family.

Just as we differed in our styles of disciplining the kids, Jackie and I differed about money. When family-finance questions arose, sparks of tension began to fly. When Jackie would return from the supermarket with her wallet at least a hundred dollars lighter, I wouldn't understand where the money had gone.

"Harry," she'd ask me, "won't you ever get used to the cost of feeding three teenagers? Or maybe you and I could stop eating?"

I also thought Jackie spent too much on clothes for herself and the children.

"What difference does it make if they were on sale," I'd say.

"Look at the total. If you buy five fifty-dollar items on sale for a bargain twenty dollars apiece, you've still spent a hundred dollars!"

Jackie would point at my closet and retort, "You like good things, too, Harry. Look at your shoes, ties, jackets."

I knew that most couples argue about money and ways of raising children — good Lord, I'd done enough family counseling sessions to know that — but when it hit so close to home, I could be just as frustrated as the next husband and father.

Once, in the middle of a counseling session with a teary wife and jaw-clenched husband, I was urging them to try a little compromise.

"Now that you've aired your grievances with each other, can you suggest how each of you, yourself, can give some ground? Can you find a little forgiveness so you can begin to work out a solution?"

As they looked silently at each other and I waited for some response, I suddenly visualized Jackie's face. She wore a mixed expression of anger and hurt — her mouth and chin were frozen in anger, but her eyes said, "You've hurt me again." I realized that I had been seeing this expression too often lately.

Why can't I be as good, as patient a husband as I am a family counselor, I wondered? Of course, the counselor puts some professional distance between himself and the people sitting across from him, I knew, but I envisioned myself on both sides of the coffee table. I remembered seeing some actor playing dual roles as twin brothers. I imagined myself acting dual roles, too, and the vision was sadly comic. I knew exactly what Harry the Counselor would say and exactly what Harry the Husband would say. Harry the Counselor, leaning back in his chair, would suggest forgiveness, tolerance, lightening up. Then I'd move myself to the other chair and sit bolt upright as Harry the Husband said, "Yes, but I have a point that she doesn't see . . ."

Knowing the lyrics didn't mean I could always sing the tune. As I refocused on the couple before me, I knew that I needed to apply the advice I was giving them to myself. If I could temper my irritation about money and child rearing, maybe Jackie and I could make some compromises. I would try to be less rigid with the kids,

I resolved. I'd ease up a bit on the money squabbles, I told Jackie that evening. And she, in turn, said she'd also try to be more thrifty.

The best times for talking about these attempts at compromise usually came when we took leisurely walks through Ten Hills, the neighborhood around Kensington Road. Getting out of the house and strolling quietly, hand in hand, through those leafy streets pulled us together again. We would also talk about how the children were faring in school and our hopes for their future and ours.

"They're each so capable, Harry. I want them to do well, to stretch their minds, to have wonderful, challenging college experiences — not the part-time, night-courses patchwork that I had — but the whole ivy-covered-campus, full-time package deal!"

"I want that for them, too, honey. I love them so much, though I'm not sure they always believe it when I'm on their backs about chores and curfews."

And we would talk about our future together after the children were off at college.

"Maybe then, Jackie, you'll be able to finish that novel of yours. You really should keep at it."

"Oh, I'll never finish it, Harry. I can't ever find the time to sit down and get all my thoughts on paper. Sometimes I'm bombarded with ideas to incorporate into the novel — usually when I'm driving the kids to school or on my way to work, or when I'm in the middle of some meeting at the office. Later, when I have a moment to write them down, those ideas are never as crisp."

"Well, in a few years our lives should be less frazzled. We won't be running in so many directions at once. The kids will be off on their own; you won't be doing so much chauffeuring, so much cooking. I may even have more time to spend with you if the church ever gets a co-pastor. Maybe we need more time together. We could wander across the country some summer by ourselves. And we won't be so consumed by work on the house. We've done nearly everything to it that we'd planned to do. In fact, we might even think about moving to a smaller place when the kids are off and grown."

Those pacific moments in our marriage, when we walked and talked about our lives together or when we shared a romantic, candlelight dinner, were refreshing and healing, but they didn't curtail a pattern that was steadily entrenching itself. Our arguments continued and, at times, grew stronger and more frequent. Something had to be done, but I didn't know how to go about it. Both Jackie and I could be stubborn. I sometimes wouldn't speak to her for a day or two. She wasn't one to turn her back silently, though. Jackie wanted to get all the differences out in the open.

"Listen to me, Harry. I have a point . . ."

"And I have a point, too. But you won't hear it," I'd say, often letting the door slam behind me as I walked out to cool off.

When Jackie's anger erupted, she'd bounce back sooner than I. Once I returned to the house after an argument and found Jackie and the children quietly laughing around the kitchen table. But their eyes were still damp and their cheeks tearstained. I knew instantly how much our argument had spilled over to upset the children, and I recognized — as they virtually ignored my presence — that the tensions between Jackie and me drew them closer to her and farther from me. "You've hurt our mother," their expressions told me. I wanted to reach out and hug them all, to wash away the tiny rivulets running down their faces, but I was still too entangled in the mean, petty threads of our argument to break free. I just walked past them and went upstairs.

At the office, Jackie's coworkers couldn't help but overhear her squabble over the telephone with me.

"I never said that, Harry! Oh, no, damn it . . . I didn't. You did."

They felt embarrassed about being witnesses to our phone fights, I'm sure, but they knew Jackie well. She'd slam the phone down, and within a few moments, she'd be joking with someone or casually asking for an aspirin. Her frequent headaches were as much a part of Jackie as her stylish clothes, her wit, and her willingness to listen to everyone's problems and lend a hand.

Jackie was also under great stress during these years because her mother's health was deteriorating dramatically. Spunky Helen Lohsen developed a brain tumor that required surgery twice. Though Jackie and her mother had been at odds almost since Jackie's birth, Jackie deeply loved her enigmatic mother. Watching her mother go through two brain operations in three years tore Jackie deeply. Her proud, always independent mother was all at once pathetically dependent.

After the first operation, Helen needed a cane with three tiny legs at the bottom. The woman who only a few years before had worn a gown and high heels to our wedding was shuffling and tottering like a stiff old lady. Then she appeared to enter a depression that, doctors felt, required admittance to the psychiatric floor of the hospital. I stopped by to see her one day, before visiting one of my parishioners in the same hospital. She was slumped in a wheelchair and didn't respond when I said, "Hello, Helen. How are you doing today?" She knew I was there, I sensed, but she said nothing and didn't raise her eyes to look at me.

"I felt so helpless," I told Jackie later that evening.

"I know, Harry. That's exactly how I feel whenever I see her now. I can't believe that is my mother, so weakened, so lethargic."

The doctors determined that she wasn't suffering depression after all but that the tumor, even though it wasn't malignant, was probably growing back. So they decided to operate again. It was déjà vu — same doctor, same room. But this time he emerged to say, "I'm sorry. It didn't go well. It's going to grow back, I'm afraid."

We knew Helen didn't have much more time to live. The once bright, often outspoken Helen conversed in disjointed phrases now. One moment she was in the real world, the next she was somewhere else — her thoughts seemed to be short-circuited. All dignity and independence had been snatched away from her.

"My mother is half gone," Jackie said. "And any hope of reconciliation with her is gone, too. I don't even know if she knows I'm here, sometimes."

Helen had to enter a nursing home, where she vegetated for a year before her death. Jackie suffered as she watched her mother slip into such a debilitated existence.

"My God," Jackie once remarked outside Helen's room. "Look at these modern medical miracles — operations and medicines for 'saving' people. Medicine creates a monster and then tells you to take it home and do something with it!"

In many conversations with the children and me, Jackie said, "If that ever happens to me, pull the plug." The children and I understood and completely agreed with her.

*　　*　　*

AFTER almost six years on Kensington Road, we decided that the house was too much for us. We'd put our hearts, souls, and wallets into it, but it was choking us financially. The strain wasn't going to let up unless we made some changes. Thomas was now in his first year of college. Christina would be headed for college the following year. John would be at home only a couple more years.

"We no longer need so much space to heat," I suggested to Jackie.

"True enough, by God! And, besides, look what we've done to this place — we made it beautiful. The job is done. There's really no more challenge," Jackie said. "And maybe we're growing a little tired of taking care of it."

"I couldn't agree more!"

We began to look for something smaller, more economical. The natural location was Bolton Hill, one of Baltimore's in-town, gentrified neighborhoods. Many of its town houses had been renovated and were too expensive for us by 1985, but a few moderately priced ones could still be found. The neighborhood held special appeal because our friends the Hobacks, my former landlords, were there. Bonnie and Paul had been urban pioneers in the 1950s, when they moved into the seen-better-days neighborhood, and they were still in the same house three decades later. When we saw a three-story town house for sale just two blocks up Bolton Street from Bonnie and Paul, our decision to move was complete. Nearly six years to the day after moving to 409 Kensington Road, on May 17, 1985 — when most Baltimoreans were at the racetrack for Preakness Day — we closed the door of the English country cottage and moved to Bolton Hill. The move could be a new beginning, a way to recharge the batteries of our marriage. Despite our disagreements about money, our love for each other was still strong. I felt we just needed to bring that love back on track, and maybe it would be easier to accomplish in a new home.

Thomas, Christina, and John seemed to accept the move without complaint. Though it was a much smaller house than 409 Kensington Road, our teenagers were rarely home, anyway, these days.

The first-floor living and dining rooms of the Bolton Hill house were rather formal, but at the top of the stairway on the second floor was a large, open room that quickly became everyone's favorite. This family room, or "middle room" as we dubbed it, at the physical center of the old town house became the hearth where everyone gathered. The previous owner had torn out the ceiling to create a doubly high expanse. A ceiling fan hung twenty feet above from what had been the third-floor ceiling. The only part of the third floor that remained was a large loft on the front half of the house. Balcony-like, the loft was separated from the upper reaches of the middle room only by a wrought-iron railing. The loft was John's domain, but he shared it with Thomas whenever he came home from college. Christina had a small bedroom behind the middle room at the rear of the house, and our bedroom was at the front of the second floor.

Jackie poured her flair for decorating into the town house. She gave the middle room an eclectic warmth. A sleigh bed in front of a corner window served as a sofa. Bookcases lined the wall under the loft railing. A dhurrie carpet of soft pastels covered most of the floor. Jackie placed my brown leather recliner and footstool in front of the exposed brick wall and hung a dozen family photographs, most taken by her, on another wall. Still more framed photos covered the tabletop next to a white wicker rocker.

Late into the evenings and on weekends, Jackie sewed pale-orange balloon shades for the bay windows in the living room and wallpapered the bathroom. The house really didn't need much work, but Jackie conceived more plans for it over the years, such as Victorian bathroom fixtures and clawfoot bathtubs.

At work, Jackie was growing more frustrated with pushing paper to review teachers' transcripts for certification by the state of Maryland. But she enjoyed the people in the office and those educators out in the counties with whom she often spoke on the phone. As much as she could, she grabbed every opportunity to get out of the office, to attend conferences or visit county school offices. But Jackie had been passed over for promotions more than once. She knew why — and if she hadn't, her friends told her often enough.

"You're not political enough, Jackie!" her close friend Carol Parham scolded her. "You just say what's on your mind. You don't play the game. You're really intelligent, but sometimes you're just too candid for your own good."

"Oh, I know you're right, Carol. But I've heard so much long-winded, hot-air chatter and read so many ever-changing regulations about teacher certification that I often wonder how much of our work filters down to helping kids in a classroom."

Jackie's impatience with the plodding education bureaucracy was sometimes unrestrained. She showed it by doing needlepoint or knitting through lengthy meetings, or she would make a pointed remark, cutting directly through rambling discussions to the heart of the issue. While the job itself wasn't totally satisfying, Jackie stuck with it because she had many strong friendships at work and because she needed the income and security.

But Jackie had more energy than the job, a family, and a new house required. So, in addition to the teacher certification course she taught at Hopkins once a week, she began to bake exquisitely rich desserts — a killer chocolate cake, glazed fruit tarts, creamy, rich cheesecakes — for a local restaurant. She wrote poetry and worked on her novel, basing characters on some friends at work. And she was forever taking photographs of the kids.

"Do you think you're going to forget what they look like when they move away?" I joshed.

"Of course not! It's just that they are growing up so fast. I love to capture their changing expressions, their maturing faces."

But the new home and all of Jackie's activities weren't helping us put the marriage back together. Everything would be fine for a while, and then, wham, we'd blow up at each other again. I didn't realize it until much later, but Jackie confided her unhappiness about our relationship to the children, her sister, Julie, some of her friends, and even my old friend Ron Bond.

Early in 1986, Jackie called Ron at the University of Baltimore, where he is a senior administrator. She asked him if he'd meet her for dinner at the Hopkins Club. Ron had heard both sides of our up-and-down relationship often enough. He thought this would be another chance for Jackie to unload on good old Ronnie, to tell him again what a rigid jerk I could be. As usual, Ron tried to play the mediator, listening to her complaints, hoping that letting off some steam might help her go back and try to work things out with me. But this time she was not just complaining about my

inflexibility with the children or my demands for tighter budget-
ing. She was talking about leaving me.

"What about the kids, Jackie? If you leave Harry, what about
them?" Ron asked.

"Oh, they're ready, as ready as I am. You know, Ron, if I'm
ever going to divorce him, I'd better do it soon, before I'm forty-
five, while I still have my body!" she said brightly.

Ron and Jackie both chuckled at that remark. That's Jackie,
Ron thought, always ready with a quick wisecrack. Yet he
couldn't be sure how serious she was. How well had she thought
this through? Was she just thinking aloud, tossing around the idea
of divorce, trying it on for size, the way any wife does in moments
of frustration? Is she telling me this, hoping I'll signal something
to Harry? Ron wondered. He couldn't be certain. But he urged
her to weigh her ideas seriously. "Why don't you and Harry give it
another good try? You've both got too much going to throw it all
away."

"Well, we'll see."

Ron's fear that Jackie might really be considering divorce was
heightened not long after their dinner. I called him at work.

"Can you come out to my office at church?" I asked him. "I
need to talk to you, and I guess I need to have you counsel me."

I may have been the professional counselor, but Ron was my
oldest friend. Professional credentials never got in our way. He
could tell from my expression how disturbed I was even before he
sat down.

"She's really serious this time," I told Ron during an intense
hour of going back and forth over our marriage's rough terrain. By
the time he left, Ron was fairly certain that our marriage was more
deeply in trouble than ever before. But a few weeks later, when he
and his wife, Mickey, had several couples over for a big turkey
dinner, Jackie and I were our old harmonious selves — upbeat,
chatting gaily with everyone, not throwing a single barbed remark
at each other. Ronnie remarked to me in the kitchen that it looked
as if we were getting back on course. "I certainly hope so," I told
him, but I knew that nothing had radically changed. We were
momentarily riding on one of our happier crests.

# Two

Incident #28396

Bertha Butler pulled on her navy para-
medic jacket, looked in on her sleeping two-year-old twins, and
left the house at 5:45 A.M. to begin another ten-hour shift. The old
fire station at Mt. Royal and North Avenue was only fifteen minutes away. As she approached the ancient brick station, few cars
rolled along the elevated expressway next to it. Wouldn't it be fine
if the whole day stayed as peaceful and quiet as it is right now? she
thought.

James MacFetrich met her by the coffee machine.

"Aren't you lucky your partner is on vacation, Bertha? You got
me today," he said, pulling at his droopy mustache.

"I'd feel luckier, Mac, if we didn't have that little ice-cream box
of an ambo today. When are they going to get the transmission
fixed on our unit? This must be the hundredth time our first line
has been in the shop."

Butler and MacFetrich: a team knit together by the necessities
of sudden medical emergencies. Five feet seven inches, lean and
angular, Bertha Butler was a thirty-four-year-old mother of six
who had worked as a paramedic for eight years. Mac — few of his
colleagues even knew his first name was James — was a thirty-six-
year-old firefighter, six feet and trim at 150 pounds. Married, no
children, with thirteen years in the fire department, he was trained
as an emergency medical technician. This Saturday he was detailed
to the medic unit, as he often was when the paramedic staff was
shorthanded.

For most Baltimoreans staggering awake that morning, March
29, 1986, would become memorable only as unusually warm for

the day before Easter. For the paramedics it would be neither a light nor a heavy day for emergency calls. The only unique thing, which they would recall years later, was that they had three CVAs that day. Odd. Ordinarily a medic team responded to ten cardiovascular accidents a month.

ONLY a few blocks from the fire station, our family was asleep under the same roof for the first time since Christmas vacation. Christina had come home from college in Philadelphia two days earlier. Thomas had returned from college in North Carolina the previous night, but Jackie and I hadn't seen him yet because he'd gone to a friend's house first. Jackie had called him there to see if he'd arrived safely — something she normally never did — but he said he'd be home late and there would be plenty of time to spend together over the weekend. I thought I heard Thomas come in sometime in the middle of the night and climb the stairs to the loft. But I'd slept so fitfully that I wasn't sure what I dreamed and what I actually heard. Throughout the night my mind had churned like a Cuisinart, as I kept replaying Thursday's argument.

"Jacqueline, this spending has got to stop," I'd insisted, waving the latest American Express bill in the air.

"Oh, Harry, as if you never spend any money! Cool off anyway. We're not talking about the national debt here. We can pay it. I get my paycheck next week." Jackie was pulling off her aerobic shoes. Forty-five-dollar ones, I recalled.

"That's not the point, that you get paid next week! Don't you see a pattern here, Jackie? We — no, you — have got to stop running up these ridiculous charges."

"But, Harry, you . . ."

"No. No more 'but Harrys.' We've got two kids in college. With John graduating from high school next year, how are we ever going to make three incredible tuitions, much less all the other expenses like getting them to and from college?"

"Harry, we've put some savings aside, right? The kids will get summer jobs. We'll make it. We always manage to . . ."

"Jackie, do I need to remind you that ministers don't make Croesus-style salaries, and you educators don't either. We both know that, but look at this bill!"

"I can see it, Harry."

"There is only one thing to do. Give me your credit card."

"What!"

"Give it to me. I'm revoking it. It may have your name on it, but the bill comes to me."

Jackie said nothing. She simply flashed those green eyes and strutted out of the room.

When I came home the next day, the AmEx card was propped up on my dresser. Victory! I thought. Maybe I'd finally made her see that her spending sprees could not go on.

I awoke Saturday morning when I felt the mattress rise as Jackie got out of bed.

"I'm going downstairs to make coffee. Do you want some?" she asked me.

"Please." I rolled over and watched her poke under the bed for her slippers. She padded out of the bedroom in one pink and one blue slipper. I punched the pillow and tried to catch a few more minutes of sleep. I knew I couldn't lie in bed much longer. Tomorrow would be Easter, and I hadn't finished writing my sermon. I'd soon have to go over to the church office to work on it. But I couldn't focus on any insightful homilies at that moment. The fresh morning sunlight wouldn't wash away the tense anger of the last few days.

I had hardly seen Jackie since Thursday night. We'd said no more than the necessary but polite "yes, pleases" and "no, thank yous."

Where is this marriage going? I asked myself for the thousandth time; as much as I love this woman, I'm afraid I'm losing her. So much distance has come between us lately. I don't see how I could live without her, but I'm so upset with her at the same time. What's this doing to our family?

As I lay in bed, I recalled the previous evening, when Jackie and Christina had gone to dinner at Bonnie and Paul Hoback's and then to an amateur production of *Amadeus*. I could have gone, too, but I had no particular desire to go with them. Our lives lately are paralleling more than intersecting, I realized.

When Jackie and Christina came home from the play, I heard them giggling downstairs like a couple of teenagers. I was somewhat envious of their closeness. When Jackie came upstairs, I asked her if she had enjoyed the play. Yes, she said, but she had shivered through the whole production. It was strange, she wondered aloud, because Bonnie and Christina had thought the theater was hot and stuffy. Bonnie had loaned Jackie a scarf to wrap around her cold hands, but Jackie still felt chilly throughout the performance.

JACKIE brought a cup of coffee upstairs to me, and I pulled myself out of bed to shower and shave. As I was dressing, I heard Jackie and Christina talking and occasionally laughing out in the middle room. After I'd dressed, I walked through the middle room and said good-morning to Christina. Her tousled blonde hair gave her a just-awake look as she leaned against one end of the sleigh bed. I headed downstairs, and, as I unlocked the front door, I heard Jackie call me from the top of the stairs. I looked up and saw not the weekday Jacqueline, smartly dressed, high heels, frosted hair, perfectly made up for work, but the Saturday morning Jackie. Uncombed hair. No makeup. A pale coffee stain on the front of the white terrycloth robe that I'd given her last Christmas. One pink slipper. One blue. It was not the most glamorous vision of my beloved, but one that would become etched in my memory forever.

"Harry, are you going to work?"

"Yes."

"When are you coming back?"

"When I'm done," I said over my shoulder, pulling the door shut behind me.

As I drove to my church office, I thought, she's turned in the credit card. She brought me coffee just as though it were any other Saturday morning. Was that intended as a small peace offering?

But I was still irritated with her. Why can't I let go of my annoyance as quickly as she can? I wondered. I tried to shake it, to toss it out the car window as I drove along. But it kept blowing back in my face like a scrap of litter that the wind won't let rest. When I arrived at church, I tried to gather some thoughts together for an Easter sermon:

Today Holy Week comes to its joyous conclusion with the glorious Easter message — he is risen! And hearing that news, we are called again to think about what new life, in Jesus Christ, means to us today . . .

We choose what we want to believe in this life, and what we choose to believe affects the way that we conduct our lives. For me, I choose to believe in Jesus Christ because I long to hear his good news of triumph, peace, and love in a world stricken with pain, anguish, and despair.

The Christian faith inspires us to believe in something grand and wonderful. It challenges us to believe that our world is greater than it appears and that our lives are much more important than we think. Simply and profoundly put, God comes to bring us life. God affirms our life by becoming one of us in Jesus. God shares our life in the experiences we all have — even the cruel end of it culminating in death. Finally, God redeems our life by showing us in his Resurrection that life is triumphant, powerful, never-ending . . .

That is the splendid mystery of Easter and our greatest challenge. And, in the greater scheme of things, it is our greatest blessing . . .

NOT long after I'd left the house, Thomas pulled on the T-shirt and pants that he'd worn the night before and came down from the loft. He hugged Jackie, gave Christina a playful poke on the shoulder, and went down to the kitchen for coffee. He came back up to the middle room with a fresh pot, poured second cups for his mother and sister, and stretched out on the rug.

"So, you seeing that same guy, Christina?" he asked. The routine had begun. At twenty, Thomas was still playing big brother to a sister only a year younger. He loved to taunt her about her current male interest, as much to relish her reaction as to criticize the poor victim who could never possibly be good enough for Thomas's little sister.

Jackie secretly enjoyed the sparring among her children. Never a mother to take sibling skirmishes too seriously, she stayed on the sidelines and jumped in only if the verbal jousting began to sound too harsh. It rarely did. Her children were so close that what drove other mothers wild as "sibling rivalry" was harmless in Jackie's view. She knew they truly loved each other, that they were one another's best friends. And she knew they valued her as a confidante. Thomas had said not long ago that he told a friend that he could, and did, tell his mother anything and everything. The shocked friend said he could never be so open with his own mother. Jackie cherished the compliment.

She smiled as Christina ribbed Thomas about how late he had come home last night.

"And John, Mom! Do you know when he came in?" Christina's voice rose upward. "You're a lot easier on him than you were on me when I was seventeen."

Jackie merely smiled.

"Are you talking about me?" John's groggy voice drifted from the loft.

"Yeah, you, baby brother."

"Let me sleep."

"You must need it since you came in at three A.M."

In the wicker rocker, Jackie pulled her legs up under her and the pink slipper dropped to the floor. She loved times like this, when the kids surrounded her. But these moments were rare now that two of them were away at college. She had begun thinking more and more of the future, after John would leave for college in about eighteen months. She thought of Stephen, now twenty-six and married just six months ago. How quickly, it seemed, he had grown up and gone off on his own. But at forty-three, Jackie hardly felt old. In fact, she usually felt energetic, ready for any new challenge. But there were some lonely, even shaky, moments when the future glared at her. Was she ready for a new watershed in her life? Would she and I share it together or separately?

The teasing routine between Thomas and Christina, punctuated by an occasional remark from John in the loft, abated, and the conversation turned to the Easter weekend. Of course we would all go to church tomorrow.

Before Jackie and the children became a minister's family, they were not churchgoers. After she and I were married, they began to attend my church with some regularity. I was proud to have them in the congregation, and after a service, Jackie would usually comment about a line in my sermon or a particular hymn. But in the past few years, Jackie's interest and attendance had waned and with them the children's. I was disappointed whenever she begged off attending Sunday service. I wanted her to reach the spiritual potential I knew she possessed. But I couldn't insist on her participation in church life — that would only push her farther away.

If my parishioners minded Jackie's absence, they never said so. But whenever she did come to church or did make a special effort at a "minister's wife" type of activity, they were charmed by her, as they had been when she staged an elaborate strawberry festival at Lochearn the preceding summer.

"MOM, what's the matter?" Christina's question was sharp.

"Oh, God, it's an incredible headache," Jackie said as she bent forward in the rocking chair and held her head in both hands.

"One of your migraines?" Thomas asked.

"This isn't the usual migraine. This came on just this second. It's so intense, so fierce! Oh, my God! No!"

John heard this from the loft. Like his mother, he suffered from headaches frequently. He knew that hers usually came on gradually, and if she took medication immediately, they could be minimized. If this one was so intense already, he knew medicine wouldn't do much good. But maybe massaging the back of her neck would. She had often done that for him, and it was the only thing that seemed to relieve the pain. John swung his legs out of bed and descended to the middle room.

"Let me rub your neck, Mom."

"God, this is awful. I can't remember ever having one this bad."

"Maybe you'd better go back to bed and lie down," Thomas suggested.

Jackie stood up slowly and unsteadily. Thomas grabbed one arm. John the other. Christina ran ahead of them and plumped up the pillows on the bed. Jackie had no sooner stretched out than she said, "No, I'm dizzy. No." And she tried to sit up. Sitting cross-legged on the four-poster bed, she held her head in her hands. John kneaded the muscles at the back of her neck. Christina stared at her mother. Thomas paced.

"Try to lie down again, Mom. Stretch back," Christina suggested.

Jackie leaned back against the pillows but again complained of dizziness and sat upright. Then she began to wobble from side to side.

This isn't right, Thomas said to himself. This is no routine headache.

"I'm cold," Jackie said, tugging a blanket tightly around her. "Oh, dear God! My arm feels numb." She squeezed her left arm.

"On, no! Oh, my God! No! I think I'm having a stroke. I can move my hand but I can't feel my arm."

The anguish in her voice, even more than her words, triggered fear in Thomas.

"Maybe we should call someone," he said.

"God, this is really a bad one. The pain! Oh, no! Oh, God, dear God!" Jackie said, closing her eyes and squeezing her temples with the thumb and little finger of her left hand.

"I'm going to call someone," Thomas announced to no one in particular.

"No, no, don't," John said, but a trace of panic in his voice only alarmed Thomas more. "Yeah, yeah, okay. Call!" John said. Thomas reached for the phone and dailed 911.

BERTHA BUTLER had just finished her coffee when the dispatcher logged in the morning's first call: incident #28396.

"Eighteen twenty-seven Bolton Street. Female with intense headache and numbness. Son sounds panicked."

At least she's not having a baby, Mrs. Butler thought. Even though she had delivered five babies in emergency situations, she always dreaded that the next call would be a difficult birth, one with life-threatening complications.

She and MacFetrich arrived only three minutes later, but to Thomas, Christina, and John those three minutes seemed infinite. Thomas ran downstairs as soon as he hung up the phone and opened the front door. When he bolted back upstairs, he found

John, tears rolling down his cheeks, pacing around the middle room. Half angry at his younger brother's unsteadiness and half sympathetic, Thomas clasped John by the shoulders and led him back to Christina's room.

"Get it together, John. She'll be all right," Thomas said. And to himself: If I lose my head, everything will fall apart. God, this isn't happening.

Christina got her mother out of the bathrobe and into a pale-blue sweatshirt and white sweatpants. Helping her mother get dressed was an automatic response. Christina knew instinctively that her mother would never go out in public, even to a hospital, in a bathrobe. After Jackie was dressed and back on the bed, Christina stood beside her and held her hand.

"My God, Christina. I think I'm having a stroke. I don't want to live this way," Jackie said, looking directly into Christina's clear blue, frightened eyes. "Remember how Hanu was near the end . . ."

"No, Mom, no. You're going to be all right." But Christina instantly pictured her grandmother — "Hanu," the kids called Helen — in the nursing home, propped listlessly in a wheelchair, gazing at nothing and talking in choppy phrases, her eyes as unfocused as her mind. Christina knew that her mother must be haunted by the same pathetic memories.

Thomas ran back downstairs and out to the sidewalk just as the orange-and-white ambulance pulled up.

"My mother is upstairs," he called out as Mrs. Butler ran up the steps after him.

"I'm so cold. Get me a blanket. I'm cold," Jackie was saying as Mrs. Butler entered the bedroom. "I'm cold. Get me a blanket. Cold."

"What's wrong, Mrs. Cole?" Mrs. Butler asked.

"I have a terrible, terrible headache."

"Is there anything unusual about your medical history?" Mrs. Butler asked as she began wrapping a blood pressure cuff around Jackie's arm.

"I've always had headaches, migraine headaches, but this isn't like those. Much more severe."

"Did you take anything for this headache?"

"No, it just came on so fast, fast."

Mrs. Butler took Jackie's vital signs. Her pulse and respiration weren't abnormal. Her blood pressure was somewhat elevated, but not alarmingly so.

"What's wrong? What is it?" Thomas asked.

"Does your mother tend to have hypertension, high blood pressure?" Mrs. Butler asked.

"Oh, no," Christina said from the other side of the bed, where she held Jackie's hand. "It's always low."

Jackie continued to sway from side to side, as though her body couldn't find a steady balance. She began repeating the same words in incomplete sentences: "Cold . . . oh, no . . . cold . . . oh, God! . . . the pain . . . so cold . . . the pain . . ."

"Mac, get me the crash box."

While MacFetrich ran downstairs and out to the ambulance, John and Thomas peppered Mrs. Butler with questions.

"Well, her blood pressure is a little high. Might be a little hypertension. But we don't know what the matter is, so that's why we're here, to get her to the hospital and find out what's wrong," was her even-toned response. But she was alarmed by the way Jackie was becoming more sluggish with each moment.

She noticed my shoes beside the bed. "Where's your father?"

"He's at his church. He's a minister," Thomas said.

"Well, maybe you'd better call him and let him know we're taking your mother to Maryland General. He can meet us there."

"Harry . . ." Jackie's voiced trailed off.

"Mrs. Cole, can you hear me? Mrs. Cole, can you answer me?" she repeated. A low moan was the only response. "Mrs. Cole? How are you? Do you hear me?"

"Yes," Jackie answered faintly. "Do you think I'm having a stroke?"

"Well, look, we don't know what's happening. That's why we're trying to get you together, to get you down to the hospital to see what's going on," Mrs. Butler said.

"I'm cold . . . cold . . ." Her voice was barely audible now. Jackie was drifting into unconsciousness.

As soon as MacFetrich returned, Mrs. Butler started an intravenous line in Jackie's arm. Thank you, Lord, for making this one easy, she said to herself as Jackie's vein cooperated and the line smoothly entered, giving Jackie D5W, a water-and-sugar solution.

"Why does she need that?" Thomas asked.

"Just to keep the vein open in case we have to administer cardiac drugs later," Mrs. Butler explained. "Here, will you help me? Please hold this IV bag."

She thought, God, these kids are going to come out of their skins. I'd better keep them busy with something.

To John, she said, "Tear this tape for me, please. I need to tape down the IV line."

Christina held her mother's head in her hands and was silent, while her brothers continued to ask frightened questions. Mrs. Butler took blood samples, filling four tubes, capping two with red tops, one with a purple top, and another with a blue one.

While Mrs. Butler pulled out an oxygen mask and covered Jackie's nose and mouth, MacFetrich hustled back to the ambulance. Pushing aside the curtain of the bay window behind the bed, Mrs. Butler watched him pull out the stretcher. C'mon, Mac, she pleaded silently, hurry up! Even though he had been gone less than a minute, she was growing more anxious. Mac placed the stretcher on the sidewalk and hauled out the folding stairchair. The vestibule of the house was too tiny for a stretcher, and because stretchers aren't used above the first floor anyway, he carried the stairchair back up to the bedroom.

As the paramedic team strapped Jackie into the chair, her legs wouldn't bend. Suddenly she was board-stiff. MacFetrich whispered to Mrs. Butler, "This lady doesn't look good."

"I know. Let's get her out of here fast." Her early calm had become sharp concern in the twelve or thirteen minutes they had been in the house. When they arrived, Jackie had been awake and alert. Now, as they prepared to put her in the ambulance, she was totally unconscious. The rapid loss of consciousness and the obvious severity of the headache set off alarm bells in Mrs. Butler's head. Trained not to diagnose, and never to tell family members any possible diagnosis, she knew the seriousness of Jackie's condition.

As the paramedics carried her down the seventeen steps to the first floor, Jackie's head lurched backward and she made a sucking noise that startled the children. While Jackie was transferred from the stairchair to the stretcher, Thomas, Christina, and John walked in circles and talked all at once.

"I'll go . . ." "You stay . . ." "Somebody's got to call Dad . . ." "Somebody has to be here by the phone . . ." "I want to go in the ambulance . . ."

In the middle of this commotion, an elegant-looking woman with black hair pulled back tightly into a bun and oversized tinted glasses strolled up the opposite side of Bolton Street. Bonnie Hoback caught sight of the ambulance.

"That can't be in front of the Coles'," she said aloud. She saw Thomas, Christina, and John shuffling around the ambulance. No Harry. No Jackie. Then she saw the paramedics swinging the stretcher around the back of the ambulance.

Bonnie walked faster. She couldn't believe that was the vivacious Jackie on the stretcher, about to be slid into an ambulance like a letter into a mailbox.

"What's wrong?" she called as she hurried across the street. The children sketched the events of the past twenty minutes for her. Bonnie's immediate reaction was to soothe them.

"No, don't call your father yet. Let them get her to the hospital and see what it is, first," she advised in her quiet, almost Southern, voice. Thomas, Christina, and John were used to Bonnie's take-charge style. When they were younger, she occasionally stayed with them when Jackie and I were away. Though they grumbled about her clean-up-the-dishes orders, they loved her like an Auntie Mame.

"Someone should stay here at the house for phone calls," Bonnie directed. "The other two go to the hospital." John was delegated to stay behind.

Inside the ambulance, Mrs. Butler was silently damning "this raggedy old ice-cream box of an ambo" because it was smaller and more difficult to move about in than the medic's first-line unit. She had already stuck three EKG pasties, or electrodes, across Jackie's chest and was attaching their wires to the EKG machine, the electrocardiograph that would monitor Jackie's heart for any abnormal rhythms.

"At least there's a normal heart rate," she muttered to herself. With a normal rhythm, there was no need to send Jackie's EKG reading ahead to the hospital. MacFetrich climbed in the back of the ambulance and secured the portable oxygen bottle. He strapped down the IV pouch and made sure the blood tubes were securely in place.

"What's taking so long?" Thomas asked when the fireman emerged from the rear door of the ambulance. "Why don't we get moving?"

MacFetrich explained that Mrs. Butler was on the ambulance radio to the hospital. She was relaying information ahead so the emergency room would be prepared for Jackie's arrival. This would save the hospital valuable time. She radioed the estimated time of arrival, and MacFetrich told Thomas, "We're ready to go now. Why don't you ride up front with me?" Mac switched on the ignition, the flashing beacon lights, and siren. Driving Jackie's Volkswagen, Christina followed in the wake of the siren's wail. John went back into the silent house that only a half hour ago had hummed with warm voices. He slumped onto the sleigh bed, his throat parched, his mind numb, his fingers combing through his white-blond hair. "She's got to be all right," he repeated over and over, between choked, frightened sobs. "They've got to make her well. They've got to. They can't let my mother die."

After several minutes, he picked up the phone to call a friend. He needed to talk to someone. No answer. He paced. The phone rang, shattering the deadly silence.

"John? What are you all doing tomorrow?" Stephen's voice was matter-of-fact. "What time are you going to church? Beth and I want to go with you." John couldn't find his voice.

"Hey, John, can I talk to Mom?"

"No. No! I mean, Stephen. . . . Something terrible has happened. They just took Mom to Maryland General Hospital in an ambulance . . ."

"What? Why?"

"We . . . they . . . don't know. She had a really bad headache, worse than a regular migraine. Then she said her arm was numb and she couldn't feel it. Thomas and Christina went with her. They're going to call Dad from there."

"Oh, my God! Which hospital? Maryland General, you said? Wait right there. I'll be right over to pick you up, and we'll go to the hospital together."

Even before he hung up, Stephen grabbed the phone book and found the number for Maryland General. When he finally got through to the emergency room and identified himself as Jacqueline Cole's son, a voice said, "We're not sure what is wrong with your mother, but maybe you'd better come down here immediately."

Every muscle in Stephen's body cringed.

ON the three-minute drive to the hospital, Bertha Butler never took her eyes off Jackie. The paramedic noticed a slight seizurelike tremble in Jackie's upper arm and shoulder. When they were a half block from the hospital, Mrs. Butler started to disconnect the EKG leads, turn off the IV, and secure the oxygen on the stretcher. As the ambulance swung into the Emergency Room Only parking bay, two nurses and a nurse's aide were waiting outside. Jackie was whisked from the ambulance stretcher to a hospital stretcher and into the emergency room.

Christina parked Jackie's car next to the ambulance and ran to join Thomas at the emergency room door.

"I'm so scared for her," Christina said breathlessly. "What happened in the ambulance?"

"I'm not sure. I could barely see her from up front. There's only a tiny window into the back. But she didn't seem to move." They raced toward the white-coats who were rushing their mother toward help, but they were suddenly stopped inside at a pair of swinging doors.

"I'm sorry, kids, but you'll have to wait out here. Could you please give the admissions desk some information about your mother?" a nurse asked.

In a monotone, Thomas rattled off Jackie's date of birth, address, occupation, and other details. His voice, he thought, sounded like a stranger's. But he could hear his own voice inside his head, repeating: This isn't really happening to us; this isn't really happening to us . . .

Christina's quivering voice broke his spell. "We'd better call Dad," she said, clutching Thomas's arm with both her hands.

WHEN I picked up the phone and heard Thomas say, "Something's wrong . . ." I was initially annoyed.

Oh, for heaven's sake, why do they have to interrupt . . . I thought.

". . . wrong with Mom . . . a really bad headache . . ."

"Thomas, what is it? A migraine? Let me talk with your mother . . ."

"No, no. I mean, it started like a headache, but it was more painful and it came on faster than any other she's ever had, she said. But, Dad . . . uh, you can't talk to her now. We're calling from the hospital . . ."

"What! What hospital? It's that bad? Why would you go to the hospital for a headache?"

"Yeah, it's that bad. Really bad. They brought her here in an ambulance. Here to Maryland General's emergency room."

"Get to the point quickly, Thomas — what in God's name is going on?" My impatience suddenly turned frantic.

"Well, we're not sure. I don't think the paramedics are telling us everything. Something was said about hypertension . . . Her blood pressure is up . . . Right after the headache started, she was dizzy and her arm went numb. That's when I called the ambulance." Thomas choked.

"Oh, good God, Thomas! This isn't just another bad headache, is it?"

"No, it's a lot worse, Dad. I think she may be unconscious."

"I'll be right there!"

As I ran red lights to get there, my knuckles were white on the steering wheel. I tried to sort out Thomas's comments — is he overly alarmed or is he trying to keep something from me? What is really wrong? How serious is this? Numbness in her arm? The mention of "hypertension" sounded like a smoke screen. What's really going on here? Unconscious? I should have asked to speak with a doctor, I thought. No, that would just waste time on the phone. I wasn't thinking straight, so I decided to pray:

God, whatever is wrong, please make this right and help the doctors to save Jackie. And, God, get me there fast!

I grabbed at any little sign of hope along the way: the sparse Saturday-morning traffic meant that I would be at Jackie's side in minutes. I had to be with her!

At the emergency room waiting area, I rushed toward Thomas and Christina. Their faces were colorless, blank.

"Where's Mom?" I threw my arms around their trembling shoulders.

"In there, but they won't let us in."

I pushed through the brown double doors anyway and looked around a huge room, fluorescently bright, a vast expanse of shiny tan linoleum. On the right side was a nurses' station under a sign saying Nurses Are Patient People. To my left, I saw a cubicle of pastel-striped curtains hanging from a chrome rod. Beneath the partly drawn curtains, a dozen pairs of legs, some in white stockings, some in white slacks. A pair of beds, with their cubicle-forming curtains pushed open, stood empty on both sides of the central one.

"That must be Jackie!" I rushed toward the cluster of legs and caught a glimpse of Jackie's head. Her eyes were closed and she was motionless. A tube was in her nose. Doctors and nurses surrounded her on every side, each one intently performing a vital task. But what were they doing? And why?

I wanted to rush up to her, touch her, hold her. I wanted to tell everyone in the white coats surrounding her, "Please, get out of my way. Leave her to me. You see, we had an argument this week. A senseless, worthless argument, about our credit cards. And now something is wrong, and I've got to make it right. I can do that if you'll simply leave her to me."

A voice behind me asked, "Can I help you, sir?"

"No. I mean, yes! Please, this is my wife and I want to know what is wrong. What has happened to her?"

The young nurse said in an even, professional tone, "Sir, if you'll wait outside, someone will be with you in a moment."

Her remark slapped me like a cold hand across the face. I wasn't in a department store, waiting to be waited on, waiting to buy a tie, waiting for someone to be with me in a moment!

I looked straight at her and said, "But she's my wife! I must see her! I must be with her! What is wrong? I've got to know!"

"Sorry, sir, someone will be with you soon. We're doing everything we can for her. Right now, please go back to the waiting area."

I walked backward a few steps and turned to rejoin Thomas and Christina on the other side of the swinging doors. We waited in silence. A vacant voice occasionally intruded with an announcement over the public address system. I wrung my hands. I paced. Thomas paced. I gave Christina my handkerchief as she sat, weeping quietly, on one of the padded vinyl chairs that populate all these sterile institutions. As a minister, I had been to scores of hospitals. All looked and smelled the same. The surroundings never meant much to me, but at this moment every detail of this place took on a sharper focus. My mind absorbed each line, color, texture — was it because I couldn't know what the hell was going on in that emergency room and I needed to fill my mind with any scrap of information?

I've never been able to tolerate waiting very well, and I couldn't abide this wait. I headed toward the doors again.

"No, Dad. Don't go in there," Christina said. "They'll call us."

"I've got to find out what's going on, Christina!" I pushed open the doors and approached the curtains. A nurse firmly ushered me back to the waiting room again. But sitting and waiting was unbearable. Christina, Thomas, and I began walking up and down the corridor leading from the waiting area to the main lobby.

Suddenly I remembered being in a hospital lobby exactly like this one, several years earlier. Gwen Moore, a young parishioner, only eighteen or nineteen at the time, had phoned and asked me to meet her at the hospital.

"My mother's here in the Intensive Care Unit and she's pretty ill."

I hardly knew Gwen's mother or father; they were not members of Lochearn. But Gwen, a quiet, sweet girl, was a very active church member who participated in our youth groups and com-

municants class. When I met Gwen at the hospital, she told me
that her mother had had a cerebral hemorrhage three days earlier.

"Now the doctors tell us she's brain-dead," Gwen wept. We
went into the hospital chapel and prayed.

After we left the chapel, I remembered, Gwen and I went up to
see Mrs. Moore in the ICU, and, later that evening, I visited Gwen
and her father at their home. They told me that they had decided
to have artificial life support systems disconnected because Mrs.
Moore was legally brain-dead. "Yes," I reassured them. "That
is the standard response when there is no hope, when someone is
brain-dead. I know what a difficult decision that is for you. She is
gone from this life now, even though her body lies connected to all
the machines. But we can believe that God is bringing her home to
be with him now. She won't be suffering anymore, and I hope that
this can be of some help and comfort to each of you."

Gwen asked me to conduct her mother's funeral at a downtown
funeral home. I was recalling that service when I suddenly heard
the announcement over the hospital loudspeaker:

"Will the family of Jacqueline Cole come into the waiting
area?" I hestitated for a moment, fearing the worst, and then
pulled Christina and Thomas toward me and braced their shoulders with my arms.

A doctor approached. He looked no older than twenty-four or
twenty-five and was built like a linebacker. His voice was too calm
and clear. I immediately recognized a tight control at work to
mask the young doctor's discomfort. I knew this must be the first
time he'd had to give a patient's family an unwanted prognosis.

"Could you come in here, please?" he asked as he motioned
toward a closet-sized room containing only a small desk and two
chairs. A room for delivering quick and dirty news. Thomas
leaned against a wall as Christina and I sat. The doctor sat behind
the desk and spread his broad hands on its barren surface.

"I'm afraid I can't be very hopeful," he began. My throat tight-
ened. I felt I couldn't swallow.

"Mrs. Cole has suffered a massive intracerebral hemorrhage
near the stem of her brain. A stroke . . ."

"No! No! God!" The three of us gasped at once.

"We actually think there were two hemorrhages, probably five or ten minutes apart. We have just done a CAT scan, and it shows significant bleeding."

I looked at and through the doctor at the same time. I couldn't believe what I was hearing. "Well, what does this mean?" I pleaded. "Is it as terrible as it sounds?" I could only begin to comprehend — I was hearing his words but a tremendous fear was blocking my way to understanding them.

"This is a very, very severe kind of stroke, Mr. Cole. I have to be completely honest with you. Patients who have this massive a CVA — cardiovascular accident — usually do not survive. This could be fatal within the hour, or the day, or at least within forty-eight hours."

"No! . . . but . . . my God!" I was dumbstruck. I glanced quickly at Thomas and Christina. Tears were streaming down their faces. Thomas's hands rested on Christina's shoulders. They both muttered through their sobs, "No, Mom, no! You can't die!"

"But, Doctor, what can you do to save her? You must save her! Can you operate?"

"The worst of the bleeding has already occurred. In a massive hemorrhage like this, the blood percolates through her head, drowning her brain in blood. We called in a neurosurgeon, and, in his judgment, surgery would be useless."

"That's unbelievable, terrible! You're saying there's nothing? Nothing you can do?" I felt a blazing heat rise from my toes to my ears. My face felt flushed, my palms clammy.

"I'm very sorry, Mr. Cole. We're moving her up to the Intensive Care Unit, where she will be watched closely," he said, rising to leave. "There's nothing else we can do but wait."

I was completely overwhelmed, swallowed up by some maelstrom that had taken control of our lives. A thousand pictures of Jackie flashed through my mind — in all of them she was alive, laughing, hugging me and the children, kneading bread with an upset child, jogging down the beach. But the one brief glimpse of her lying motionless in the emergency room cubicle kept pushing the other images away.

Thomas and Christina were clinging to each other, quietly sobbing. I put my arms around them, and we staggered through the waiting area.

"We'd better go home and tell John and call Stephen," I said, choking back tears. Save Jackie, please, God. Please don't take her away from us! I prayed silently.

Of all the emotions rushing through me, the strongest was to pull the children to me, to forge the tightest bond we could create, because if we could be together for Jackie, she wouldn't leave us.

ACROSS the emergency room, Bertha Butler had just returned from her second emergency run of the morning. She noticed a tall man in a tan trench coat, his arms around Thomas and Christina.

"Is that Mrs. Cole's husband? The reverend?" she asked Mitchie, the nurse's aide who had been at the door when Jackie was brought to the ER.

"Yeah. Such a shame."

"What's happening with Mrs. Cole?" Mrs. Butler asked.

"It's real bad. A big bleed. Doesn't look like she's going to make it."

"I thought it was bad, the way she lost consciousness so fast. She sure didn't follow the textbook on CVAs. No slurred speech. No paralysis. Just, bang, she was out," Mrs. Butler said. "It's so pitiful. Those poor kids. She's so young, too. So much life could have been ahead of her still."

Three

No More Than 48 Hours

"Are you going to be able to drive, Dad?" Christina asked me as we walked out of the emergency room. Here she was showing concern for me! And I wanted to console her — she looked so wounded and fragile.

"Yes, honey, but what about you? Can you drive Mom's car home by yourself?"

"Sure, but Dad I'm so scared!" She tilted her head into my chest, and when she stood straight again, her forehead bore a red imprint where she'd pressed against my coat button. Then she pulled Jackie's key ring from her pocket and walked slowly toward her mother's car.

Thomas collapsed into the front seat of my car. I cried and yelled and pounded the steering wheel as I started the engine.

"We can't lose her, Thomas! She can't die!"

Thomas answered me with muffled sobs. "No, no, she can't . . . Please, Mom, please . . ."

The car seemed to drive itself home. I barely saw the streets, my vision was so clouded with grief. I kept glancing in the rearview mirror to see if Christina was still following us. I was anxious about her driving even this short distance alone, in such pain, and I felt that we all needed to stay connected. If another driver dared to cut in between us, if I lost sight of Christina, we'd fall apart altogether. Surely that was irrational, I knew, but nothing was making any sense, anyway. Nothing was in proper perspective. Our world had spun upside down. Jackie might not even be alive by the time I got home.

When we turned the corner onto our block, I caught sight of

John running down the front stoop and into the street. Stephen and Beth were pulling up to the curb. I parked in the middle of the street parallel to Stephen's car. Christina stopped just a few feet behind me. Everyone jumped out of the cars simultaneously. The tears on our faces confirmed the fear on John's, Stephen's, and Beth's. We spoke all at once, gagging on the words, broken answers crashing against terror-filled questions.

"Mom . . . stroke . . . massive inner cerebral something . . . I don't know . . . they don't know . . ."

"Oh, God, NO! NO! . . . why? . . . impossible . . ."

"Probably won't survive, the doctor said . . . NO . . . NO . . . NO . . ."

"Die? . . . Within forty-eight hours? . . . She can't die! . . . No, God, no! . . ."

"Mom cannot die! . . . I want my mother back . . . I want Mom . . ."

If anyone witnessed our hysteria in the street, we didn't notice. Our whole block, even the whole city, seemed lifeless except for the six of us wailing in front of our house. The spring sunshine washed the red brick facades of the town houses and warmed the cobbled sidewalks, but it couldn't — nothing could — dry our tears.

Once we went inside, we tried to comprehend what was happening. I wanted to comfort the children and answer their questions, but I couldn't. I had no understanding of what had happened in the past few hours.

"I don't know what to say," I began, trying to force a calm tone into my own voice, but it came out thick and leaden. I repeated to Stephen, Beth, and John what the doctor had told us. "I know they're doing everything possible at the hospital to keep Mom alive. I want to pray for her now, kids. Let's ask God to save her from this stroke, to heal her, and to give us strength right now."

Each of us was silent for several minutes. As I prayed for God's mercy and grace, I looked around the living room at the children with their heads bowed and trembling. They were like matched pairs: Stephen and Thomas, the older two with their dark hair, the big brothers who had always played protectors to the younger two; Christina and John, their vulnerability barely hidden behind the translucent curtains of their pale skin and hair. Jackie was the center of their entire lives long before I came into this family, I thought. How can they survive without her? How can I? Is this really happening, dear Lord? I wondered.

My eyes caught the stairway, and I recalled the fresh memory of Jackie in her white robe and mismatched slippers — only a couple of hours ago. How that vision burned in my mind! How could I have not been home when the stroke hit her? Was there something I could have done to help her?

Stephen sat on the floor and stared at the floorboards. Beth crouched next to him with her arm around the small of his back. "She's got to make it. She's got to pull through this," Stephen said. His words were determined and strong, but the expression on his face revealed his agony and disbelief: it's impossible — I cannot be losing my mother.

John kept repeating over and over, "I want my mother back." I put my arms around him and tried to calm his trembling.

I was standing silently, hugging John and staring at the others, praying for them as much as for Jackie, when my mind sluggishly shifted gears. There are a lot of people who love Jackie, who need to know what's happened to her, I realized. They must be told of this horrible tragedy. I urgently needed to share our pain and to seek their comfort. I picked up the phone and dialed Jackie's sister and father, my mother and brother, Ron Bond and other friends. Everyone reacted with shock and disbelief: "No, not Jackie! A stroke? How can that be? I'll come right away to be with you." I phoned Bonnie and asked her to walk to the house to stay with the kids while I returned to the hospital — I had to get back to Jackie.

As I sped to Maryland General, I realized that someone else would have to take over tomorrow's Easter service for me. I'd call Louise Bailey, my secretary, from the hospital. Louise would take care of everything, I knew. For the first time in sixteen years, I would not show up to lead a service in church. Practical plans for tomorrow melted away quickly as I tried to grasp the cruel paradox that Jackie might die at Easter. Easter! The glorious day of Resurrection. New life, new hope, the most sacred day in the Christian year. I thought of some verses from the Book of Psalms that I'd planned to read at the opening of the Easter service:

"This is the day the Lord has made. Let us rejoice and be glad in it . . . This day is a holiday of the Lord's own choosing; greet this day with rejoicing, greet this day with triumph."

Please, Lord, let me greet tomorrow with rejoicing, with triumph. Please heal Jackie. Roll this stone away, just as you rolled the stone away from Jesus' tomb. Let her live! I prayed.

I RETURNED to the hospital and headed for the emergency room without thinking. The waiting room was empty, so I rushed through the double doors. The center cubicle was unoccupied, its striped curtains opened, the sheet on the gurney perfectly smooth. For a moment I thought this day had been a nightmare and I had just awakened. Then it hit me: Jackie has already died! She died while I was driving here . . . the doctors called home but I'd already left the house . . .

But a nurse broke in: "Mr. Cole? Your wife has been taken up to the Intensive Care Unit on the second floor. The elevator is across the hallway."

As I stepped off the elevator, I looked left, then right. I felt totally lost. The ICU appeared at the far end of the hall to the right. I walked across a long expanse of speckled-tan linoleum toward a central nursing station, a wooden island in the center of the room. On the front of the island, a row of cupboards and drawers wore hand-lettered labels: Blood Tubes, Angiocaths, PRN Adapters — all the paraphernalia of caring for the dying. I shuddered. I looked around the edges of the room, searching for Jackie. Tiny glass cubicles lined both right and left walls. I felt cold and afraid. She must be in one of those glass cages, I thought. I was wary of looking too closely for fear of finding her, yet I desperately needed to see her.

JESUS! This man looks just like Jesus Christ, I thought as a doctor approached. With the beard, the straight dark hair parted down the middle and flowing to the top of his collar, the intense face and deep, serious eyes, he resembled every portrait of Christ on every frontispiece of every hymnal I'd ever opened.

"I'm Dr. Tad Pula. Are you Mr. Cole?" he asked, extending his hand. "I'd like to talk with you, but you might want to see your wife first. She's in room fourteen, over there."

Even before I was through the open doorway of her cubicle, I was weeping at the sight of my beloved Jackie. A plastic tube emerged from her nose. Another tube was in her mouth. Her face was still. Her eyes were closed. Her arms lay on top of a sheet. An IV tube connected her pale-blue vein on the inner side of one arm to a bottle hanging from a pole next to the bed. Her chest rose and fell with every puff of air from a respirator on the other side of her bed. It uttered a soft wheezing sound, but I couldn't look at the machine or at the monitor that sent little green scribbles scrambling across its screen. I was only peripherally aware of the technology hooked to Jackie.

I held her hand and wept. "Jacqueline, Jacqueline. I love you so much. Be well. Be strong, honey. Don't leave me. Don't leave the children. Please, God, save Jackie. Save my wife," I implored aloud. "Save Jackie."

I stroked her hand and kissed her forehead and cheeks. Jackie's face gave no response, had no expression. She looked as if she were asleep, but I could see that it wasn't a peaceful sleep. Her body didn't looked relaxed under the sheet. She looked frozen. A beautiful, icy still life.

I stood next to her and held her hand in mine, unaware of everything but Jackie's immediate presence. Time did not exist for me. There was no hurry to do something, to go somewhere. I simply was with Jackie.

"I'm here with you, honey. I will always be with you, no matter what happens. I love you and I will always love you. God loves you. So many people love you. Everyone's praying for you. We want you to get well. We can't let you die. We can't let you leave us!"

Dr. Pula appeared in the doorway and asked to speak with me. We walked in silence out of the ICU to a small conference room that would become familiar to us.

"I cannot tell you why this happened to your wife, Mr. Cole," Dr. Pula began. "She was apparently a healthy woman of forty-three with only a medical history of headaches, I understand."

"Yes. Jackie often had migraine headaches, but that was all. She was . . . is, I've always assumed, in great health. She doesn't smoke. She's always dieting, always working out. She does Jane

Fonda and Joanie Greggains videotape workouts in the morning and usually again at night. Jackie's mother died a couple of years ago of a benign brain tumor, but I don't know of anyone in her family who's ever had a stroke, certainly no one as young as Jackie. I can't understand this. Is it really as bad as the doctor in the emergency room told us?"

"I'm afraid so, Mr. Cole. I should explain. I'm head of the Division of Neurology here, and I was called when Mrs. Cole was brought to the ER. We saw immediately how massive this stroke was. As you may have been told, she lost consciousness rapidly. It was less than a half hour, I believe, from the time she was alert and awake and complaining of a severe headache until she became unconscious, comatose.

"We're doing everything we can. We have done a CAT scan, and it showed a very large hemorrhage. Mrs. Cole has already been seen by the neurosurgeon, who feels that surgery wouldn't offer any chance of a meaningful result."

"But, Doctor, what actually happened to Jackie? What caused this stroke?" I pleaded.

"We don't know exactly what caused Mrs. Cole's stroke. But there are two kinds of stroke: one where there's a blockage of an artery that supplies blood to the brain and the other a hemorrhage, or rupture, of the blood vessels. Hers was a hemorrhage, a bleeding stroke. And it was a subarachnoid one, meaning the intracerebral blood vessels — those within the cerebrum — ruptured and the bleeding extended into the subarachnoid space, the space around the brain, and then into the ventricular system. The ventricles are the normal fluid-filled chambers that all our heads are filled with. So the hemorrhage was more than just local. The blood went not only where it wasn't supposed to be locally but also burst through the surface and spread all around. It was inside the brain and outside the brain in the ventricular space.

"I'm sorry if this sounds too technical or detailed, but you should know that this is a most serious kind of stroke and her vital signs are quite unstable as a result," Dr. Pula said as he ran both hands from his temples through his hair, revealing a high forehead.

"I appreciate what you're trying to tell me, Dr. Pula, but what

does this all mean? Is it absolutely certain that she is going to die?"
I blurted.

"The vast majority of patients who have this kind of stroke die
within a few hours. She may survive the day, or even into tomorrow, but I would suggest that you bring your children down here
and notify relatives and friends of the seriousness of this."

His intense hazel eyes told me more than all his words. I cringed
— the worst-case scenario has arrived, I thought. First she's taken
to the hospital with a headache. Then it's a stroke. Now it's the
worst possible kind of stroke. A killer stroke! Can this be real? I
asked myself. Can it possibly get any worse? My heart utterly
sank.

I was torn. I wanted desperately to stay with Jackie, never to
leave her, to will her back to health despite the tragic prognosis
Dr. Pula had just spread before me. But I also needed to be with
the children. They had to be told these details, how poor the
outlook was, and how soon we could lose her. I would race home
and bring them back to the hospital so they could be by her side.

When I reached home, I felt instinctively that if I could embrace
our children tightly, our combined strength would help save
Jackie. I gathered Christina, Thomas, John, Stephen, and Beth
upstairs in the middle room. I asked them to sit down and listen to
what I had to say. I wanted to set a stage that would comfort them,
a stage where I could control their reactions, where I could give
them some strength to withstand the news I was about to deliver. I
hesitated and then forced myself to utter the words.

"Mom has had a very, very bad stroke, and it is very likely that
she . . . that Mom is going to die fairly soon." I choked on the
word "die." "We need to go and see her and say good-bye."

John's face was expressionless. Stephen's and Beth's were
infinitely sad. Christina screamed, "No!" as she jumped out of her
chair and ran downstairs and out the front door. Thomas ran after
her to bring her back. I felt an instant, stinging hurt. I couldn't
shoulder their pain. I wanted to pull Christina back — Don't run
away! We must stay together for Mom!

For the first time, I was fully aware of how out-of-control this
day had become. How unrealistic to think you can control their
reactions, I told myself — You're not in the driver's seat here,

Harry! You cannot save Jackie. You cannot guide or comfort or help your children. You are utterly helpless!

I know myself pretty well — when I feel helpless or without control of a situation, I can get very angry. I went into our bedroom, pounded the bed with both hands, cursed, and yelled until most of my anger was spent.

"God, what has happened here?" I demanded. "What have you done? Listen to me! I'm talking to you and I am angry. I want my wife back now."

THAT Saturday was the longest day of my life. I walked through the unwritten script of calling everyone who cared about Jackie to tell them about her stroke.

One of the most difficult calls to make was the one to my mother. My father had entered a nursing home only two months ago, and I dreaded bringing Mother more bad news.

When she had first met Jackie, Mother had withheld her opinion, but I knew she was apprehensive about my involvement with a twice-divorced mother of four. But as she and Jackie got to know each other, they grew close. Mother loved the children and came to see Jackie as the daughter she never had.

I called Mother and began, "I have some very bad news. It's about Jackie." She gasped as if she instinctively knew what I was about to say. After I had delivered the grave details, Mother said, "Oh, Harry, I am so sorry. I don't know what to say." I could hear her crying softly. "I'll meet you at the hospital right away."

But Mother was so distraught that she couldn't drive, so her sister and brother-in-law, Evelyn and Jack, brought her to the hospital. When I first saw her in the hallway, she struck me as regal, dressed in a black suit, her hair snow-white, her back tall and straight. Mother's strength had just begun to emerge this past year, as my father's Alzheimer's disease wracked his mind, finally necessitating a nursing home, and then he developed prostate cancer. As his mind and general health declined, Mother's inner compass found direction. She took charge of everything — the banking, house and automobile maintenance, medical insurance forms — things she had never had to do earlier in their marriage. I'd proudly witnessed Mother's strength grow in recent months, but when she walked down the hospital hallway toward Jackie, I had never seen her so lost, so fragile. She had come to the hospital to comfort me, but her face revealed how utterly forlorn she was. I crumbled. We held on to each other and wept.

My brother, Wayne, arrived, followed minutes later by Sid Venable, our family doctor for over thirty years. Sid examined Jackie and consulted with the doctors and nurses. He could offer us no more hope than Dr. Pula had.

"I'm so sorry for all of you, Harry," he said, with tears in his eyes, "but intracerebral hemorrhages are almost always fatal."

Jackie's father and Julie, with her husband, Sam, and son Andrew had arrived, weeping and hugging the children. Everyone entered Jackie's cubicle briefly to hold her hand, kiss her, and say a final good-bye. Then each emerged to join the rest of us, milling through the hallways on this anguished deathwatch. No one knew what to do, what to say. After a while Wayne went out for hamburgers, chips, and sodas for everyone. We ate in silence.

While I was consumed with despair and anger, I was also concerned about the children's reaction to seeing Jackie dying in the ICU. As I brought them back to the hospital that afternoon, I feared that the whoosh of the respirator, the tube in her nose, all the mechanisms hooked up to her, would frighten them even more than my earlier explanation of her condition. But I realized as soon as they walked into the ICU that they barely noticed the machinery. Their eyes focused only on Jackie's lifeless face. They saw her as dying and didn't notice the "life-sustaining" equipment attached to her. They froze at the doorway, seemingly afraid to enter her tiny ICU cubicle, and stared at her closed eyes. A nurse with curly brown hair encouraged them to touch her, hold her hand, kiss her forehead.

"It's okay," she said. "Lots of times, family members are reluctant at first to touch a patient because of the tubes and things, but it's good to touch her. And talk to her. Even though she is in a coma, we don't know that she can't hear you."

Forty-eight hours. Forty-eight hours. Those seemed to be the only words racing through my mind. The doctors said she won't live forty-eight hours. This visit could be the last. As visitors slowly left, each one knew that there would probably be no visit tomorrow. Yet no one verbalized that unspeakable thought.

"Good-night. I'll call you if anything happens. Please pray for her," I said to everyone as they left. My voice was flat. The words just spilled out, like coins from a change-making machine, as though they were the exact words required in this situation. But I felt emotionally wrecked and my emotions were jumbled and mismatched to my words.

The nurses had kindly let us overextend visiting privileges; we'd had too many people in and had stayed beyond normal visiting hours. But they eventually started to usher us out gently. I went into Jackie's cubicle for one last visit alone. "I love you, my darling. I will always love you. I want you to know how very much you mean to me. And know that God loves you and will always be with you. I will be back tomorrow," I told her, as I held her hand and kissed her forehead.

But I knew that I might very well not return tomorrow. The phone might ring in the middle of the night. We might never see her alive again. I backed out of her doorway slowly. I wanted nothing more than to stay with her, to hold her hand through the night, to hold on to her so death wouldn't take her away. But a nurse touched my arm and said, "Good-night, Mr. Cole. Go home and get some rest. We'll take good care of her here."

We returned home to wait. Ron Bond had come to the hospital and came home with us to stay through the night.

Back at the house, he sat with us. It reminded him of a wake. He watched me wander from room to room, occasionally making a phone call or answering the phone. Each time it rang, everyone stiffened with the thought that the hospital was calling with final news. But the hospital never called. Near midnight I went up to the loft to be with the children. They were watching "Saturday Night Live." Tom Hanks was the host. No one laughed.

I dreaded going into our bedroom. Yet I was utterly exhausted, physically and emotionally. I first tried to sleep on the sleigh bed. I couldn't. Christina had fallen asleep on the loft floor, so I tried to sleep in her room. I couldn't. About 4:00 A.M., I finally went to our bedroom and lay down on the still-unmade bed where Jackie and I had slept the night before, where she had waited for the ambulance as blood vessels exploded in her head. I tried to imagine what happened that morning. But I couldn't visualize it. Instead my mind raced with memories of a healthy, live Jackie in action, racing into the surf each summer, sweating through the daily aerobic workouts, running up the stairs to the loft. The home movie in my mind reeled off visions of her stirring a steaming pot of homemade soup to cure all our winter colds, bending over the children when they were younger and helping them with their spelling homework. I recalled her encouragement when my doctoral work seemed overwhelming. I could see her typing my thesis and beaming with pride when I was finally awarded my degree. I thought of all the walks we'd taken, hand in hand, when we'd talk about her "spiritual potential," as I called it. I could almost feel her smooth hand in mine.

Suddenly I wept openly. Everything about Jackie was absolutely vital to my existence — and it was gone! I was an abandoned child, crying out for comfort. I heard my own voice echoing inside my head, I'm alone . . . I'm helpless . . . I'm heartbroken . . . I'm bereft . . . I'm desperately alone . . . without Jackie. Jackie means the world to me. Please, dear God, bring her back to life. I'll do anything if you'll wake her up and heal her. We have so much still to do.

And that was the most painful thought — that sudden realization that we had no future, no chance to perfect our marriage. I saw how all our bickering had been so trite, so meaningless. But through all that, we'd shared a sense of promise. I was always waiting for the moment when everything would come together — and I was positive it could someday — when the pettiness would fade away and we would reach a perfect love. That dream, that hope was vital to me. Now that dream was evaporating in an Intensive Care Unit, and I was devastated.

Throughout the restless early-morning hours, I simultaneously pleaded with and raged at God. Like an Old Testament patriarch, I was fiercely angry with God for letting this happen to Jackie. If the patriarchs could argue with God, why couldn't I? This was no time for quiet, contemplative prayer. Some people may think that ministers never rant and rave before God, but in times of personal crisis, I act like anyone else. On this night, I couldn't simply toss up my hands and say, "Okay, Lord, this is all in your hands — though deep in my soul I knew it was — so take care of things for us, and I'll see you in the morning."

Long ago, at the beginning of my theological training, I accepted the idea that God is omnipotent. God provides. God is all-powerful. I believe that with all my being. And on this night, my "dark night of the soul," I retreated deep into that basic belief. If God is all-powerful, then why did he do this? Why? Why Jackie? My strongest, purest, most primal reaction was rage at this God I'd always believed to be providential. As I prayed and pleaded, begged and bargained with God — I heard nothing.

"God, why are you silent?" I demanded aloud. For the first time in my life I felt that God was absent. There was no hope. No presence of God. Nothing.

As dawn broke, I was still awake. The clock radio went off at 6:00 A.M., as it did any other day. The first sound I heard was the hymn, "Break Forth, O Beauteous Heavenly Light." For a fraction of a second, I thought, this is a dream. Jackie hasn't had a stroke. I lay in bed, listened to the hymn, and thought of the irony of our situation. It was Easter morning, and Jackie was in a deep coma, her brain flooded with blood from a massive hemorrhage. I prayed intensely for Jackie's resurrection. Oh, dear God, it would be so right for her to wake up on Easter. It would be a perfect way to redeem this terrible tragedy.

THE phone began ringing early as friends heard the news from other friends and called to offer prayers and condolences. Each caller expressed disbelief: "Why Jackie? How could this have happened to her of all people, only forty-three years old and in such perfect health?" I had no words to console them or to counter their incredulity. I simply thanked them for their concern and prayers and asked them to keep Jackie in their prayers.

A number of my colleagues called to tell me that they and their congregations would be praying for Jackie at Easter services that morning. Many of them used the same words that I had so often used to console others whose loved ones were dying. I knew the words, knew how and when to say them, but I never expected them to fall on my own ears.

"We're praying for Jackie, the children and you, Harry. None of us understands why this has happened, but we believe in God's love and goodness. He will give you the grace and strength you need in this time of such great grief. But we know that life is eternal, and you have the assurance that Jackie will be with God." I appreciated my colleagues' consolation and prayers, but the role reversal jarred me. I'd never been "ministered to" this way before. I wasn't used to feeling helpless or dependent, and I certainly wasn't accustomed to the gravity of a situation like this one.

The house began to fill up by midday, as relatives and friends came to wait with us on this death vigil. Everyone spoke of Jackie in the past tense — "She was so wonderful . . ." "She was such a true friend . . ." "She was so creative" — it was as though she had already left this world. And in my mind, she was beginning to leave me, even though I knew she was hanging on by means of a respirator, drugs, IV fluids.

I shuttled back and forth between the house and the hospital several times. When I was at the hospital, I felt useless, almost in the way, as nurses surrounded Jackie, adjusting tubes and IV lines, watching monitors, checking neurologic signs by looking into her eyes. But as soon as I'd return home to be with the children or to report to family and friends, I'd feel cut off from Jackie and want to hurry back. At least the hospital is only three minutes away, I thought, grateful for even this small blessing.

EARLIER in the week, Jackie and Bonnie Hoback had planned Easter dinner at our house. They had shopped and prepared several dishes. The refrigerator was jammed. My mother, Bonnie and Paul, Jackie, the children and I were to sit around the dining room table for one of those lavish holiday meals that Jackie loved to create with all the silver, crystal, and linen. But after she visited Jackie with me early that Easter morning, Bonnie hurriedly rearranged the plans. Instead of setting the table for a joyous dinner, she set out a buffet for the mourners who came and went. As I watched her keep busy by shuttling platters and bowls back and forth from the kitchen to the dining room, I noticed tears sliding down her cheeks.

Jackie always called Bonnie "my city mom." Bonnie and Paul

had no children, and they had treated me as a son ever since I graduated from seminary and rented their third-floor apartment. When I first introduced Jackie to them a dozen years ago, they embraced her as a daughter.

"Oh, dear God, why couldn't it have been me instead of Jackie," Bonnie cried. "I've had a long, rich life, but Jackie still had so much ahead of her, so much love and talent to give. Just before I came over here, I was gazing at the charcoal sketch of Paul that Jackie did a few years ago. I just stared and stared at it, remembering how she coaxed him into sitting still long enough to finish it — it's the best picture of him, too. She really captured him. And I thought about how we'd always have Jackie with us, in our memories and through that picture . . ." Bonnie's voice caught. I hugged her as she wept against my shirt.

Julie came by the house before going to the hospital. As she hugged Christina and the boys, she noticed a framed cross-stitch on the wall at the top of the stairs. Years ago their aunt Thelma had embroidered the child's prayer "Now I Lay Me Down To Sleep" and framed it for Jackie and Julie. When they were very young, it hung over the double bed that they shared.

Julie remembered how much that embroidered prayer had meant to Jackie. She had asked for it a few years ago when their father was selling the house and dividing up household things after their mother's death. Julie removed the cross-stitch from our wall and told me she wanted to take it to Jackie. When she walked into Jackie's cubicle, she propped the frame against the wall.

"Jackie, I've brought you Aunt Thelma's cross-stitch, 'Now I lay me down to sleep. I pray the Lord my soul to keep. If I should die before I wake, I pray the Lord my soul to take.' "

Julie kissed Jackie's cheek and left, thinking she would never see her sister again. But despite the piercing pain she felt and saw on the faces of Christina and the boys, Julie knew that Jackie would take some comfort from the innocent child's prayer. And if Jackie died before she awoke, the Lord would surely take her soul.

BY Easter Sunday evening, the anger I'd expressed to God the night before had vanished. I began to think that perhaps God

wouldn't bring her back on Easter, but at least he hadn't completely taken her away, either. Jackie was still with us.

Though I still didn't comprehend why this had happened to
Jackie, and to us as a family, I was moving away from the spiritual
abyss of the previous night toward an attempt to resolve this crisis.
I can't save her medically, but I can try to enlist God's presence, I
thought, so I asked several of my closest friends in the Presbyterian
ministry and Ron's Episcopal priest, Noreen Kraley, to pray with
me. Ron and Noreen met me in the tiny chapel on the first floor of
Maryland General on Easter Sunday evening. We knelt, and Noreen led our prayers:

> "O gracious God, on this day when you have shown us
> your love and salvation by your son Jesus Christ's Resurrec-
> tion, have mercy on Jackie, on Harry, and on their children.
> Strengthen them with your gracious assurance of your pres-
> ence in their lives. Reassure them of your love in this, their
> darkest hour. Bless them with your mercy and peace. Let
> them know that you redeem suffering and loss and that you
> give us eternal life, in Jesus' name. Amen."

Four

Intensive Care

Nurses Nancy Hart and Brenda Flentje were on duty in the Intensive Care Unit when Jackie was brought up from the ER. They worked with Jackie continuously, monitoring her vital signs and trying to stabilize them, putting a hypothermia blanket under her to lower her temperature. Nancy even removed Jackie's nail polish to keep an eye on her circulation.

On admission to Maryland General, Jackie's temperature was 103, her pulse was 86 and regular, and her blood pressure was not particularly high, 160/90. But throughout the first afternoon, her heart rate kept dropping down to the twenties and thirties. When they went off duty at 7:00 P.M., Brenda and Nancy expected to find Jackie's bed vacant the next morning.

Yet Jackie survived the night. And she survived Easter Sunday. By Monday morning, I had given up hope of an Easter resurrection, but I began to think that there might be a better outlook than the doctors originally painted. The critical forty-eight-hour period had passed. Jackie's vital signs were somewhat more stable. Perhaps she will survive this stroke, I dared to think. Now I waited, prayed, and hoped. I stayed by her side hour after hour those first days, looking and praying for rays of hope. I squeezed her hands, tickled her feet (and felt almost foolish doing so), stroked her arms, and talked aloud to her, all in the fervent hope that some sensation would arouse a response.

Occasionally she moved a leg or an arm. Each time visitors saw such a sign, they ran out to the nursing station to announce the news bulletin. But each time, Brenda or Nancy or another nurse would explain that these weren't deliberate actions. Jackie wasn't controlling those motions. If she stiffened an arm or leg, for instance, a nurse would patiently point out, that was called "posturing," an involuntary motion that is a sign of a deep coma.

Julie had formerly worked as a vocational rehabilitation counselor and knew more about strokes' effects than other members of our family. Julie's way of trying to cope with her sister's condition was to query doctors and nurses. She didn't like to bother them, but when she did have a question about Jackie's treatment or status, she politely prefaced it with, "I guess I'm an information person, but could you please tell me . . ." If she could get a handle on some concrete information, Julie felt, she might be able to understand what was happening, what to look for, some clue as to what might happen next. So Julie posed questions like, "Has the swelling in her brain reached its peak? When will it subside?" But she found the doctors reluctant to give definite answers. Perhaps they don't really know, or don't want to be pinned down to a specific prediction, she thought.

Julie also read Jackie's medical chart whenever she visited. When Julie first read "decerebrate posturing" on the chart, a shudder of fear ran through her. Julie knew that decerebrate posturing was a sign of one of the deepest, worst kinds of coma. When someone suffers a hemorrhage in the brain, one measure of the severity of damage is the person's level of consciousness. Sometimes a patient may be alert and awake, perhaps have a headache or be nauseated, may not be able to move an arm or leg, but will still be able to interact with people. Those are the "better" kinds of stroke.

Others who sustain a hemorrhage in the brain may seem to sleep in what is called a "lethargic" state. If no one talks to the patient, he or she may drift off but would wake up if spoken to or shaken. Still others are in a "stuporous" state of consciousness. They aren't able to talk, but if a doctor attempts to determine their level of consciousness by giving some painful stimulation, such as pinching a shoulder muscle or putting pressure on the forehead, they will fend the doctor away with an arm motion.

And then there is coma, the state of being unable to respond purposely to stimuli. If a doctor pinches a patient in a coma, the patient is unable to make a purposeful response such as pushing him or her away. This was Jackie's state, but comas can range from "shallow," in which a patient may yawn or have some spontaneous facial movements, to brain-dead. Various signs indicate the depth of a coma. And that is why those words "decerebrate posturing" scared Julie. She remembered her training: the brain consists of cerebral hemispheres with which humans think. Then there is the brainstem, which controls vegetative functions — waking and sleeping, the heart's beating. If a hemorrhage causes damage to the brainstem, the patient not only is comatose but also has abnormal involuntary movements — posturing — in response to pain. If a patient stiffens and extends the arms when pinched, that is decerebrate posturing and that indicates damage to the top half of the brainstem, where consciousness is controlled. Decerebrate posturing signals nearly the worst kind of coma. The only state worse would be no posturing at all. If Jackie showed no posturing, it would mean that her whole brainstem was out — she would be brain-dead.

WHENEVER new patients are brought into the ICU, nurses focus primarily on their medical problem: this one is a "bleed," that one is "chest pains." But from the beginning, the nurses seemed drawn by a particular poignancy to Jackie. She was more to them than a "big bleed." Forty-three-year-old wives and mothers aren't supposed to be big bleeds. Like the nurses themselves, Jackie was at the peak of her life, with a family who loved and depended upon her, a future to fill. From the first day Jackie entered the ICU, the nurses related to her as if she was more than just a medical diagnosis. As I watched them busily caring for her, collecting her blood samples and specimens, doing neuro-checks for gag reflexes, checking her pupils, making sure her airway was clear, suctioning secretions building up in her endotracheal tube, bathing her, turning her, toileting her, adjusting her feedings, IV tubes, medications, they often talked to me — and directly to Jackie herself — about how aware they were that she had a loving family and friends. "You have so much still to live for, Jackie," more than one of them said.

And the kids! They broke the nurses' hearts. Nancy Hart had first seen Thomas and Christina outside the ER that Saturday morning when she went downstairs to the soda machine. Earlier Nancy had heard a code called over the public address system: "ERT-ER," the code calling the emergency resuscitation team to the emergency room. But Nancy knew no more at that point. She just thought, "Who are those poor, distraught, weeping children?" But after Jackie had been brought to the ICU that afternoon, Nancy realized the connection. Her first vision of Thomas and Christina stayed with her throughout the afternoon as she cared for Jackie. This isn't supposed to happen to a young mother, Nancy thought. Those kids need her; just on the sensitive edge of adulthood, what'll they do without her?

BY Monday, from all over the country, old friends whom I hadn't seen since our seminary days were phoning me, offering their prayers and those of their churches, and saying they'd call other seminary friends to ask for even more prayers for Jackie. I took great solace in this.

"I feel so helpless, Harry. I wish there were something we could do to help you and your family," Naomi Palmer, one of my parishioners, said when she appeared at the door with a huge platter wrapped in foil. "You have our prayers, of course, and we'll be bringing by more food so you and the children won't have to worry about shopping and cooking. I know this isn't much, but at least it's a little something we can do. You and Jackie are so dear to us, you know."

I thanked her and told her how much we appreciated her prayers and her offerings of food. Over the coming days, the members of our church brought us so much food that the refrigerator was packed, and Bonnie had to store the overload at her house.

While it seemed that all of Jackie's friends in and around Baltimore had called to offer prayers and condolences, there was one person who didn't know what had befallen Jackie. I had to reach her. Maureen Ricker, Jackie's best friend, was a tour director on a cruise ship somewhere in the Pacific. I picked up the phone and asked the operator how to contact Maureen's ship.

Maureen had never received a shore-to-ship call before, she later told me. When she got the message to go to the radio room, her alarm antenna went up immediately. It was like receiving a call in the middle of the night back home, and she thought something must have happened to her family.

"You'd better sit down, Maureen," I began. "Something dreadful has happened to Jackie."

"Jackie? What in the world . . ."

When I explained that Jackie had suffered a massive stroke and wasn't expected to live, Maureen was stunned into silence. I thought for a moment that the phone connection had been broken.

After several seconds, she said, "I can't believe this, Harry. Not Jackie . . . Look, I'll be in Los Angeles tomorrow, and I'll come straight home."

"Good. Listen, Maureen, I can't hear you very well. This is a poor connection, but," I nearly shouted, "you'd better hurry. There isn't much time, I'm afraid . . ."

Maureen called an airline as soon as her ship docked and reserved a seat on the next plane to Baltimore. On the flight east, Maureen tried to gauge the urgency she'd heard in my voice. Strokes can range from mild to deadly, she knew; just how bad could Jackie's be? She wished she'd had the presence of mind to press me for more details, but the ship-to-shore connection was so faint, anyway, she told herself. Yet, as fearful as she was of the unknown facts about Jackie's condition, Maureen wouldn't allow herself to think that Jackie might not be alive when she landed. "Jackie's always there," Maureen kept repeating to herself. "Jackie has always been there for me, for Harry, for the kids. She's a rock, the one you could always depend on for support." Maureen remembered how Jackie had held her hand through the breakup of Maureen's marriage and divorce. She could hear Jackie's voice reassuring her that "this, too, shall pass. You'll get on with your life. It will get better." And it did, largely because Jackie's friendship helped sustain her and cheer her at the darkest moments.

Other passengers on the long flight east were watching a movie, but Maureen couldn't look at it. Her mind was churning with memories of Jackie. She clearly saw Jackie the first day they met. Maureen was working for the Maryland Department of Education, with Miss Rice in the teacher certification division, when Jackie came in for a job interview. Eleanor Rice had risen higher in the state education hierarchy than most women of her generation. She was secure enough about herself to wear her 1940s hairdo with a hairnet. In strode Jackie with stylish, frosted hair. Maureen thought that the two women couldn't have contrasted more sharply — the older, unmarried woman whose career and church work filled her life and the young, divorced mother, raising four children alone, at the beginning of her career.

Miss Rice asked Maureen to sit in on Jackie's interview and later asked Maureen what she thought of Jackie.

"Her credentials on paper are more than acceptable," Miss Rice said. "Do you think she can handle the job and not let her family responsibilities interfere? For example, if her children get sick, will she get behind in her work?"

"No, I don't think so. She seems a very determined, motivated person," Maureen said.

"She struck me as confident and capable, too," Miss Rice said. "I think we should give her an opportunity." Maureen saw a parallel in Miss Rice's hiring Jackie: the older woman had overcome workplace bias against women in her day, and now, in the late sixties, when it was rare for a woman to support herself and four children single-handedly, Miss Rice wanted to give Jackie a chance. And Maureen was rooting for Jackie from the sidelines.

Miss Rice had turned out to be correct, Maureen remembered. Jackie mastered the complex state regulations so quickly that Maureen wondered if she had a photographic mind. Whenever a school administrator brought a thorny certification problem to Jackie, she found the most workable solution.

"Jackie's not your usual bureaucrat," someone in the office once remarked. "She deals with people, not paper." No other bureaucrat Maureen had ever worked with could cut through red tape as efficiently and with such good humor as Jackie. Her caring about others drew fellow workers to Jackie when they had personal problems, too. At least once a week someone would be huddled at Jackie's desk to confide an anxiety about a difficult child or a marital problem. Jackie was known throughout the office as a good listener and a no-nonsense friend who gave straight, unvarnished advice. Her own life's experiences have forged her into becoming empathic and honest at the same time,

Maureen thought; she can really feel for people because she's been there herself.

WHEN Maureen walked into the ICU on Tuesday night, the monitors and machines pulled her eyes almost magnetically toward them so she couldn't focus on anything else. Her ears rang with their hums and whooshes and beeps. Perhaps they were pulling her senses away from Jackie, she wondered, because the sight of her friend, hooked up to all this machinery, was just too painful to witness. For a brief moment, she squeezed her eyes closed and tried to shut everything out: This is a dream, she told herself. This is a bad dream, and we'll all wake up. Jackie will wake up. All this machinery will fall silent and vanish. And we'll all be back at Harry and Jackie's house, laughing as I tell them about the silly tourists on my last tour.

But Maureen opened her eyes again, looked directly at Jackie, and wept. It was no dream.

Over the years, Maureen and Jackie had shared secrets, dreams, laughs, and tears. Theirs was a deep, honest friendship of two women whose many dissimilarities complemented each other. Where Jackie's style was sometimes flamboyant, Maureen's was more reserved. Where Jackie gave off bursts of bustling energy; Maureen was evenly paced — her walk was slower, her voice more level. But they shared many traits, too, and one was a tenacious will not to give up.

When Maureen went home from the hospital Tuesday night, she was still dazed. She continued to hear the noises of the life-sustaining equipment long after she left the ICU. But when she returned the next morning, Maureen had awakened from the shock of seeing her stricken friend hooked to monitors and tubes.

"Good morning, Jackie! It's time for perfume-of-the-day!" Maureen announced brightly, as if Jackie would hear her, sit up in bed, and applaud.

"Today it's your favorite from Germany — 4711." Maureen opened the turquoise-and-gold bottle and dabbed some on Jackie's arm a few inches from the tape that held an IV tube in place. She rubbed a few more drops on Jackie's neck.

"Now all the nurses will be jealous, and the handsome young

residents and interns will be turned on," Maureen continued. "Yes, I brought Harry some of the liqueurs he likes, and I brought you more perfume, the way I always do when I come home from a cruise. But you'll have to wait till tomorrow for another fragrance. Maybe we'll have L'Air du Temps day tomorrow."

Maureen didn't say it aloud, but her inner voice added, And maybe if you smell enough of this perfume, you'll come out of this damn coma!

A friend of Maureen's on the ship had told her about a neighbor who had a stroke. The friend had read the newspaper aloud to the neighbor every day she was in the hospital. When the neighbor recovered, she remembered hearing her friend read the paper. So Maureen swung into action. She would bombard Jackie with talk, music, scents, touch — anything that might evoke some response. She told me to bring down Jackie's favorite books — we would read aloud to Jackie. She asked her brother to get a tape recorder. I brought meditation tapes to Jackie's cubicle, and Maureen brought tapes that she thought might jolt Jackie — Julio Iglesias, Willie Nelson, love ballads that Jackie and Maureen used to play on the car tape deck when they drove to education conferences.

"I admit I'm kind of surprised at that choice of music, Maureen. I guess it's just not my taste," I said.

"That's okay. It might strike some chord in her," Maureen told me. "It might hit something inside her, and maybe she'll move!"

Every day Maureen visited Jackie and talked about significant memories that they shared. For example, Maureen would launch into a monologue about a conference they'd attended:

"Remember that workshop you led, Jackie? Remember how more people came to your workshop than any other? And when it was over, they filled out their evaluation forms with the most favorable comments possible — you were almost embarrassed about being more popular than the other presenters. And remember how we kidded you that the higher-ups would think you'd packed your workshop with all your friends?"

SUDDENLY Maureen jumped. Alarms rang. Something's wrong, the machines screeched. Nurses came in from the nursing station. To Maureen, and to every visitor who first heard these alarms, they signaled an emergency. But to the nurses, they were routine. An alarm rang if an IV bottle needed refilling. If someone accidentally brushed against the side of Jackie's bed, a cable to the cardiac monitor or a tube to the ventilator might become jarred and a bell would go off, startling everyone in the room except Jackie. But Jackie just lay there, her chest rising and falling to the rhythm of the ventilator, as if nothing had happened.

ON the same day Maureen arrived, charge nurse Vanessa Ajayi returned to the ICU after a maternity leave. Just before taking her leave in January, Vanessa had cared for a twenty-nine-year-old mother who died after going into respiratory, and then cardiac, arrest soon after giving birth. Vanessa was only two years older than that young mother.

Vanessa gave birth to a son in February, and when she returned to work on April 1, she found Jackie dying in ICU. Vanessa was shocked. It seemed as though her son's birth would be framed by the deaths of two young mothers. She couldn't help but think, It could be me.

Vanessa had been a nurse for eleven years and had seen many comatose patients, but only four or five as young as Jackie. She's so pitiful, Vanessa thought as she read Jackie's chart and learned how poor her prognosis was. She had survived the first critical period. Perhaps it was safe to say she had survived the stroke itself, but nobody really expected her to live through the week.

For Vanessa Ajayi, taking care of Jackie was not just another nursing challenge. Vanessa saw Jackie as a young woman who could do nothing for herself but who was nonetheless a real person. Even though she had never known that real person in a conscious state, Vanessa talked to Jackie as if they'd been friends for years, often sharing her thoughts aloud: "The doctors aren't getting any hope, but they're medicine people, Jackie. They look at medical signs and symptoms. We look at people signs and symptoms. That's the difference between doctors and nurses. I believe the last say isn't the doctor's or nurse's anyway, Jackie. If the Lord wants you to stay, he has a reason."

Near the end of the week, some of the nurses began to think that there might be some hope for Jackie. Her vital signs were more stable — she was still hanging on! As they bathed and turned her, they were aware that she had taken good care of herself. She was fit, trim, and had a strong heart. Every day, hour after hour, as I stood by, watching them care for her, I heard the nurses talking aloud to Jackie, telling her what they were doing: "I've got to turn you now, Jackie, or else you'll get godawful bedsores . . ." Even though she was in a deep coma, she might be able to hear them, and any stimulation was better than nothing.

By the end of the first week in ICU, Jackie seemed to have settled into a continuous sleeplike coma. She continued to posture, especially when nurses turned her, but I understood that these were involuntary movements, and they gave me no hope.

Jackie's tiny cubicle was filling up with cards, needlepoint, even a stuffed rabbit that Andrew, Julie's son and Jackie's godchild, brought on Easter. Visitors poured into the ICU, but their presence began to cause some conflict. The nurses recognized that Jackie had many sources of support from family and friends, but they still had to care for her at least thirty minutes of every hour or two. The ICU staff liberally bent the visiting-hours rules for us, but, though they didn't like to do so, they occasionally had to shoo visitors out so they could attend to Jackie.

The children also urged me to curb the number of visitors for Jackie's sake.

"Mom wouldn't want everybody walking in here and seeing her like this," Thomas said.

"Only family and close friends should be allowed," Christina added. They knew how Jackie felt about herself. The last thing she would want, the kids argued, would be to be seen without makeup and nail polish, with her hair limp, lying motionless like this, by people from her office or by my minister friends.

But I believed in numbers, in community. There is a power in community, in everyone's sharing and giving, that to me symbolized strength and safety. The more people who cared, and who came to show that they cared about Jackie, the safer she would be, the safer we would all be, I believed. Seeing people come to visit Jackie made me feel very supported, and I needed that.

The kids prevailed, though, when they convinced me of what Jackie herself would want. "Everybody else can still pull for her, pray for her, without marching into the ICU," John said. So I gave the head nurse a short list of visitors who could be admitted. Ron made the list as "close family friend." And he indeed was. Ronnie came to see Jackie every day.

Jackie's dear office friends Carol Parham and Adolphus Spain visited often, carrying word of Jackie's condition back to the office and bringing cards and little gifts back to her ICU cubicle. The impact of Jackie's stroke on her circle of friends was enormous. The initial shock and disbelief that this could happen to Jackie — of all people — gave way to tears and prayers and silent stares at her empty desk. A Bible study group of department employees, many of whom had only passing acquaintance with Jackie, included her in their prayers and asked their individual congregations to pray for her.

Whenever Adolphus returned to the office after a hospital visit, he was besieged with, "How's Jackie?" "Any change with Jackie?" He was particularly struck one afternoon when an office janitor approached him.

"How's Mrs. Cole?" Sampson asked with tears in his eyes. "I do miss her. She always had a big smile and hello, and she was always asking how my family was doing. Such a shame this had to happen to Mrs. Cole." Adolphus had no good news to report, but he thought, my God, I never realized how many lives she's touched.

SEVERAL days after the stroke, Ron urged me to seek another opinion about Jackie's condition. To Ron, and to many Baltimoreans, Maryland General was just another hospital, but Johns Hopkins was the city's preeminent medical institution, the one that put Baltimore on the medical world map.

"My God, Harry, Dr. Pula is younger than we are!" Ron said after first meeting him. "He may be head of neurology, and he may be terrific, but why don't you call in someone from Hopkins to look at Jackie?"

"Well, I think Dr. Pula's very good. And I've also talked to other doctors on the staff, the emergency room doctors as well as Sid Venable. They're all saying the same awful things. My God, I've seen her CAT scan picture — the inside of her head is totally white, like overexposed film, all white from the blood that has filled her head! It seems to me that all the evidence is self-authenticating. And everyone here seems to be doing everything medically possible to keep her alive. But, if you want me to look for a Hopkins opinion, I suppose it can't hurt."

So I called Dr. Howard Moses, an older, well-known neurologist at Hopkins, who had diagnosed and treated my father for Alzheimer's disease. While Dr. Moses examined Jackie on the Wednesday following her stroke, Ron and I waited in the ICU waiting room, a square space populated by three plastic plants and tan-and-brown vinyl chairs pushed against each wall. Pushed to the walls, I imagined, to leave plenty of open space in the middle of the room for visitors to pace. Ron and I sat and stared at the tan floor tiles patterned to look like marble. Everything in this room — fake marble, fake plants — is as unreal, I thought, as my life right now.

Anyone passing by might have mistaken Ron and me for a couple of expectant fathers because the sign over the door said Fathers' Waiting Room as well as ICU Waiting Room. An unintended irony, no doubt, by a planner who designed this shared waiting room halfway between the maternity wing and the ICU wing, between birth and death.

When Dr. Moses finished examining Jackie, he told me, "I'm leaving a few suggestions for Pula." He wrote up a report for Dr. Pula, concluding, "Cannot improve upon your formulation and management. Prognosis poor. But worth trying. Good luck." He had concurred with Dr. Pula that an angiogram was not needed but another CAT scan should be done, and he suggested reducing the Decadion, a steroidal drug given to reduce the pressure, caused by the stroke, in Jackie's head. I was neither encouraged nor discouraged by Dr. Moses's visit, but Ron was reassured, now that a "Hopkins man" had seen Jackie.

A few evenings after her stroke, Ron and David Ash, another close friend, were leaning against our kitchen counter and talking with me about some "realities" that I'd have to face soon. They asked me if my insurance was covering Jackie's hospitalization costs. I hadn't looked up the details — I hadn't even considered it because I was solely focused on whether Jackie would live another day — but I told David and Ron that I knew that Jackie's state employees' medical coverage was maximum. That was a relief, David mentioned, because a day in an ICU unit could cost $1,000 to $2,000, depending on various machines, treatments, and consultations.

But their questions did remind me that I had an immediate financial problem. A big tuition bill of Christina's was due, and we had planned to draw on Jackie's state employees' credit union for it. Only Jackie had access to the credit union, though. How could I pay the tuition?

Jackie and I had never obtained a power of attorney for each other. We'd never even written our wills. And certainly the idea of a living will, setting forth our wishes about artificial life support measures in situations like Jackie's, had never seriously crossed our minds. Even at the time of Jackie's mother's illness and death, we barely gave it a moment's notice. After all, we were far from old age, infirmity, and death, we thought. We lived our lives in the busy present. Details like writing wills weren't a priority, but we'd get around to those things eventually. We had plenty of time . . .

David, an attorney, called another lawyer friend more expert in this area who said power of attorney wouldn't apply because Jackie was comatose and unable to grant it, but he suggested that I obtain legal guardianship of Jackie's property in order to carry out her fiscal business. David told me not to worry; he would begin the process to obtain guardianship the very next day.

 Five

Guardianship

By the end of the first week of Jackie's coma, I was totally distraught. And confused. A stroke as massive as Jackie's was supposed to kill her, yet she survived. Still, there was no sign of improvement in her condition, either. What did this mean? I asked doctors and nurses, who couldn't give me specific answers. Everything was still wait-and-see. What did this portend? I lay in bed, night after sleepless night, asking God, "What's going on here? Please, Lord, make yourself known. And please bring Jackie back to us."

Christina had wrapped herself in Jackie's white bathrobe Easter Sunday and Monday and walked around the house in a stupor. She said hardly a word. On Tuesday she abruptly announced, "I'm going back to Philadelphia today. I'm not doing any good here and I'm missing classes. I think Mom would want me to go back to college and keep going."

I wanted Christina to stay with us, but she seemed to need to get away in order to cope. Without Jackie to hold us together, I feared, we were splintering apart. John retreated to the loft, where he lay silent for hours in his hammock and listened to music. Stephen grieved with Beth at their house, but we saw them at the hospital each evening. Thomas stayed home on an extended Easter break, but he needed to return to his college work, too. At the end of the week, when I took him to the railroad station, we embraced and cried silently.

"I desperately don't want you to leave," I told him. "But I know you need to get back to school. I'll call you if anything changes, and you call us whenever you need to talk. It would be especially good if you could talk often with John and Christina."

"I will, Dad," he promised, and I was instantly reminded of him as a fourteen-year-old, promising to look after his younger brother and sister when Jackie and I would go out for the evening. Thomas will always fill the big brother's shoes, I thought sadly.

As he looked back at me from the railway platform and waved slowly, Thomas's face was a portrait of pure anguish. If only I could do something to wash away his pain . . .

I MET with Dr. Pula nearly every afternoon in the small room off the ICU. We were almost immediately on a first-name basis. He patiently answered my many questions in detail. When I asked about Jackie's coma, he explained that patients like Jackie are likely to be in a continuous sleeplike coma for a few weeks, usually not more than a month. Then, if the patient has survived other complications, her condition would take on what appears to be sleep-wake cycles. A patient might open her eyes or blink or yawn, but she's really not awake or focusing or responsive. In fact, this continuous sleep-wake condition is usually called a "vegetative state." Life can go on in this vegetative state because the brain still activates the autonomic nervous system to carry on the mechanical functions like heart pumping and waste elimination.

"Complications, you said? Just what complications might arise?" I asked. That question opened the floodgates. Dr. Pula explained that a comatose stroke patient lying in bed constantly, sustained by various technological means such as the respirator, can develop numerous complications. For instance, pneumonia is not unusual in people who have been on a respirator for a period of time. Anytime a line is inserted into the body, an infection can set in. A urinary tract infection could develop from the catheter, for example. When infections develop, they can then spread to the lungs or bloodstream; other complications could be skin ulcerations or blood clots developing in legs. . . . I wished I hadn't asked. I didn't want to hear any more.

By the second week of Jackie's coma, she had followed the predicted pattern: staph pneumonia attacked one lung and soon spread to the other. Dr. Pula told me that this was one of the complications of intubating a patient. Jackie had been intubated immediately upon entering the hospital because she needed to be hyperventilated mechanically, to have the ventilator breathe rapidly for her in order to help her respond to the massive hemorrhage that was damaging her brain.

In intubating a patient, a tube is run from the ventilator through the mouth, down the trachea, and into the lungs. A stroke patient like Jackie often has difficulty swallowing. Instead of properly swallowing secretions into the esophagus, she would aspirate them into her trachea and then into her lungs. Normally, when a secretion goes to the wrong place — down the wrong pipe — people cough, and the lining of the trachea helps move the secretions back up. But that doesn't happen if there is a tube down the trachea. The result is that secretions, and bacteria in them, get into the lungs, and pneumonia often results. By April 10, twelve days after her stroke, Jackie had pneumonia in both lungs.

Dr. Pula told me that although the pneumonia would be treated with antibiotics, the tube still shouldn't be left in for a long period because other complications could result. Vocal cords could be damaged, and the trachea itself could soften. If a patient survives the coma and the tube is removed, the patient may not be able to speak correctly, and the trachea may no longer be competent.

That seemed academic to me — I had no reason to expect that Jackie would survive the coma. But I was devastated by the news of her pneumonia. What else could possibly go wrong!

Dr. Pula suggested that the tube could be removed and a tracheostomy could be done. An incision would be made directly into the trachea at the base of the neck, beneath the vocal cords. A shorter tube would be placed through this hole to connect the respirator to her lungs. Jackie's blood pressure and pulse had not been very stable as a result of the hemorrhage's damage to her brainstem. But by the end of the second week of her coma, Dr. Pula and other doctors thought she was stabilized enough to consider a tracheostomy the following week.

MAUREEN remembered the story of Patricia Neal, the actress who had suffered a near-fatal stroke caused by an aneurysm, a weak spot in an artery wall that burst in her head. Ms. Neal's stroke occurred in 1965, a year after she won an Oscar for her role in *Hud* with Paul Newman. She overcame astounding odds to regain her mobility and her speech, and she went on to act professionally again. Maureen recalled that a book had been written about Ms. Neal and her husband, the writer Roald Dahl. Maureen was determined to find the book. After calling almost every library and bookshop in Baltimore, Maureen finally located a copy in Dundalk, the gritty, industrial neighborhood in southeast Baltimore. She brought "Pat and Roald," by Barry Farrell (Random House, 1969), to the hospital and read parts aloud to Jackie and me. If Patricia Neal could make such a triumphant recovery, Maureen reasoned, so could Jackie.

"But that's a different situation," I told her after I read the book myself. "Patricia Neal didn't have the same kind of massive cerebral hemorrhage that Jackie did. Her aneurysm didn't occur in the same place as Jackie's hemorrhage. Her doctors were able to operate immediately to remove blood clots and to close the aneurysm, and she came out of her coma in a little over a week."

I didn't want to crush Maureen's hopes completely, but I wasn't about to grab at such comeback stories. Not in light of what all the doctors were saying about the seriousness of Jackie's condition. I wasn't going to inflate hopes only to have them cruelly dashed.

Maureen spent hours with Jackie, talking to her, being nearby, telling her what a fighter she was. "What we see is such a frail vision," Maureen told me during one late afternoon visit, "but underneath that, I believe, Jackie is still the fighter she's always been. She has a strong will, always has. There are times when Jackie looks to me like she's fighting to breathe almost in spite of that ventilator that's breathing for her."

The same day that pneumonia was discovered in Jackie's lung, Maureen had to leave Baltimore to return to her ship. Maureen's vigil had helped me enormously. She'd been as supportive as possible in an impossible situation. But after ten days at Jackie's side, Maureen reluctantly realized that she needed to return to her job. The ship was still in port at Los Angeles, and Maureen could fly back before it embarked on the next cruise to Mexico. She and I talked about her predicament. What good was she doing here now? she wondered. For all her determination to jolt Jackie back to consciousness with talk, music, and perfume-of-the-day,

Maureen's spirits began to sag. In just ten days, she had watched Jackie's medical condition deteriorate and she saw no improvement in her neurological state.

"This is one of the hardest decisions of my life, Harry. But maybe I'd better go now and come back later, when I might be needed more," she told me as we were having a drink and waiting for sandwiches at a bar across from the hospital on Antique Row.

"I don't know, Maureen. I wish you could stay. I know Jackie would want you here. I don't know how much your talking to her is getting through. I don't know what might be helping and what is just going down a deep, dark drain. But I'll try to keep up your share of the talking and reading and playing music. Of course you have to get on with your life. I'm selfish in wanting you to stay on, but having you here has been a great support for me and the children. Maybe having Jackie's best friend here is like having a part of Jackie here, too."

In my desolation over losing Jackie, Maureen provided a ballast for me.

"But if you need to go, I understand. And I know what you mean about being needed more later. Yes, the children will certainly need you if . . . when, they lose their mother. They're really close to you, I know. They'll need all the support they can get. I know I can't give them everything they need now. I understand how they're feeling, but it makes me so upset when they turn away from me. I try to talk with them about it, but they're so lost without Jackie. I'm trying but I know I can't be both parents for them. I want at least to comfort them, but they — Christina and John especially — run away or fade into their own silent world. I feel locked out." My eyes teared.

"I know, Harry. I know. But you have to remember that Jackie has been their whole life. She's been the dominant force in their lives since they were born. And now she's being stolen from them. Nobody, not even you, can give them everything they need right now. It will take a long time. They'd be starting to move away, to separate from you and Jackie at this point in their lives anyway. It's just that it should have been gradual, and this has been so sudden, so cruel," Maureen said.

On April 10, I picked Maureen up and drove to the hospital so she could visit Jackie one more time. Her eyes were so flooded with tears that she saw Jackie's lifeless face as a pale blur. Maureen dabbed a drop of Joy on Jackie's neck and kissed her forehead.

"Good-bye, Jackie. I'll be back soon." And Maureen backed out of the room.

I drove her to the airport in silence. The departure area was packed with noisy vacationers bound for a week in the Jamaican sun. Every face wore a smile. Every hand seemed to hold a beach-bag jammed full of sun lotion, straw hats, sunglasses, and pulp novels. Maureen and I stood like refugees on a sorrowful island in this sea of cheery strangers.

When boarding was announced, I hugged Maureen and said, "Thank you, Maureen, thanks so much for being here, for all you've done for Jackie — not just these ten days, but for years. And thank you for helping the children and me, for standing beside us with your love and encouragement."

As she walked away, Maureen turned and flashed the thumbs-up sign.

"She's going to make it," Maureen called out over the crowd noise. I wished I could be so sure. All I felt was a tremendous void.

DURING the first two weeks of Jackie's coma, I spent all my waking hours at the hospital with Jackie or with the children when they were at home. I didn't go to Lochearn at all. The church took care of itself as everyone came together to handle services and church business. The Session, which is the church's board of directors, told me that I was not expected to preach, that I should take care of myself and my family first. The elders took turns leading Sunday morning worship. Several women of the church fine-tuned a schedule of volunteers who would bring us food each day. They even arranged for someone to come in and do housework for us.

On the third Sunday after Jackie's stroke, I drove to Lochearn and walked slowly into the church. Parishioners greeted me with embraces and simple, heartfelt expressions of "I am so sorry." No one asked after Jackie's health; they all knew how poor it was.

I felt a bit disoriented as I headed toward a rear pew rather than the front of the church, but when a silver-haired woman softly asked me if I would sit with her, I gladly joined her. As I sat next to her, I was reminded of sitting in church next to my grandmother as a boy. I again felt the security of knowing I was cared for, not only by her but by the fellowship of the people around me in church. My church was ministering to me, I realized, and I took great comfort in being a part of that fellowship. One of the elders, Sam Poist, preached and led us in pastoral prayer, which was devoted largely to Jackie, the children and me:

" . . . God's love sustains us and relieves suffering. This is a terrible, terrible tragedy, but it is in God's hands. We certainly hope and pray that Jackie will get better and will be returned to the loving arms of her husband. And we know that through God's love, something good, something redemptive will come out of this."

Throughout this ordeal, the members of my church supported me with their prayers, their love, their fellowship — all of which gave me strength and solace without which I don't think I could have survived.

As I had each night for the past two weeks, I entered Jackie's cubicle the evening after Maureen left, drew the curtains, turned out the light, and closed the door. As I pulled a chair up next to Jackie's bed, I held her hands and began to talk to her.

"I wonder whether you can hear me, Jackie? Will you ever be able to acknowledge my words . . . I love you so very, very much, my darling. I want you to know that. I am praying for you. Just about everyone we know is praying that you will recover. Even people you don't know — people in many churches across the country, and even in Scotland — who have heard about what's happened to you. You are in their prayers, too."

But on this particular Friday evening, I felt that I had to add something I hadn't said before. I apologized again and again for not being with Jackie that Saturday morning when she had the stroke. I begged her forgiveness for being angry with her about the credit card. Earlier that day, I had looked at the card, still propped up on my dresser where Jackie had left it. When I'd first seen it there, two weeks ago, I thought I'd won a victory by making her return it. But how hollow a victory that was now! How silly, how petty a fight ours had been.

"I love you more than anything in the world, Jackie. I want you back. I need you. The children need you. Please, please don't leave us. You're kind and you are good," I told her as tears streamed down my cheeks. "You never realized how good, how wonderful, you are. You never understood or believed that, but you are so wonderful, so good."

I held her face against mine and kissed her cheeks and forehead over and over again. As my tears fell on her face, I kissed them away.

"God loves you, Jackie. And the spirit of Christ lives in you. You are God's child. He loves you and will redeem your suffering. Whatever is to come, it will be all right."

One of my fellow ministers had urged me just a few days earlier to loosen my tight grip on the strands of hope that Jackie might recover. I suppose he wanted to help me adjust to the eventuality of Jackie's death. "Give her up," he'd said, "but give her up to God and let him work his will."

I hadn't been able to accept that. Not then. I didn't think I'd ever be ready to give her up. As strongly as I believed that if she died, she would have eternal life with God, I was not emotionally ready to let go of my wife.

But on that Friday night of the second week of her coma, I discovered that I was ready. I'll never know why I was ready on that particular night. Perhaps each night had brought me one step closer to the realization. I only knew the time had come. All my bargaining with God, all my mourning, all the pain, all these complicated medical machines — none of it was bringing Jackie back to life. Despite the tubes and wires hooked up to her body, I tried to hold her as best I could, and I tried to explain it to her.

"I'm losing you, Jackie. The doctors are giving us no hope. I have to give you up, Jackie. This is the most difficult thing I've ever had to do. I love you so very much, but I don't have the right to keep you if you need to go. And . . . I think you need to go . . . and I think I need to let God bring you home with him."

I sat with her a few moments longer, then I leaned over her and held her as close to me as I could, and said nothing. I kissed her lips, left the room, and walked out of the ICU without saying my customary good-night to the nurses on duty.

When I arrived at home, no one else was there. It was the first time, I realized, that I would be alone in the house since Jackie's stroke. I went upstairs to the middle room and turned on the stereo. The local public radio station was playing Pachelbel's Canon in D Major. Jackie and I had listened to the piece many times and loved it. For both of us, it symbolized beauty, continuity, perfection. It was music God would listen to or compose himself, I'd once said to her. But that night in our empty house, it symbolized Jackie herself: she was the beauty, the continuity, the perfection that I was giving up.

As the music reached a crescendo, I turned the volume as loud as the dial allowed. With the sound reverberating through the whole house, I felt both strength and a sense of calm wash over me. I stretched back in my recliner and glanced toward the wall covered with family pictures. My eyes fastened on a single, striking photograph of Jacqueline. Her sparkling green eyes stared directly through the camera's eye and into mine. A flapper's sequined cloche was tight on her head. The camera's flash had caught several sequins that shot back bright rays of light. What a perfect way to capture Jackie's essence, I thought, as I sat transfixed by her image. Everything that came her way Jackie gave back, just like the light reflecting from her eyes and those sequins. The love that the children and I gave her, she gave back ten times over. The talent and intelligence that God had given her, she gave to the children. The trust and confidences others gave her, she returned in loyal friendship.

I leaned back in the recliner and closed my eyes until the music ended. Then I opened my eyes, stared into Jackie's photograph, and said, "Thank you, Jacqueline."

I went into our bedroom, got on my knees, and prayed aloud. I told God that I would fight and bargain for her life no longer: "I give her up to you now."

For the first time since her stroke, I slept through the night without one wakeful moment.

* * *

EARLY the next week, Jackie was scheduled for the tracheostomy. The pulmonary specialist had also detected in one lung an empyema, or abscess of infection caused by the pneumonia. A chest tube would have to be inserted surgically to drain the abscess. The tube would be inserted Tuesday, April 15, the same day as the tracheostomy.

Moving Jackie to the operating room was considered too risky and unnecessary, so the tracheostomy and chest tube insertion would be done in her ICU cubicle. At 3:15 P.M. both procedures were completed uneventfully. The chest tube was in and the endotracheal tube was removed from her mouth and throat. The doctor and nurses were cleaning up when the alarm of Jackie's cardiac monitor suddenly went off.

"Look at this!" Vanessa Ajayi exclaimed. "V-tac!" Jackie was going into ventricular tachycardia, a dangerously abnormal heart rhythm, or arrhythmia, of 100 to 300 beats a minute. A heart in ventricular tachycardia beats too fast to deliver enough oxygenated blood to meet the body's needs and can be fatal.

"She's losing blood pressure," Vanessa said, as she slapped paddles onto Jackie's chest to give her heart an electrical shock. The first shock failed to steady the heart rhythm or restore pressure, so the nurses alternately pumped Jackie's heart and applied electrical shocks. And they "bagged" her by putting an oxygen mask over her new tracheostomy.

"Come on, Jackie! Help us! How dare you do this when we're trying to pull you through! You're not helping. Come on!" Vanessa demanded.

Jackie was resuscitated within fifteen minutes. Dr. Pula, as her attending physician, was immediately informed, and he called me right away.

"Cardiac arrest? Is she stable now? How much more must she take?" I asked him. "What more can go wrong?"

"She is stable now, Harry, but it does seem like there's just one hurdle after another, doesn't it?" Dr. Pula didn't say so until much later, but Jackie's latest crisis was another example of many he had witnessed — as soon as one medical management decision or treatment is accomplished, some new menace pops up. It was one of those days when Dr. Pula felt that disease was laughing in his face.

After Jackie was resuscitated, Vanessa reflected for a while and concluded that Jackie just didn't care any more. Many times when she turned Jackie or exercised her legs and arms, she had explained, "Now, Jackie, we're exercising you so you won't be stiff and crippled when you come out of this coma." But Vanessa sensed Jackie's resistance. "I think you can be mean and stubborn when you want to, Jackie!"

But during V-tac, Vanessa thought, Jackie wasn't being stubborn any longer. She feared that Jackie was actually pulling against their attempt to save her life. As angry as she was at Jackie for "trying to leave us," as Vanessa told Jackie, another part of Vanessa could understand why.

"You're probably tired of this, aren't you, Jackie? Over two weeks of being laid up like this. You can't do anything for yourself. How would I feel if I were like that? I'd probably want to die."

Word of Jackie's cardiac arrest plunged our family deeper into desolation. Julie visited her sister every day.

"As I watch the monitors and tubes and listen to the whooshing ventilator, all I see is the person of Jackie slipping away," Julie told me one day in the hallway. "In there, Jackie is a body lying on a bed, hooked to machinery. This isn't my sister."

Early in Jackie's hospitalization, Julie had brought in a framed photograph of Jackie in her wedding dress. Julie placed the picture on the small bedside table so that every nurse and doctor would see who Jackie really was — smiling, eyes open, vibrant. Jackie the person, not Jackie the comatose body.

During one visit, before Jackie's cardiac arrest, Julie had felt particularly close to her sister. "If I could just give you all my strength and energy," Julie told Jackie, "if I could climb in bed and hold you, head to toe, and transfer all my strength to you by osmosis, I could keep you alive. I could make you live." Julie knew it was an irrational, desperate fantasy because nothing else was working.

But by the third week, after the pneumonia, the empyema, and the cardiac arrest, Julie began to wish Jackie would let go of her life. She knew her sister had a strong will. Yet Julie saw a woman full of infection, weak, immobile, hooked up to machines, a woman who had lost all means of communication. Jackie was losing any semblance of the person she really was. She was a body to be manipulated by professionals, Julie thought. "They're trying to keep this body alive with their antibiotics, ventilator, chest drain, IVs, cardiac monitor. Jackie is becoming less and less a person. The only purpose she's serving is fulfilling medical interests and expertise. There's really no other purpose except for the medical people to do their job. It's such an insult to her," Julie grieved, "to her body, to her self, to her person, to her dignity."

Julie valiantly tried to maintain Jackie's dignity. Just as she brought in Jackie's photo, she also brought in perfume. Not for the same reason Maureen had brought it, as a stimulus to awaken Jackie, but simply because Jackie loved perfume. Perfume has always been important to Jackie, so why not treat her as the person she is, with the things that were important to her, Julie reasoned as she sprayed Jackie's wrists. The nurses also began squirting perfume on Jackie and around her room, but for other reasons than Maureen's or Julie's. The empyema draining from Jackie's lung gave off a horrible odor that filled the tiny room.

One afternoon when Julie was visiting, the nurses asked her to wait outside for a while so that they could bathe and toilet Jackie and change her sheets. Julie walked to the quiet, private end of the hall to wait. During those twenty or thirty minutes, all her thoughts about the loss of Jackie — Jackie the person — overcame her, and Julie wept freely. She decided that she didn't want her sister to go on in this condition. "Oh, how you'd hate it if you knew what was happening to you, Jackie," she cried aloud.

When she reentered Jackie's room, Julie glanced at the photo of the vivacious Jackie. Then Julie took her sister's hands, looked at her passive face, and implored aloud, "Would you please let go, Jackie? Would you just give it up? It's okay to let go of your life. Would you just give it up? It will be all right."

"Who am I to give such assurances?" Julie later told her husband, Sam. "But if it's possible for her to let go of this wretched life, lying there the way she is, then I wish she would. She wouldn't want to go on like this if she knew what had happened to her."

CHRISTINA and Thomas were both home from college for the weekend. Christina continued to wrap herself in Jackie's white terry robe when in the house and change into regular clothes only when we visited the hospital. The day after Jackie's stroke, Thomas had gone to her jewelry box and pulled out an almond-sized silver scarab that she had worn on a neck chain years ago. He placed it around his neck and told me he would never take it off. For both Thomas and Christina, wearing an item of their mother's close to their skin seemed to pull her close, almost to unite her with them again.

That weekend, three weeks after Jackie's stroke, I asked Julie and all the children to meet with Dr. Pula and me at the hospital. Before we met him in a conference room, we crowded into Jackie's ICU cubicle. Nothing had changed. She looked as immobile and lifeless as she had for the past three weeks. I knew how much it pained the children to see her like this. It was a sight they would never get used to, no matter how often they visited. We kissed Jackie and talked to her for a few moments, telling her how much we each loved her, and then we left, arms around each other, to meet Dr. Pula.

We listened quietly for nearly an hour as Dr. Pula described Jackie's condition: the pneumonia raged in her lungs, infection from the pneumonia swam through her bloodstream and could infect other organs such as her liver, her kidneys, her heart. The antibiotics were not yet winning. The empyema was being drained from her lungs, but it was not responding well to antibiotics either.

"The state of her coma has changed, as normally happens after a few weeks, from a continuous sleeplike state to a vegetative one," he explained.

"And how long could that go on?" Stephen asked.

"It could continue indefinitely if her other physiological complications can be brought under control," Dr. Pula answered softly.

"And that cardiac arrest?" Thomas said. "Could something like that happen again?"

Her cardiac arrest had certainly been a scare but was not likely to happen again, Dr. Pula assured us. It had probably occurred because her body, besieged with so many other problems, couldn't withstand the additional stress of the tracheostomy and insertion of the chest drain at that moment.

Dr. Pula had done most of the talking, with the children asking a few more questions about Jackie's care. Julie and I had heard much of this information before from Dr. Pula, other doctors, and nurses. Then Stephen asked the toughest question of all.

"Do you think she can recover? I mean, with the best medical care, all the machines she is on, the antibiotics you're giving her and everything — she has a strong constitution, you know. She's young still. Her heart and lungs were certainly well exercised . . ." Stephen asked, almost pleaded.

Dr. Pula ran his hands through his hair and replied that, in his best opinion, chances were very slim that Jackie would awaken from her coma. It was not just a deep coma; the cause was important to understand — the worst kind of massive cerebral hemorrhage. She would most likely die — no one could say just how soon or how far in the future — Dr. Pula concluded, but as long as the medical complications could be managed, she would continue to live with the respirator aiding her breathing, the cardiac monitor keeping watch on her heart, the IVs filling her with antibiotics, and the nasogastric tube delivering water and nourishment.

A bleaker picture couldn't have been painted. We now faced a major, painful decision: artificial means could prolong Jackie's presence among us probably for months and months, maybe years, if she continued to receive the current high level of care. But for how long, for what reason, if she was never going to recover to the full life that she had always desired?

If Jackie continued to linger in the coma and, despite the other complications, managed to hang on by artificial means, what options did we face? The respirator could be turned off if court permission were obtained. The hospital wouldn't turn it off at our request, though, because she was legally still alive: she was not brain-dead, Dr. Pula explained. Her brainstem showed activity and she had no underlying terminal disease. She could be moved from the ICU to a regular room, and nature could take its course while Jackie was kept as comfortable as possible. But we were not ready to make that decision yet — not just three weeks after the stroke.

"It doesn't seem that we need to make any decision today, do we?" I asked.

"No, I'm not urging you to," Dr. Pula said. "I just want you to know Mrs. Cole's condition, what is likely to happen, and what possibilities you may have to face in the future."

"But, Dad," Thomas turned to me, "we're talking about maybe disconnecting those artificial life supports, those machines — pulling the plug — if she stays in this coma indefinitely and doesn't improve, right? If she just lingers like this for a long time, as long as the machines and medicines keep her body alive, but she still doesn't wake up?"

"That's right, Thomas. If the doctors can keep the pneumonia from killing her and fight off other complications, Mom could remain like this for a long, long time, I'm afraid."

"No, she'd never want that," Christina said. "She always said she'd never want to be kept alive by machines. Remember what I told you she said when she was having this stroke? She looked right at me and said, 'Christina, I don't want to live this way.' We all know what she meant. She didn't want to live an awful half life like Hanu did at the end."

"I agree," Julie added. "We all know Jackie wouldn't want this to go on for months, or perhaps years. Harry, it's an awful decision to have to make, but if her condition doesn't eventually change, we're going to have to do what she would want us to do — stop those machines that artificially prolong her so-called life."

"I know, Julie. I know that's what she'd want us to do," I said. "We may eventually have to face up to that."

"Well, if we went to court and got permission, would we turn off everything?" Thomas asked. Dr. Pula patiently explained that in some cases the respirator alone is withdrawn, and in other cases all supports are withdrawn because some patients manage to go on even without the respirator.

"What would we do, Dad?" Christina asked.

"Oh, I haven't even thought about the specifics, Christina. I suppose we might ask permission to turn off the respirator and stop the antibiotics. I don't know about the feeding tube. What do you think?"

The children said nothing for a few moments. The idea of withdrawing food and water from their mother was too emotionally complex to comprehend. Finally, Julie spoke. "It seems to me that if we end artificial life supports, we end all of them. We don't pick one, two, or three, A, B, or C."

"But if we were allowed to withdraw just the respirator and she continued to live without it, should we then disconnect the naso-gastric tube?" Thomas asked.

"This is very hypothetical, Thomas. But, well, if it gave her any more chance at recovery, even the most remote, I don't think we would withdraw it," I said.

"But the feeding tube is an artificial support just like the respirator," Julie added. "It's a mechanism used because she can't swallow in this coma. Just as the respirator is a mechanism to do her breathing for her, the feeding tube gets nourishment into her because she can't do it herself."

"But not yet," Stephen said. "It's only been three weeks. Yeah, I know what she always said about these situations. I know she wouldn't want to go on like this, without any ability to talk to us, to know what's going on, without any improvement. But I think we should wait longer." Beth nodded in agreement.

"I agree, Stephen. Believe me, I'm in no hurry to make such a momentous move. But I think we'd better get used to the idea that the time may very likely come — we don't know when — when we'll have to face this decision," I said.

"Well, Dad, we all know what Mom would want us to do for her. If things don't change, if it doesn't look like she'll get better," John suggested, "I think we'd all agree what the decision should be. So maybe we ought to put the timing of the decision in your hands. You're most in touch with the doctors. You're the one who'll know when the time comes."

"That makes sense," Julie added. "I think we all want Jackie spared the long, drawn-out, undignified dying that my mother went through. I know Jackie would feel she was putting a tremendous emotional burden on the kids and you, Harry, to watch her linger, not alive in any real, conscious, human sense. She may not be feeling anything herself right now. In this coma, she's not feeling pain, but she would hate to put the family through years of watching her vegetate in a hospital bed or nursing home. She wouldn't want the living to suffer for her. If she could know what's going on right now, she'd shake her finger at us and probably say, 'Don't keep me alive by these damn machines! You know I don't want that.' She'd hate knowing how helpless you'd feel watching her go on and on like this because she felt that same helplessness when Hanu was dying."

We each remembered and talked about Jackie and Julie's mother for a few moments. Helen Lohsen had been a fiercely independent woman. In the 1960s, when she held a good job with the state government, she suddenly decided that she wanted a Mercedes-Benz. So she traded her old Chevy for a Mercedes. When she wanted a fur, she bought herself a full-length mink coat. But she wore sneakers, long before they were fashionable as career women's streetwear, with the mink when she went to the A & P early in the morning to take advantage of the day-old bakery sales.

For several years before she died on the Lohsens' fortieth wedding anniversary, in 1980, Helen was anything but independent. After she was first operated on for a benign tumor in her head, her brain swelled. The resulting hemiplegia (paralysis of one side of her body) left her with very little movement or feeling on her left side. In the eighteen months between that operation and a second one, Helen became much more passive. The independent life of making her own decisions, driving her own car, working, was finished. After Helen's second operation, her husband tried to take care of her at home. But after a week, John realized he was incapable of caring for her alone. She entered a nursing home, where she remained for a year until she died. During that year, she was either in a wheelchair or in bed. Her speech was intact, but her memory was so disjointed that normal conversation was impossible. Her thoughts and words had no continuity as she flitted from moment to moment, making bizarre comments. Her thought process resembled unhooked railway cars, bumping into and bouncing off each other, barely staying on the track.

Watching her mother's mind and body slip away like that had been particularly painful for Jackie. Even though their relationship had always been strained, Jackie loved her mother and hated to see her deteriorate.

Jackie had always been a woman of action. If something went wrong, she jumped to fix it. At the office, when a handicapped young woman suddenly had a seizure, everyone froze as the woman lay on the floor. Everyone but Jackie. "Get back. Move the furniture out of the way. Call a doctor . . ." Jackie instantly took charge as she fell to her knees to help the young woman.

But in her mother's final years, there was no useful action for Jackie to take. An inability to take some action, to make things right, frustrated Jackie enormously. She had often remarked that she never wanted to live the kind of existence that her mother had suffered at the end of her life. Jackie saw it as an indignity to her mother and as a tremendous burden to those who loved her.

"If I ever become like that, pull the plug," Jackie had said more than once. Everyone in the family knew that a vision of Helen in the nursing home must have flashed through Jackie's mind when she thought she was having a stroke and said, "I don't want to live this way."

I knew that Jackie would despise that condition, too, but I was also beginning to believe that the medical technology was just prolonging the inevitable, which, to me, was Jackie's joining God in eternal life. All those tubes and machines keeping Jackie only technically alive were getting in God's way — God's way of working out his will. And God's will, I believed, was to bring Jackie's life to a meaningful conclusion that we could all eventually understand. Her life would be significant beyond her death, and we would be able to see and comprehend that significance.

In my theological training, I had taken a number of ethics courses. But I never expected that I'd have to make an ethical decision of this magnitude in my own life. Did I, did anyone, have the moral right to turn off artificial life support, to end another's life? Could I "play God" in effect, by seeking an end to Jackie's life, as empty of meaning and purpose as it now was? I had always been taught to believe that God gives us the freedom to exercise our wills as we choose in our lives. I also believed that when we have to make difficult choices in which something important could be lost, such as self-esteem, friendship, or even another person's love, something greater, something of a higher good, the peace and strength and knowledge of God is gained.

Over the years, I had often discussed various ethical questions with fellow seminary students and ministers, but always on an abstract, academic level. Now the questions were intensely personal: Would I take some action that would bring about my wife's death? Could I assume that moral responsibility? I called several of my closest, most trusted friends in the ministry to discuss the ethics of a decision that I knew I'd soon have to face. One was Jim Rissmiller, a close friend since our seminary years, who was now pastor of the Community In Christ Presbyterian Church in Greensboro, North Carolina.

"Jim, I don't know if there is any moral 'good' in this situation. But even if there is some good that I can't see right now, is there perhaps a greater good in freeing Jackie from this condition, of freeing her to join God, by withdrawing her artificial life support systems? Do you think I can make the right, the moral, decision to end her suffering? I think we both understand that suffering often has a meaning. But Jackie's suffering is so pointless! She's suffered a major hemorrhage; she suffers indignity to her body every day in that ICU, and she's totally unaware of her suffering — what possible good is it doing her? What can she learn or gain from this? I have no hope she'll recover and see no sign that she's about to receive any relief from suffering by going on like this.

Jim and I ran up a number of phone bills discussing our situation. Jim's approach was to begin with broad questions and then hone in on the important, specific ones:

"Harry, what I think we need to look for in any situation is how do we do the least harm to achieve the highest good? What do you see as the most good you can do for Jackie while causing the least harm?"

"Jim, I don't know how any more harm can be done to her than has already been done! She's only technically alive because machines are breathing for her and tubes are feeding her food, water, and antibiotics. She has lost the ability to communicate, to relate, to have any sort of human interaction or intimacy or growth.

Maybe I would be doing the best thing by stopping artificial life supports because it would attain a higher good — her eternal life with God. I know she would find a peace that she certainly doesn't have here on earth now. But what I'm struggling with is the decision that comes down to this: can I justify my actions in helping to cause Jackie's death?"

"Well, Harry, if you do make that choice, I think it's wrong for you to believe you're 'killing' Jackie. The stroke is what's killed ninety-nine percent of her. Maybe it's more accurate to say you are putting an end to her artificially prolonged life because — after all — isn't that what the machines are doing, prolonging her life and postponing her death?"

"It seems that way, Jim. They certainly aren't restoring her health. Her chances of recovery from the stroke, the coma, and all the resulting complications are so extremely thin — I don't see how the medical technology is doing anything other than postponing her inevitable death."

"I know you don't, Harry, and I know how much you love Jackie. But, whatever you decide, I also know you will make the most appropriate decision that will somehow bring good out of this terrible tragedy. No one can give you a neat formula to apply here. You must make the most difficult decision of your life, but I also know that God is present in your life and will give you guidance and wisdom to make the best decision for Jackie. And after you make that decision, whatever it is, God will bless you with the solace and strength to live with it. My church and I will be praying earnestly for Jackie and for you."

Throughout this period, the decision I was approaching was more a theological one than a medical or legal one. I was not only Jackie's husband who deeply loved her, but an ordained Christian minister, and I couldn't divorce my interpretation of Jackie's situation from my theological training and beliefs. So I continued to turn to fellow ministers to discuss the decision facing me.

Herb Valentine, who is the executive director of our Presbytery, was another minister who provided a great source of support while I thrashed through the question of whether to withdraw Jackie's artificial life supports. One afternoon Herb came by the house to make a pastoral call before going with me to the hospital.

"Harry, this is in God's hands. We all hope and pray, of course, that Jackie will get better. But if she does not, you have the knowledge that God loves each and every one of us. He doesn't abandon us in our darkest hours. His love for Jackie and for you will guide you."

"I do believe that, Herb. And I pray for that. I don't know when I will be ready, if I will be ready, to decide to withdraw life support systems. But I do believe God is present in our lives, though I'm trying to understand where God is at this moment."

"Something good, something meaningful will come out of this terrible, terrible tragedy, Harry. Something redemptive will come out of this — we will see that — because it is God's way to bring about redemption."

I thought for a moment about what he said and responded, "You know, Herb, I've believed for a long time, since seminary I suppose, that life is lived between extremes. At one end there is immense suffering and pain, immense evil. But at the other extreme, God is there with all his love and forgiveness and mercy and peace and grace. When we're confronted with evil, when the agony and suffering are overwhelming, we ask ourselves, Where do we go with that pain? And the answer for me is toward God at the other end. We run toward that end, God's end, to escape the pain. That's the Christian journey. The goal is to overcome the pain and suffering by turning to God and believing he can bring it to a meaningful end.

"If Jackie dies, she would be at the end of that journey. She would be over the edge, beyond suffering. She would be with God."

"Yes, Harry," Herb assured me, "she would have eternal peace, and you would know that Jackie lives eternally with God."

"And she deserves that, Herb. Right now, in that coma, she is not living the kind of life she wanted to live, or the kind of life that I believe God wants her to live. There's no growth, no communication, no intimacy, nothing that gives life meaning. With each day, it is more and more difficult for me to understand how or why God would want her to go on like this."

DURING those weeks my mind had to do some quick gear shifting from major ethical/theological questions to practical ones. In the third week of Jackie's coma, I learned from her friends at the state education department that I should hurry to get her retired from her job. If she died before retiring, her benefits would be roughly one-third to one-half of the amount they would be if she died after retiring. The only way she could retire would be for me to obtain legal guardianship and apply for her disability retirement.

These were horrifying thoughts, ones I had absolutely no desire to deal with, but I knew I had to look out for the best interests of the children. It was my duty to see that they received whatever benefits Jackie had earned in more than a decade as a state employee. But I would have to act quickly, I learned, because the state system required that an employee retire by the last day of the month or else wait until the end of the following month. It was already early April. The guardianship process normally took about six weeks, David Ash told me. No one knew whether Jackie would survive the day, the week, much less the month of April. But if I didn't obtain guardianship before May 1, then I would have to wait until June 1 to retire Jackie, and no one really expected she would still be alive by then. David contacted the Master of Equity section of the Baltimore Circuit Court, which appointed an attorney, Leo Ottey, to represent Jackie's interests. F. Lee Bailey wouldn't have been a more fortunate choice. Leo had two qualifications that helped speed the guardianship process: he had known David at law school, and he was thoroughly familiar with the process because he had formerly clerked in the Master of Equity office. Once David explained Jackie's condition and the need to expedite the guardianship petition, Leo pushed it through as rapidly as possible. He had to interview me, the children, and Julie to ascertain whether I was a suitable guardian or a charlatan. I found some of his questions a petty nuisance in the midst of a tragedy that was shattering our lives, but I realized he had to ask them.

Leo also asked Dr. Pula for a statement about Jackie's condition. Dr. Pula wrote:

To Whom It May Concern: I examined Jacqueline Cole yesterday, 4/21/86. Mrs. Cole is completely disabled and unable to make any decisions for herself because she is presently comatose. She has been comatose for three weeks due to an intracerebral hemorrhage. It is likely that her clinical condition will not change for an extended period of time.

Another letter from a house-staff doctor, worded exactly like Dr. Pula's, was also attached to the petition.

On April 23, David, Leo Ottey, and I appeared before Judge Thomas Ward to present the guardianship request. In his written petition, David had asked the court to make me the guardian of Jackie's property. But David verbally amended the petition at the hearing and asked Judge Ward to grant me "guardianship of the person" as well. David was looking toward the future — the immediate future, he feared, after talking with Jackie's physicians. I would need guardianship of Jackie's "person" to make any crucial medical decisions about her level of care, perhaps even a decision to withdraw life support systems.

At the conclusion of David's and Leo's presentations, Judge Ward signed the petition, making me the guardian both of Jackie's person and of her property. Judge Ward ruled that Jackie "lacks sufficient understanding or capacity to make or communicate responsible decisions concerning her person because of a disability . . . being in an indefinite comatose state of unknown duration resulting from a massive stroke."

The judge's order also stipulated that "the guardian may consent to medical or other professional care, counsel, treatment, or service for the disabled, except that this Court must authorize any major surgery or any other medical procedure that involves a substantial risk to the life of the disabled." Judge Ward also added the requirement that I would need to get court approval to move Jackie to "a different place of abode." Presumably a nursing home.

David and Leo sliced the legal process of obtaining guardianship to several days. With certified copies of the guardianship papers in hand, I immediately rushed from the courtroom to the state office building. I had to get the papers in that afternoon because the state retirement agency's medical review board would meet the next day for the last time that month. The fastest way for me to get across town was to take the subway. I couldn't believe I was actually doing this — dashing across town, like a character in a movie, to come in just under the wire. Another surreal scene, I thought. But as I sat on the bench and waited for the next subway train, a wave of relief swept over me. At least this is one thing I've been able to do, I realized; it may be a small achievement, but I've done it for Jackie. It's what she would want me to do. Throughout this drawn-out nightmare, I've felt so helpless, so unable to act, and this is the first thing I have actually accomplished for Jackie. I was grateful for that.

When I returned home exhausted late that afternoon, I couldn't face the empty house. I headed down the street, where I knew Bonnie and Paul would offer me comfort. When I walked into the living room, Bonnie was sitting on the black moiré sofa with her friend Alicia. Bonnie didn't rise to embrace me as she usually did, and she said nothing for several seconds. The silence didn't register with me until Alicia asked, "Are you going to tell him?"

Bonnie looked up, dry-eyed but particularly drawn, and said softly, "Harry, my mother died this afternoon at one-fifteen."

I pulled Bonnie up to her feet and wrapped my arms around her. I could say nothing but "I'm so sorry, I'm so sorry . . ." I could feel doom pressing down on my head, my shoulders, my back. I squeezed my eyelids shut and felt the world go dark. Death was surrounding us! I am experiencing death right now, this very minute, I thought. This news of the death of Bonnie's mother was surely a harbinger of Jackie's death. And here in Bonnie's living room, it was more convincing than all the doctors' somber words at the hospital. When I opened my eyes, I noticed my tears falling over Bonnie's shoulder and onto her polished wood floor.

Bonnie's mother had been ill for some time and two days after Jackie's stroke had entered the ICU room next to Jackie's. Bonnie had been doing double duty, first visiting her mother and then going into Jackie's cubicle, where she fixed Jackie's hair. Bonnie had disapproved of the way the nurses combed it straight back, so she would rearrange Jackie's hair to curl down on her forehead. Then Bonnie would read *Out of Africa* aloud to Jackie, day after day. I had wondered whether Bonnie would finish the book before Jackie's death.

JACKIE was officially retired for "ordinary" disability, as opposed to "accidental" disability, on the state employees retirement form. What a choice, I thought. Her last payroll statement became effective April 30, with the comment that she had accumulated sixty-one hours and six minutes of annual leave and eleven hours and six minutes of comp time. At any other time, I might have been amused by the precision of the bureaucracy's minute-counters, but on that twenty-seventh day of Jackie's coma, I only wished that I could capture those seventy-two hours and twelve minutes and wrap them up with a satin ribbon as a gift for Jackie. How I longed to present her with seventy-two hours and twelve minutes of conscious, full life! I'd sweep her away from the ventilators and tubes and take her to a beautiful place, perhaps an isolated beach, where I'd tell her how much I loved her. I'd put my arm around her shoulder and pull her close to my side again as we'd walk along the sand. I'd be able to hear her voice, her lilting laugh. I'd be able to see her eyes sparkle again . . . I pushed those thoughts away. Wishful thinking. There could be no seventy-two-hour-twelve-minute vacation from reality. This wasn't one of those "escape cruises" advertised in the travel section of the Sunday newspaper. Those were hours and minutes that were lost to Jackie forever.

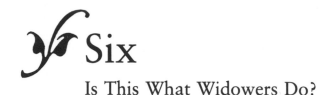

Six

Is This What Widowers Do?

Despite her dire prognosis, Jackie was treated like other patients who spent long weeks in bed. Maryland General's physical therapists and ICU nurses exercised her muscles to prevent atrophy and weakness. They put splints on her hands, wrists, feet, and ankles to prevent contractures. Should she miraculously come out of the coma, they didn't want her joints to be so stiff and contracted that they were useless.

Another danger of lying immobile was the possibility that Jackie's feet would "drop," or become flaccid through lack of use. Before the foot splints went on, ICU nurses thought that one foot already was beginning to drop, so they suggested that I bring in a pair of running shoes to support Jackie's feet. I went home and retrieved the shoes that she'd worn every time she worked out to a video tape. But when I returned with them, the nurses said that a high-top shoe would give her greater support in the ankle. I didn't question the nurses — it was something to do, a small gesture of helping Jackie, and there were so few of those opportunities left.

I went to a shoe store and selected a pair of white high-top Reeboks. As I opened my wallet to pay for them, the clerk admired my wedding band, with its serpentine curve of tiny diamonds.

I'm losing it, I thought, as I desperately fought back tears. How do you explain to a shoe-store clerk that these new Reeboks are for your dying wife, the wife who gave you this ring just eight years ago? Or do you even want to explain it to a stranger? I didn't. I thanked the clerk and quickly left the store.

When I returned to the hospital, I put the immaculate white

shoes on Jackie's feet. For the first time in weeks of visiting her, I laughed.

"These look ridiculous, Jacqueline! If only you could see yourself with these brand-new shoes poking straight up under a hospital sheet!"

But for each rare moment like that, there were thousands of sad, poignant, often excruciating ones. When I came downstairs to the kitchen one morning, I looked in the refrigerator for something to spread on my toast. Nothing but margarine. Then I noticed a nearly empty jam jar pushed to the rear of a shelf. The label read, in Jackie's fanciest script, Color Me Raspberry.

I spread the last teaspoon of raspberry jam on my toast and remembered how Jackie had put up so many preserves last summer. This was the last jar of all those she'd made. When I finished my breakfast, I washed out the jar carefully so the label would remain intact. I dried the jar and placed it on a high shelf. Another ending, another finality, another "last thing" of Jackie's.

Our friends were wonderful about trying to help me ward off loneliness. A day didn't go by without someone asking me to lunch or dinner. But Jackie's very absence made her present at each meal. One Saturday, our friends George and Candy Webb, with whom Jackie and I had often gone out to dinner, met me for lunch at Chiapparelli's, one of our favorite Italian restaurants. Seated at a table set for four, the three of us were acutely aware of that fourth, hauntingly empty place. Jackie belonged there! George made a toast, "To Jackie, may she return to us to complete the foursome." George knew as well as I did how unlikely that possibility was, but he offered the toast with genuine hope.

During those weeks of Jackie's coma, I frequently went to my mother's for dinner. I needed her company, and her need to be helpful to me was partially filled by feeding me.

Just two months before Jackie's stroke, my father's Alzheimer's disease had reached a crisis. I was in my church office that frigid January day when Mother called — Dad had threatened to hit her. As I rushed to their home, I realized that his deteriorating mind had reached the point where he couldn't live at home any longer. He had been in and out of hospitals and nursing homes for his Alzheimer's and for prostate cancer. Each time he seemed a bit better, he'd come home. I'd known the day was coming when he could no longer live at home, but Mother, Wayne, and I had been postponing the inevitable as long as we could. I wasn't ready to accept the fact that my always-strong father needed more help than we could give him. Perhaps none of us is ever ready to face the pain of having to commit a parent to institutional care. From counseling several of my parishioners, I knew that assuming responsibility for a parent — in effect becoming a parent to one's own parent — is an awkward, sad midlife predicament. But I didn't realize how deeply sorrowful it could be until I had to take that step with my own father that January day.

Mother had also called my uncle, who arrived shortly after I did. It took both my uncle and me to remove my father physically from the house. He was six feet tall, like me, stubborn, and stronger than I expected. We had to force him into the car so that I could drive him to the hospital, where I had him admitted to the psychiatric unit until I could find a bed in a nursing home a few days later. As I left my father in the hospital that January afternoon, I thought that nothing could ever again bring such sadness into our family's life. Even his death couldn't be as painful as this, because death is a passage to eternal life. But commitment to a hospital ward because of Alzheimer's seemed far worse. Little did I imagine that afternoon that a far greater tragedy was only two months away.

After my father entered a nursing home for good that January, Jackie and I tried to give Mother extra support by spending more time with her, getting her out of the house, and taking her on outings. And after Jackie's stroke, I tried as best I could to continue seeing Mother often, usually for dinner. As she began clearing away the dishes one evening, I became totally overwhelmed with emptiness. She and I had been eating at a table with two conspicuously vacant chairs. The two most important people in our lives weren't where they were supposed to be. I held Mother as she stood next to me and wept as I hadn't done since I was a little boy.

"I'm losing everything I love, Mom."

"Yes, Harry, and so am I."

*　　*　　*

ON a Sunday soon after Jackie's stroke, I visited the First and Franklin Presbyterian Church, where we'd been married. I entered and took a seat in a rear pew. The church held so many memories. I was overcome with grief and had to leave before the service ended. On my way out, a parishioner asked, "How's Jackie?" I broke into tears and quietly asked, "Pray for her."

Another Sunday after church, when I arrived at the nursing home to visit my father, I found him sitting listlessly before a bowl of vegetable soup. I pulled up a chair and began spoon-feeding him the soup.

"Do you know, Dad, that Jackie is in the hospital?" He offered no response. "Do you remember Mother and I told you what happened to Jackie?" He nodded slightly, wordlessly.

Can it get any worse, I wondered? Here I am, spoon-feeding my father, whose mind barely comprehends the reality around him. And after I finish feeding him this soup, I'll drive to the hospital to visit my comatose wife! How much more can I lose?

I ate dinner alone one April evening at an Inner Harbor restaurant that had often bought Jackie's rich, elegant desserts. After dinner, I strolled along the warm, damp harbor and watched couples walking arm in arm. Everything in the present reminded me of Jackie in the past. Suddenly I was struck with a thought that erupted out loud:

"My wife is going to die! My wife is going to die!" I turned abruptly and ran toward my car. Startled couples stopped and stared at me, shaking my fists, crying and shouting, "My wife is going to die!" My frenzy seemed to gush from a deep well of pure fear, the fear of losing Jackie. I felt the fear pumping through my legs and I ran faster toward the car. My lips tasted salty from the tears washing my face. When I reached the car, my tears were spent. I felt so empty, so hollow that a breeze off the harbor could have knocked me over. I took several deep breaths and turned on the ignition. I'm losing it, I thought on the drive home, I'm losing everything.

WHEN I visited Jackie in the ICU, I focused exclusively on her medical condition. I needed to know exactly what was happening, what her blood gases revealed, how the pneumonia was progressing. But when I wasn't at the hospital, I tried to do some church work, though the elders and others stepped in to help and urged me to take care of myself and my family first and foremost. There were several marriages that had been scheduled for those weeks, but I simply could not perform them. The pain was too great.

When I marry a couple, I become very involved with them during premarital counseling. Over a span of weeks, as we talk about the meaning of marriage and their hopes and goals, I come to know them well and share their joy in forging a future together. That is one of the happiest, most satisfying aspects of my ministry. But how could I become as involved as I should be in the joyful union of a young couple when my own union with Jackie was dissolving as she lay dying in that coma? I just didn't have the emotional wherewithall to marry anyone. Other ministers took my place at the altar. But I was able to perform a few baptisms — bringing a new baby into the Christian community was a joy that could push my daily despair aside for an hour or so. And I did continue to visit some of our elderly and ill church members to bring them Communion in their homes and hospital rooms.

After visiting Jackie and trying to attend to my church work, I filled the rest of my time with mundane activities like taking Charlie, our Lhasa Apso, on slow daily walks along the brick sidewalks of Bolton Hill. I tried to imagine the future as I walked. There was no doubt in my mind that Jackie was going to die. What was life going to be like without her?

This is what widowers do, I realized. They take long walks with their dogs through lovely neighborhoods. They wear gray wool sweaters and tweed jackets like I'm wearing, and they walk their dogs to give an illusion of substance and direction to their lives. But they are seventy-two or eighty-two. I'm only forty-two.

Do they stare at couples and try to make some sense of their own solitary existence? Do they meander around the neighborhood and think of what was, what could have been, or what might be? Do they mourn? Do they cry? I mourned, and occasionally on these walks, I'd suddenly burst into tears. I didn't care who noticed.

I often stared at people on the street and wondered who they were, what their problems were, whether they were happily mar-

ried, or unhappily married. Do they know what they have? I wondered. Are they aware that they are building a relationship with
someone else? Do they know how precious that is, how little time
we all have to build what we want, to give what we want to give to
someone we love? I thought of Jackie, alone and dying. I cherished
all the beautiful, caring things about her — her upbeat sense of
humor, her ability to inspire confidence in others, especially the
children. I remembered her making homemade soup for the kids
when they were sick. I pictured her helping them with their
homework and taking them to work with her when they were little
and had a day off from school. She always made sure they had a
book to read or drawing materials to keep them busy while she
worked. I thought of her creative eye, her artistic black-and-white
photographs of Bolton Hill buildings and trees, her paintings and
sketches of the children. All of the cherished gifts that Jackie had
given us were suspended in my memory, just as she lay suspended
between life and death in that hospital bed.

SEVERAL of my minister colleagues were great sources of support
at this time. As we discussed the spiritual and ethical dilemma of
Jackie's situation, the question of suffering always arose. What
was its meaning and purpose?

"I know suffering is a part of life, a part of being human," I said
once to Bill Hug, one of my fellow pastors. "And I know that
God redeems our suffering. But, Bill, suffering has taken on a new
meaning for me in these past weeks. Medically speaking, Jackie
isn't suffering any physical pain or discomfort, because she can't
feel anything in that coma. A doctor can pinch her, poke her, pour
ice water on her! She won't feel it. She won't respond to the pain.
But I do think she is suffering by being in this condition. She's
suffering the loss of awareness, the loss of her self, her ability to
feel loved, to give love, to communicate with us . . . to think . . . to
speak. She's suffering the loss of basic human dignity when strangers bathe her, catheterize her, poke her with tubes. I know she
would despise that if she could see what's happening to her!"

"Yes, it is suffering, Harry. And you and the children are suffering as well. But you know that suffering has a purpose, no
matter how painful it is. Something good will come from this

suffering, God shows us that. And," Bill said confidently, "whatever happens, you know that God loves you. He loves Jackie and the children. If Jackie doesn't recover, God will give you the strength to endure. You have had the blessing of eight years of marriage to Jackie and you still have the children. Even in this brief time, Jackie gave you so much by giving you your wonderful family. Jackie dispensed grace, didn't she? To you, to the children, to me, to everyone." Bill spoke of Jackie in the past tense, as everyone was already doing.

Grace, I've always thought, is a gift from God, something we haven't earned, don't deserve, but something we need and cannot refuse because God is forever wanting to give it to us. God had indeed dispensed grace through Jackie. She was always giving someone something, a hug to the kids when they most needed it, a kiss to me when I least expected it, an encouraging word to a teacher, a willing ear and sound advice to a friend. How could I, how could the children ever endure the loss of Jacqueline's graciousness?

Meanwhile, I waited for God to dispense grace in our direction, either by an improvement in Jackie's condition or in the form of guidance to help me reach the decision looming before me: would I seek withdrawal of her artificial life supports?

I recalled an evening in seminary when a group of us asked a favorite professor if he believed in the devil. No, Dr. Balmar Kelly did not, but he said he did believe there was "an intelligent power of evil. I am too much of a twentieth-century man to believe in the devil, but I do think that this intelligent power of evil is at work in the world."

I thought that made a great deal of sense. Evil is real and insidiously involved in seeking to do cruel, destructive things to good people. It was this intelligent power of evil — not God — that struck down a lovely forty-three-year-old wife and mother. Not long after Jackie's stroke, I was given a copy of Rabbi Harold Kushner's book *When Bad Things Happen to Good People*. Like Rabbi Kushner, I don't believe that God causes our suffering, but God helps and sustains us in times of crisis. As Psalm 121 says, "I lift mine eyes to the hills, from where does my help come? My help comes from the Lord, maker of Heaven and Earth."

No, I don't think God does cause our suffering. For me, God is the ultimate power of goodness and love, of mercy and grace. God suffers with us in times of tragedy and loss. Both Christianity and Judaism introduce us to the idea of a God who suffers as well as creates. Jesus Christ suffered crucifixion in the New Testament. In the Old Testament God is made homeless and goes into exile with his exiled people. He weeps as he sees what some of his children do to others of his children.

On the first night of Jackie's stroke, I felt nothing of God's presence in my struggle to understand what had happened. During those sleepless hours of my dark night of the soul, I thought that God was absent. With the dawn of Easter and Jackie's survival of those first critical hours, I began to sense some inkling of God's presence. Though I couldn't understand it rationally, I took it on faith, the faith I have held since childhood Sunday School, that God would redeem Jackie's suffering even as he did for his Son and as he has for so many others. I continued to pray for signs of his grace. I began to see that I needed to challenge and withstand — through faith and prayer — that intelligent power of evil that was attempting to take Jackie from us and destroy our family.

I read the Book of Job and many of the Psalms over and over, particularly Psalm 23: "The Lord is my shepherd; I shall not want. / He makes me lie down in green pastures. / He leads me beside still waters; he restores my soul. / He leads me in the paths of righteousness for his name's sake. / Even though I walk through the valley of the shadow of death, I fear no evil; for thou art with me; thy rod and thy staff, they comfort me. . . ."

I HAD another meeting with Dr. Pula and a young resident who occasionally treated Jackie. The resident suggested that the time to make a decision about Jackie's future was coming.

"No, that time isn't here for me yet. I'm not at the point where I'm ready to make a decision," I explained, and I went on to vent my frustrations.

"While you're working toward medical resolutions, I am trying to find an acceptable spiritual solution to this entire dilemma," I began.

"I'm trying to find what I think is the 'kairotic' moment in which to decide what's best for Jackie. In the Old Testament, the idea of the *kairos* referred to a particular moment when God saved the Hebrews, as when he delivered them out of Egypt. In the New Testament, it refers to God saving us in Jesus Christ. I don't mean to preach to you, but I need to explain what this means to me," I told the doctors. "*Kairos* in our situation refers to my recognition and acceptance of the fact that Jackie's life is in God's hands — no matter what action we decide to take. For me to demand Jackie's return is unnatural. It would be like pushing mountains into the sea. My response right now is to put Jackie's life in God's hands, even if that means giving her up."

I realized that the young resident wasn't the least bit interested in what I was trying to say. Dr. Pula looked intense.

"Well," I concluded, "I'm just saying that I believe that there's a time in the course of life when God acts, when God resolves something, and that's what a kairotic moment is. But I'm also saying that I don't think that moment has arrived yet."

"So we will continue to give Jackie the same level of care?" Dr. Pula asked.

"Yes," I answered. "But for now I want to leave whatever resolution that may come in God's hands. I want her care and treatment to continue as it has been."

"Absolutely," Dr. Pula affirmed. "If this is what you want, this is what we'll do."

STEPHEN visited his mother every evening after finishing work and his classes at the University of Baltimore. As he stared into her face, she sometimes seemed to express a grimace, while at other times her eyes moved underneath her closed lids.

"She looks like she's dreaming, doesn't she?" Stephen remarked one evening.

"Perhaps, Stephen. But I don't see how she could be, really, in that deep, deep coma. According to some of the articles I've been reading about coma, it's thought that people don't dream while they're comatose."

As he stared at his mother's face, Stephen's expression was hopeful. But when he looked away, he couldn't help but see the tubes attached to her body, and he would choke. I put my arm around his bent shoulders. But Stephen allowed his sorrow only brief entry. If one part of this deathlike portrait could cheer him, it was the splints. To Stephen, the splints meant that the medical people weren't entirely giving up on his mother. Neither was he.

"I know you're strong, Mom. I know you can pull through this," he repeated aloud, evening after evening, as he squeezed her hands.

In all the empty hours of visiting Jackie, memories filled Stephen's mind. He remembered her holding his hand and taking him to school the first day. He remembered her laughing and playing with him in the waves at the beach, summer after summer. He recalled how she used to fuss about what the kids ate. She was always so busy with work and with driving them from place to place, why didn't she just heat up frozen dinners? he wondered. But she would have no junk food for her kids! She was vigilant about their nutrition, and she took extra time to see that they ate fish and chicken, eggs a few mornings a week instead of cold cereal out of a box, plenty of orange juice and hearty soups in winter, fresh fruits and vegetables year-round.

Each of Jackie's children brought to her ICU room special memories and secrets they'd shared with her, as each grappled painfully with losing her. While Stephen was the strongest in his belief that she could recover, the younger three came closer to accepting the prognosis that she would not survive the stroke damage, the coma, and the other complications. With their mother-centered world crumbling around them, they were uncertain of most things. But they knew one thing for certain: Jackie wouldn't want to live in this state indefinitely.

For Thomas, one of the most difficult parts of visiting her was the sight of her hands. He knew how much Jackie's lovely hands meant to her. Right after the stroke, they were clawlike. Now they were imprisoned in splints. Her nails were cut short and unpolished. They weren't her hands, Thomas thought. She would hate to see her hands like this.

Whenever Thomas dragged himself back to college after a weekend visit, he left his heart and mind in Baltimore with his mother. He sat through his classes, he turned the pages of his engineering books, but nothing really registered. He kept thinking,

My mother could have just died. She could be dead right this minute. Isolated and alone, though his roommates tried to support him, Thomas felt loneliness crushing his chest and heart. He took long, solitary walks, often late into the night. He had once smoked, then stopped, but now as he walked, he smoked Camels. On these walks, he often listened through headphones to instrumental New Age music. Its beauty and intensity reminded him of his mother, and some of the more melancholy songs matched his mood. He fingered Jackie's scarab on the chain around his neck. Before falling asleep at night, he'd remove the scarab to gaze at its Egyptian hieroglyphics and talk to it. The scarab represented Jackie's spirit to him, and talking to it was as close to talking with Jackie herself as Thomas could come.

A friend had told him that a scarab was a good-luck symbol: when one has bad luck, he or she gives the scarab away and, in turn, gets rid of the bad luck; but the person to whom the scarab is given receives good luck, rather than the giver's original bad luck. Thomas wondered if the scarab's passing from Jackie's neck to his would bring them both good fortune. Given all he knew about Jackie's condition, he doubted that it would.

After Thomas heard of Jackie's cardiac arrest, he phoned me.

"I'm going to come home and stay," he said flatly.

I forced my voice to sound calm and soothing.

"I know it's very hard to be so far away, Thomas, but maybe you'd better stick with your classes as a way of keeping yourself on track for a while."

"But my studies are meaningless right now," Thomas replied.

I knew his mind was made up, and it would do no good to insist that he stay at college. He returned home, and I wrote to his dean to explain the circumstances and ask permission for Thomas to withdraw for the semester. When he moved back home, Thomas took it upon himself to keep our lives together as best he could. He tried to support John and me, letting us unburden ourselves on him, comforting us at our weakest moments.

"C'mon, John, I'll go to the hospital with you," he would say at precisely the right moment. Thomas sensed just when John was feeling so depressed that he couldn't face another trip to the ICU alone. And when I was especially absorbed in a sorrowful silence,

Thomas seemed to appear from nowhere with "How are you feeling, Dad? Want to talk about it?" Thomas was trying to do what he knew Jackie would want him to do — be strong, be helpful.

Christina tried to cope with the loss of her mother by plunging herself into her work, as if filling her thoughts and time with schoolwork would crowd out the hopelessness of our tragedy. But on weekend visits home, Christina walked in a silent funk and looked as pale as Jackie's white robe, which she continued to wear. She brought home a copy of a letter Jackie had written to her, with a copy to Thomas, just two months earlier, when the space shuttle *Challenger* exploded. Jackie rarely wrote letters to Thomas and Christina at college — the telephone suited her better. But she had been so moved by the *Challenger* disaster that she shared her thoughts on paper.

"I couldn't believe it happened. It was like the day President Kennedy was shot — everyone remembers exactly where they were, what they were doing, when they first learned of the tragedy. I suppose I paid more attention to this space flight than others because a teacher was aboard. Working with teachers every day gave me a bond with Christa McAuliffe. In a way, we were all riding with her. It was such a significant symbol for education. . . . I feel so badly for her children, her husband, her students . . ."

Thomas and Christina carried Jackie's now dog-eared letter around, folding and unfolding it until the ink paled on the crease lines.

At the hospital, Christina stared at Jackie and wondered about her bizarre gesture the day before the stroke. When Christina came home for the Easter break that day, Jackie picked her up at the train station and found her hurt and annoyed. The fellow whom Christina had invited home for the weekend had told her at the last minute that he wasn't coming. Jackie tried to cheer Christina by taking her shopping. At an antique shop, Jackie picked up a string of cloudy glass beads. "Do you like these, Christina?"

"Yeah," she replied without enthusiasm. Jackie bought them.

Jackie always saved gifts for the occasion and wrapped them in pretty paper and ribbons. But this time she gave the unwrapped beads to Christina as they were walking out of the shop.

"Here, happy birthday, sweetie. You know, that guy is a foolish fellow for not spending his time with you!"

Christina's birthday wasn't for two more weeks. "Why did she do that? She never gave birthday presents early like that," Christina wondered as she replayed the scene over and over.

Christina finished the semester and kept in touch by phone. But every time I called her or she called me, I grieved that I had no good news to report.

John stopped by the hospital nearly every day after high school and often brought a friend with him. The nurses were struck by the sight of two young, vulnerable kids, bookbags slung over their shoulders, in the midst of a unit where most patients were old and dying. John's schoolwork was suffering badly. His teachers and counselor called to let me know that they were aware of how heavily Jackie's condition was weighing on John. I appreciated their concern, but none of us knew how to help him. I tried to get him to talk with me.

"Is there anything we can help you with, John? I know this is such an awful time for all of us, but what can we do to help each other? Can I help you review for tests or anything? I want to help you if I can. Or can we find a tutor to help you catch up with the work that has slipped?" But my attempts at getting him to talk and my offers of help with his schoolwork were met with a brief, "No, thanks, Dad."

Every morning when Jackie was in the hospital, I fixed John's lunch for school. Ham and cheese, every day. And I tried to cook breakfast for him as Jackie had. I scrambled eggs and placed them in front of him. He poked at the eggs in silence, usually leaving more on the plate than he ate. I knew I was no short-order cook — the eggs were either too runny or too rubbery. I sensed resentment on John's part that these were not his mother's eggs, but I wanted to show him some continuity in our shattered lives. Damn it, if his mother wasn't here to fix his breakfast, I was! Both of us skirted the eggs issue in awkward silence until John finally said, after many mornings of miserable eggs, "These are bad, Dad. These eggs are just bad!"

When John and I were alone in the house all week long, I felt an acute pain each time I saw him and tried to talk with him. John was incredibly lost without his mother. He was depressed and unengaged. He retreated into silence up in the loft, where he lay in a hammock and listened to music. I couldn't reach him. Though he sometimes talked on the phone with friends, he seemed not to want to talk to me at all.

"You and I will suffer more than anyone else, John, because we need Jackie more than anyone else," I tried to tell him. "I think we could help each other if we could just talk about it. I wish you could talk to me about your pain and let me share it with you."

"I'm sorry, Dad. It's just so hard to talk about it. What can I say — I love my mother and I want her back!" Then he'd stride up the stairs, two at a time, to his lonely loft.

Jackie and John used to paint together up in the loft. I thought of them, creating, learning, growing together. Now that was gone. John had no mother to share his artistic talent, his love of life. John and Jackie are so much alike and he needs her so badly, I thought. There's no one to fill that wretched, jagged hole in his heart. At seventeen, he's nowhere near ready to lose her, especially so suddenly. And I'm powerless to console him. I prayed that, in time and with God's grace, John would find peace and strength.

One evening, when I'd almost given up hope of consoling John, he asked me out of the blue: "Dad, I've got to ask you something."

"Sure, John, anything." I was thrilled that he'd opened a conversation after these weeks of near silence.

"Are you going to get married again?"

I was dumbfounded.

"John, I'm married now. To your mother. I don't ever want to *not* be married to her. But, I suppose, I would think about that again someday, after . . . if . . . after she died. . . . But if she should die, I want you to know this: I want you to know that you are my son and you will always be my son. I love you very, very much. And we will always be together."

"Okay, Dad. Thanks." And we hugged.

BY the fourth week of Jackie's coma, I desperately needed to discover God's will in all this. From the evening I'd listened to Pachelbel's Canon and stared into Jackie's photograph, I had given her up — I thought. But as time passed and she languished in the ICU bed, seemingly unclaimed by God, I grew more restless. When was God going to take Jackie? Our family, our friends, parishioners, my fellow ministers and their congregations and I were all praying that God would bring our suffering to a merciful end. I turned to Scripture again. Job had his boils. He lost his family and his sheep and oxen. I also read the Psalms. David suffered when he felt forsaken by God. I have something in common with them, I thought. Jackie remains with me, yet I've lost her. There is no resolution to this tragedy.

I have always prided myself on the ability to find resolutions to life's dilemmas. As a counselor and minister, I've enjoyed a great deal of satisfaction from helping others to solve their problems. Whenever I've counseled a couple with marital difficulties, or comforted a widow who has lost a lifelong partner, or helped an unemployed father find a job, I have felt useful about helping them to overcome their troubles. But in the face of Jackie's critical condition, I was at a loss for myself. Living with ambiguity isn't something that I do well. And this was more than an ambiguous situation. It was becoming a spiritual crisis of major proportions for me. I had to find another answer. Over these four weeks, my only answer had been to let God be God. But now I was beginning to wonder if God wasn't waiting for me to do what was necessary.

JACKIE'S infections were still raging when an internist told me that he planned to put Jackie on a new dose of antibiotics. The treatment would take six weeks.

My God! Six weeks! How did this happen? We have to put up with this for another six weeks? Who knows if Jackie will live another six weeks? This is ridiculous! It's just another attempt to come to an acceptable medical resolution, I thought. From the day of the stroke, the doctors have told me she has very little chance to survive; then once she survived that first weekend, they told me her chances of recovery — given the severity of the stroke, the pneumonia, the empyema, the cardiac arrest, and other possible complications — were infinitely small. Never in a million years is she going to come out of this, so even if they do cure the pneumonia with these six weeks of antibiotics, we'll be back to square one, a brain that drowned in blood and doesn't work! I was deeply frustrated by what I saw as a futile attempt to reach a medical resolution.

After so much time, so many doctors examining and treating Jackie and her increasing complications, this had become a drama — a theater of the absurd. We're all up there on a stage, going through our motions, saying our lines in a script that someone else wrote for us, and never knowing if or when the curtain will drop. But this is my wife's life, our life, I thought, and God is at work here . . . somehow.

I poured these thoughts out to another minister friend, Judith Michaels, pastor of the Waverly Presbyterian Church. Judith had been coming to see Jackie about twice a week. If she came in the late morning, Judith and I would then walk across the street for lunch, where I did more talking than eating. Judith has always been a great listener. From working with her on Presbytery committees, I knew she had a way of focusing in on a problem and bringing a rambling conversation back on track.

As I let my thoughts flow, Judith would ask practical questions such as "Do you have confidence in the doctors, Harry?"

"Yes, I do. I've talked to a lot of them. I've seen her CAT scan. I've talked to all the nurses, too. But this has become more of a theological question for me, Judith, than a medical or legal one."

"Well, what is the theological question?"

"The question is whether I, as a husband, a Christian, and a minister, have the right to . . . I hate the term, 'pull the plug,' but that's what I'm facing: do I pull the plug for Jackie? Based on what the doctors say, I have no hope for her recovery, certainly not a recovery where she'd be lucid or communicative. So I have to ask myself: what would Jackie want me to do? What does God want for her? I know, because she said it many times herself, that she would not want to go on living like this, living a 'life' maintained by machines. I don't think God wants her to live like this either. She's lost, Judith. She's lost to the children, to me, and to herself — she can't do anything, she has no capacity for growth, intimacy, love."

"I hear you, Harry. And you want to free her from this? You want to bring some good out of this?"

"Yes, Judith, even if it means losing her in this life. The kids lose their mother, whom they love and need so much, and I lose her — I can't imagine life without Jackie. But I think I may have to face that reality. I will have to make the ultimate sacrifice: letting her die so she can move out of this limbo to an eternal life with God. That seems to me to be the only way good can triumph over evil here and God's will be done."

"That would be the greatest sacrifice, Harry. Giving up the one you most love in this world. I'll pray that God will give you wisdom and strength to make the right decision."

I ALSO talked to Maureen about the sense of loss I was feeling. Whenever her ship docked in Los Angeles or Mexico after a ten-day cruise, she called to see if there was any change in Jackie. I told her there was no improvement, and when I told her about the plan to try a new six-week course of antibiotics, my sense of its absurdity burst: "It's crazy, Maureen. It's another attempt to find a medical resolution, when she's so far away from us that she'll never come back! It's like pulling a jack out of the car trunk when the whole damn car has broken down!"

Maureen knew exactly what I meant.

"Talk about absurdity! Unreality! Here I am on this ship, Harry. A cruise ship is the complete opposite of reality. These passengers are here to escape reality. Everything's got to be up and bright on board, so I have to smile at them even when I'm thinking of Jackie. And I think about her all the time."

Jackie's other dear friends, Carol and Adolphus, were as distraught as Maureen. The only difference was that they saw Jackie nearly every day. When he first saw her on Easter Sunday, Adolphus was anguished by the sight. Jackie's back was arched, and her hands were clenched like claws, signs of posturing. She looks so rigid, so stiff, so deformed, he thought. As tormenting as the sight was, Adolphus wasn't put off by it. He talked to Jackie, held her hand and patted it. His father had suffered a stroke, and he knew that someone in a stroke-induced coma may very well hear others talking. So he spoke words of encouragement to Jackie.

Carol was much more pessimistic than Adolphus from the outset. Ten years earlier, Carol's mother had suffered an aneurysm and multiple strokes. Carol watched helplessly as her mother lay, hooked to a respirator, in a nursing home for nearly a year. Carol could only imagine the same future for Jackie. Much younger and stronger than Carol's mother, Jackie might languish like this for years, Carol realized. The first time she saw Jackie in the ICU that Easter weekend, Carol prayed, "Lord, take her home. I don't want to let her go, but I don't want her to go through what my mother did." Carol visited Jackie each lunch hour in the early weeks, but each time she saw Jackie, she became more firmly convinced that Jackie shouldn't have to vegetate on artificial life supports for months or years.

I was waiting for the nurses to finish attending to Jackie one noontime, when Carol appeared in the doorway.

"Look at that, Harry! They're changing her diaper, throwing her leg around like a chicken wing! Can you imagine what Jackie would say about this — this unbearable assault on her person-hood, her dignity!" Carol exploded.

Jackie's body had begun to bloat because of the steroids given to reduce the swelling in her head. Carol hated to see this happen to her friend. It just wasn't Jackie. Not the Jackie she had always looked up to as a big sister, who boosted her self-esteem and encouraged her to lose weight and get in shape, who bluntly told Carol to change her hairstyle and dress up. This wasn't Jackie, the dear friend who stepped in when Carol's husband had been in a life-threatening accident and offered to take care of Carol's children — and fixed Carol's family buckets of chicken soup — until the crisis passed.

Whenever Carol visited the ICU, I saw in her face, in her tear-filled eyes, how much she hurt. She told me it was an ache that others couldn't understand because they hadn't been through it as she had with her mother. "I can't bear to see this repeated," she said. Carol found herself grieving for a lost friend, even though her friend was technically alive. Her visits to the ICU became less frequent. Instead, she spent her time with our children, sitting with them outside the ICU, or driving them wherever they needed to go, or drinking coffee with them in our kitchen. Carol tried to help them accept the unacceptable. "Your mother brought you up to be strong, independent kids. As hard as this is for you now, you will survive losing her. You'll heal. You have each other — God, I don't know of any other brothers and sisters who are as close as you are. And you will always carry with you the talents and qualities she encouraged in you. She was always so proud of you."

PEOPLE at the office had been asking when they could visit Jackie, but Carol and Adolphus put nearly everyone off. They knew that the children didn't want everybody to see their mother in this condition because she herself wouldn't want it. Adolphus and Carol agreed with the kids and protected Jackie from too many visitors. They became the news couriers, carrying word of her condition back to the office. But on one occasion, Adolphus brought along Jean Sorrentino. Jean had been particularly close to Jackie because, as mothers, they shared the joys and trials of raising children. Jean and Jackie constantly reassured each other about their worries and decisions, their children's behaviors, and all the everyday parental dilemmas for which no textbook exists. When Jean was concerned about her older son's getting a divorce, or her daughter going two thousand miles away to college, she found Jackie to be an empathic listener, a real friend.

The sight of Jackie lying immobile, almost in a fetal position, with her bright eyes closed, shocked Jean. She was about to turn and run out of the room, but she noticed Adolphus take Jackie's hand and talk to her. He's behaving as if Jackie is really there! He's practically trying to put words in her mouth, Jean thought, as he urged Jackie to respond to his questions. Jean was moved by Adolphus's devotion, his faith in Jackie, his belief that she might hear his words or feel his hand squeeze hers. Jean's initial shock was quickly replaced by an overwhelming feeling that life was mysterious and fragile. How much people need other people to survive, Jean thought. She took Jackie's hand and told her friend that she was missed greatly, that everybody was pulling for her, and that she hoped Jackie would recover soon.

"I miss our long talks, Jackie. I miss seeing all those pictures of your kids that you always bring to work. You've got to get better and start taking more pictures of your kids."

As they were leaving the ICU, Jean said to Adolphus, "I don't know if it was real or imaginary or just wishful thinking, but I felt some semblance of contact between Jackie and me in there."

JULIE and Carol were already acknowledging the futility of prolonging Jackie on artificial support. Given her experience with her mother, Carol had no reason to hope. Julie had reached the conclusion that Jackie was serving the sole purpose of letting medicine do its job. No one tried to push me toward a decision, but when I talked with Julie or Carol, or my friends in the ministry, the same questions always arose: How long can we prolong Jackie's inevitable death? When do we determine when to end this pointless suffering? When does living take precedence over dying? How long must everyone suffer as we watch her stay alive in only the technical sense, only alive because these machines are breathing for her and feeding her?

I was becoming increasingly convinced that a medical resolution was not feasible. Yet I continued to pray that God would reveal his intentions. What is he attempting to do here? I wondered. The frustration of not knowing grew as painful as watching Jackie linger on in her coma. At the end of the first month, whenever I considered Jackie's medical facts, my mind churned with "-lessnesses:" hopelessness, meaninglessness, powerlessness, uselessness . . . With the infection spreading from Jackie's lungs through her bloodstream, defeating the antibiotics, and the continuing vegetative state of her coma, how much longer could this tragedy go on?

Julie was wondering the same thing. On one of her afternoon visits to Jackie's cubicle, Brenda Flentje came in to check on Jackie's IVs. Julie had often spoken with Brenda and found her as approachable as she was professional. No one else was around, so Julie decided to ask Brenda a question that had been troubling her.

"What happens when somebody 'pulls the plug' and disconnects a respirator? Does the patient die right away?" Julie asked.

"Oh, no, death is not immediate," Brenda explained. "Some patients can continue to breathe on their own for a while. Some, like Karen Ann Quinlan,* live for years in a coma after the respirator is disconnected. And if a feeding tube is disconnected, death is not always immediate, either."

"Oh," Julie replied softly. "I guess I assumed that as soon as the plug was pulled, that would be the end. It hadn't occurred to me that Jackie might live a little longer."

Suddenly Julie was more confused and saddened than ever. If the respirator were withdrawn, it was possible that Jackie could linger for years, like Karen Ann Quinlan. But if the feeding tube were removed, she would surely die, but not immediately. Dear God, why must we have to make such harrowing choices? she pleaded silently.

---

* In 1976 the New Jersey Supreme Court granted the father of twenty-one-year-old Karen Ann Quinlan permission to turn off her respirator, after she had lapsed into an irreversible coma. She breathed unassisted for nine more years and died on June 11, 1985.

# Seven
Toward a Decision

Throughout the first month of Jackie's coma, I tried to read everything I could find about stroke and coma. I needed to know exactly what was going on medically, to be certain that I thoroughly understood Jackie's condition and treatment. The more facts I gathered, the better I might cope with her condition, I believed.

But near the end of that first month, after the lung abscess, pneumonia, and cardiac arrest had forced their way into the picture, and after the children, Julie, and I had that long Saturday talk with Dr. Pula, I realized that medical knowledge about Jackie's condition provided more than a method of coping. It was an absolutely necessary prerequisite to making the most wrenching decision: whether to disconnect Jackie's artificial life support systems or prolong this tragedy indefinitely. I believe that I was close to that decision from a theological perspective, but I didn't dare ignore any medical aspect, particularly if I were to decide on life support withdrawal and follow legal channels to do it. So I filled four sheets of yellow legal paper with questions for Dr. Pula, who patiently answered each. When he finished, he said, "Harry, now you know as much as anyone about stroke and coma. You ought to take your boards."

Dr. Pula had recommended that I read *The Diagnosis of Stupor and Coma*, by two leading authorities on coma, Drs. Fred Plum and Jerome B. Posner. I found it anything but encouraging. The authors cited their own experience with a group of coma patients. "Among 45 patients who were vegetative at the end of one week, 13 later awakened and five had satisfactory outcomes. Even after being vegetative for close to two weeks, eight patients awakened and one recovered to the level of a moderate disability, his chief difficulty being intellectual losses that precluded his return to work. For patients who remained vegetative after two weeks, however, the prognosis became uniformly poor."

The phrase "uniformly poor" jumped off the page at me. That meant Jackie! Her coma was now in its fourth week. I read on:

"Twenty-four such individuals survived to one month and of them only five were alive at the end of the year. Three remained permanently vegetative; the other two had overwhelming neurologic limitations as well as incapacitating mental impairments."

I wanted to slam the book shut, but I made myself read the next paragraph. Plum and Posner cited another study, this one of 110 "chronically vegetative subjects." Only 3 percent of them recovered and survived for three years, and — here was the clincher — none was able "to resume activity as a social human being." Dr. Pula also loaned me an article on "persistent vegetative state" from a neurological journal, which said the "possibility of regaining independence is negligibly small" after a month in coma.

After all my reading, I went back to Dr. Pula with the bottom-line question. "Tell me, Tad, is this hopeless?"

"It's not hopeless in the sense that it would be if she were brain-dead. Jackie isn't brain-dead. She still has brainstem reflexes, and the EEGs show there is some brain activity. If she had no brainstem reflexes and the EEGs were flat, she would be brain-dead.

"While Jackie's overall medical condition has been one hurdle after another — the pneumonia, cardiac arrest, lung abscess — you could say that her neurological condition has plateaued by now. When she came in, her pupils weren't reacting properly, which wasn't a good neurological sign, but the rest of her brainstem reflexes were relatively good. Over the past couple of weeks, she hasn't lost the rest of the brainstem reflexes, so it isn't a situation of one thing going one day, another thing going the next, and yet another going on day three.

"But Jackie's overall condition from the beginning has looked very bad. It has been a fight for life from the word go. It's highly unlikely that she will regain consciousness, and highly unlikely that she will have the combination — and I stress 'combination' — of surviving the stroke and the other medical complications and regaining consciousness."

"Can you give me any statistical prediction of her chances that are more encouraging than the material I've been reading?" I asked.

"That's difficult because there aren't enough numbers, not enough incidence of people surviving massive cerebral hemorrhages like Jackie's, who survive the stroke and go on to regain consciousness and then — if by the remote chance they get that far — survive complications like pneumonia.

"If you want to pin me down to numbers, I'd have to say her chances of surviving the stroke, the coma, the complications — and returning to a meaningful life — are *one in a million*. And I say that, not so much based on hard statistics, because there aren't any, but to indicate that it's a tremendous long shot that she'll return to a relatively 'normal' life," Dr. Pula explained.

"So, even if she could beat those long-shot odds and come out of the coma, what would her condition be?" I asked, fearing the worst.

"Well, the best medical evidence we have would indicate that, even if she regains consciousness, she probably will be very, very dependent. Many patients who have massive strokes need chronic-care facilities."

"You mean nursing homes?"

"Yes."

Jackie in a nursing home — I shuddered at the possibility.

"You mean, she wouldn't be able to take care of herself, even take care of her bodily functions?"

"Most likely, she wouldn't."

"That's exactly what she wouldn't want, Tad. She would hate to be dependent on others. She'd detest the loss of dignity, the loss of independence."

"From what you've told me about Jackie's expressed wishes," he said, "it's highly unlikely that she would have the kind of life she would deem acceptable if she should regain consciousness and survive the pneumonia. But for now, I think we should continue to do what we're doing for her."

I OFTEN shared my thoughts with Ron Bond and David Ash — from the small, daily frustrations to the big, cosmic agonies. I talked with them about my concern for the kids, how they were withdrawn, lost, how I felt helpless to heal them. We talked, too, about practical matters: how would I manage to send the kids through college on my income alone? I'd probably have to take huge loans, maybe sell the house. And we talked about the big question: just because medicine has given us the means to prolong life, must those means be used simply to keep a body breathing if there's no realistic hope that life will return in any truly meaningful sense? Would I dare play God by trying to end this artificially supported "life"? Or would I be acting, as God might want, to free Jackie from her ICU prison of respirator, IV nourishment, chest-tube drain, antibiotics that weren't working, anyway — to free her to move from this tragic place on earth to a peaceful, loving place with God? Could it be an act of love, of grace, of faith, to take an active part in letting Jackie go? In all my talks with other ministers, we all reached the same conclusion: there was no clear-cut formula for this situation. Church doctrine provided no ready answer. I would have to find my own, most appropriate, response, my fellow ministers counseled, and God would surely guide me with his grace.

During one of our many discussions, I made a point of asking David's professional advice about what legal avenues I might follow if and when I might reach some decision about withdrawing artificial life support systems. David was direct and detailed:

"You'll have to go to court, Harry. I've had no direct experience with a case like this before, but I've done some checking. It's unfortunate that Jackie didn't write a living will to indicate what she'd want done in a situation like this. The Maryland living-will law was enacted just a year ago. But even if she had written one, it might not apply because we would have trouble proving that her condition is 'terminal.' Under Maryland's "Life-Sustaining Procedures Act," as it's called, the living will applies to patients who have an incurable injury, disease, or illness certified to be a terminal condition by two examining physicians. And the doctors have to determine that the patient's death is imminent. That means death will occur whether or not life-sustaining procedures are used to prolong the dying process. But if she'd had a living will, it might strengthen the position in court that she would have wanted life support withdrawn in her present condition. Well, that's moot anyway because she never wrote one. Then, there's another factor: she is not legally dead, because there's some brainstem activity, right?"

"Yes."

"So, the law says you're not dead if the brainstem still functions. That means you can't just tell the hospital to turn off the machines. And you can't do it yourself unless you want to face a murder charge. And remember, under the provisions of your guardianship, you need the court's permission to approve or authorize any procedure that could affect her life.

"But, as her legal guardian, you could seek a court order to disconnect artificial life support systems on the basis that she, herself, would have wanted them withdrawn in these circumstances. That's what I understand happened in the Karen Ann Quinlan case. The New Jersey court granted her father, as her guardian, permission to disconnect her respirator based on her right to privacy. In other words, a person has the right to refuse treatment as part of her right to privacy. If the person can't exercise that right because she is comatose, her legal guardian can. It's sometimes called 'substituted judgment.'"

I heard David's words and I tried to absorb their meaning, but I couldn't respond because I was having great difficulty integrating those hard, cold judicial facts into my emotions.

"I can't tell you what to do, Harry. It's your decision. All I can give you is my legal opinion about your options. I'll stand by you, no matter what you decide."

ON Tuesday of the fifth week of Jackie's coma, I awoke and realized that it had been a month to the day since her stroke.

What more can I do? I asked myself. I've tried pleading and

bargaining with God to revive her. I've placed her in God's hands and waited for him to take her home. The doctors do everything they can, yet nothing changes. If anything, things get worse.

My innate need to resolve problems was festering, just as my hope was waning that God would rescue Jackie, either by awakening her or by letting her die. A month after her stroke, there was no question in my mind that Jackie would die. Everything the doctors said pointed to her death. But when? I felt a sense of anticipation. Her impending death was becoming a momentous event in my mind. I was beginning to feel a note of completion, even excitement, about the ending of Jackie's tragedy. She would soon be free. She would join God in an everlasting peace. Good would finally triumph over evil and suffering.

During a late-evening visit, I was startled to see Jackie open her eyes — only partially, but indeed open. Two black coals, like the eyes of a corpse. There was no spark of life in them. I shuddered and called a nurse, who explained that Jackie was not doing this voluntarily. Comatose patients sometimes do this, just as she sometimes blinked when she was moved. It's called "coma watch," the nurse said, "just like posturing, it's involuntary. Don't get your hopes up, Reverend Cole. It's not a good sign."

Later that week I attended the funeral of my father's closest friend of fifty years, Frank Armiger. In the nursing home, my father was unaware of Frank's death. I wasn't sure the Alzheimer's allowed him even to remember his friend's name. After Frank was buried, I walked across the cemetery in a chilly drizzle to my own family's plot. I stared at the graves of my grandparents and great-grandparents. Several grave sites remained in our family plot. I chose two. One for Jackie. The other for me.

My mind filled with conflicting visions. I suddenly recalled Jackie on our patio at the old Kensington Road house. The kids were all away with friends that night, and we'd had a romantic candlelight dinner outside, that balmy summer evening. Jackie was so lovely and so loving as we talked about our future.

"What do you suppose we'll be doing in thirty years, Harry?" she'd asked.

"Probably baby-sitting our great-grandchildren."

"I wouldn't mind that — but not too often," she laughed. "I'd like to travel a lot, wouldn't you? I'd like to pack up my camera, rolls and rolls of film, and a sketch pad, too. And you and I could travel around the country. You could be an itinerant preacher." Her voice was serious but the glance she shot me was full of teasing.

"Maybe we'd go to Europe. There's so much I want to see and do. No porch rocking chair for me, thank you!" She covered my hand with hers and squeezed.

I wanted that memory to spring to life, to happen night after night. I loved her so much, and I ached at the thought that we would never have moments like that again.

The burial of Dad's friend slapped a dose of cold reality in the face of my pain and sorrow: Jackie and I wouldn't have a future together. As I walked back across the cemetery, my mind filled with thoughts of funeral arrangements for Jackie. I considered who would do the service, what music should be played, who would eulogize my wife. I realized sadly that I would soon have to select a casket.

WHEN I met Dr. Pula in our familiar conference room the next day, he noticed a difference in me. I was holding myself taller and straighter. I seemed less reflective and inquiring. I didn't stretch back in the chair, ponder, and ask questions as usual. I was more forthright and definite. As close as we'd become, Dr. Pula was too professional and reserved to ask outright, "Harry, have you had an inspiration or revelation?" But he told me much later that he'd wondered whether the change he sensed in me had a spiritual source. At that moment, though, he broached the subject with a simple observation and question:

"You seem a bit, umm, what shall I say, different, more definite? What's on your mind today, Harry?"

"You know, Tad, this has to stop," I said. "This cannot go on."

"Well, Harry, I don't know that anything has to change today or this week or next week in terms of Jackie's treatment. You know she's on a new antibiotic and the lung abscess is draining . . ."

"No, it's different now. It's been over a month. It's one thing after another," I said firmly. "I think we need to stop all these futile attempts at a medical resolution."

"I'm not so sure, Harry, that that's really the best thing to do. In fact, I'd like to continue our current level of supportive care. That's my game plan," Dr. Pula suggested. "Maybe as the weeks roll by, we might be less aggressive about adding additional things if new complications arise."

"No, that's not good enough. Maybe I am different today, Tad. I don't know. I'm too deep in this to see objectively any day-to-day changes in my own perceptions. I'm not sure why today is the day I've decided that enough is enough. These decisions come slowly. They evolve over time. For more than a month, we have been watching Jackie die. We have no hope that she'll recover. You've told me yourself that even if, by the remotest chance, she should come out of this coma, she's going to be severely disabled, dependent on others for her feeding, toileting, bathing, dressing.

"Each day builds on the previous one, I suppose. Day after day, I've been praying and thinking about what I am to do here. All I see is death closing in on us. Maybe it was the funeral I attended yesterday that has nudged me to the brink of this decision. That funeral was one more reminder of Jackie's death — I even began thinking of her funeral arrangements! I can't explain the timing. But I know now that I can no longer stand in the way," I affirmed. "We are just postponing her death with these medical techniques and machines. I am convinced that God doesn't want her to go on this way, month after month, comatose, hooked to a ventilator, catheter, IV tubes, chest drain. And neither would she. Neither would Jackie! This isn't a life. It's hopeless. Futile. Pointless. There's nothing redemptive in this suffering.

"All this high-powered medical technology isn't curing her. It's just holding her back from eternity, from peace with God. I think we need to give God and Jackie a little leeway here — I want her to be transferred out of ICU to a regular private room, at least."

"Harry, I understand your point of view. I agree that a patient has the right to determine her own treatment. I accept your right to speak for her in these circumstances, that what you're asking is in accordance with her wishes. I don't think your statement that 'enough is enough' is unreasonable. But when you say 'we need to stop all these futile attempts,' I have to tell you that I cannot legally or professionally authorize withdrawal of life support measures."

"I know, Tad. And I know that you want to do what's best for Jackie as much as I do. I know you can't switch off those machines and pull the tubes. That's why I am talking to my lawyer about going to court for permission to have these artificial life support systems turned off."

As Dr. Pula and I had come to know each other over these weeks, each recognized that the other was very strong-willed. Each held firmly to his own ideas and beliefs. We jostled like gentlemen until our polite negotiations ended at an impasse. Dr. Pula agreed that Jackie could be moved out of ICU soon, but he was definite about continuing the antibiotics, the respirator, chest drainage tube, and IV feedings.

EACH night when I visited Jackie alone, I told her how much I loved her. "I love you more than life itself, Jackie. It is absolutely vital to me that you know that God loves you and so do I," I repeated as I held her hand, kissed her, and cried. "I have always loved you, Jacqueline! And I will forever.

"I don't know if you can hear me, if you can comprehend my words, in this distant coma. But I pray that you can. I love you and I am going to act for you, not for myself, when I go to court to end this. I will make the ultimate sacrifice for you, to give you up forever.

"As much as I can't imagine my life here on earth without you, I have to give you up now, and I want you to go home with God. You'll find eternal peace with God very soon. In heaven, you'll know all God's secrets. All the questions you've ever had will be answered. You'll have no doubts, no fear of anything, no insecurity. You'll be completely at peace. All the hurts and disappointments you've known in this life will be taken away. You will have that indescribable joy and peace and oneness with God. You'll see God's face and know that he loves you. I am absolutely certain of that, Jackie, my love."

*　　*　　*

ON Tuesday morning, May 1, I looked at the calendar, ripped off the April page, and tore it to tiny shreds. How I wished I could rip the entire month out of our lives.

The next day, Jackie was moved from the ICU to a private room on the sixth floor, 638. Coincidentally, her final payroll statement came that day. Another ending. I was becoming accustomed to endings. But at least events were beginning to move. I almost felt relief at having reached a decision to go to court. Ever since the first long meeting with Dr. Pula, when the children and Julie agreed to put the decision about possibly ending Jackie's life support systems in my hands, I had tried to weigh several factors separately: What was best for Jackie? What would she want? What was best for the children? Where was God in all this, and what did he want me to do? It was difficult to deal with these questions individually, because they all blended into one another. Yet I tried, in my many silent and solitary moments, to consider every option as I worked my way toward the most appropriate and fitting decision for Jackie's welfare.

Whenever I approach the task of making a major ethical decision, I go back to the writings of H. Richard Niebuhr, the late American ethicist at Yale Divinity School, whom I had often studied in Christian ethics courses at seminary. Niebuhr offered a standard of moral credence and direction that made sense to me. For Niebuhr, the basis of ethics is that everyone is responsible for his or her own behavior and decisions. To Niebuhr, and to me, ethical decisions allow wide latitude. There's no prescription for how a responsible person should act in one set of circumstances or another. Instead of rigid rules, ethical decisions are made within a two-way relationship between man and God. But to make decisions, we respond to an idea for a desired end. To whom are we responding? To whom are we responsible? God. God is the object of our responsibility. If I sought withdrawal of Jackie's artificial life supports, I would be making an ethical decision to reach a desired end — the end of her pointless, futile existence in a limbo caused by a massive stroke — and I would make that decision with full responsibility toward God.

I reread Niebuhr's *The Responsible Self* and focused on his statement "Responsibility affirms — God is acting in all actions upon you. So respond to all actions upon you as to respond to His action." When I considered how God was acting in our lives, I considered another of Niebuhr's ethical standards: that humans need to make a fitting response to God's actions. A fitting response makes us accountable for our reaction to God's action. What appropriate response could I make in these circumstances? The more I thought about it, the more convinced I became that the fitting response was not to prolong Jackie's inevitable death by keeping her on artificial, mechanical means. The fitting response would be to disconnect those machines and tubes and allow her to die.

ON a raw, gray Saturday afternoon, five weeks after Jackie's stroke, I drove to the Witzke Funeral Home. The cloying fragrance of carnations filled the silent emptiness of the place.

I had been conducting funeral services for years, but I was totally lost about what to do for Jackie's. My friend Russell Witzke walked me through the procedures. I nodded my assent to everything that Russell suggested. But I firmly stated that I wanted no viewing, no visits to the funeral home. We would have a simple, private service for the family and closest friends. Later we'd have a memorial service for everyone who loved Jackie and wanted to celebrate her life with us. I told Russell that I would talk to Jack Sharp, my old friend and minister of Govans Presbyterian Church, who would conduct the service. Then I walked heavily into the casket room. I selected a richly polished cherry casket because it was simple and dignified.

"That's just right for a beautiful lady," Russell said quietly. I signed some papers confirming the arrangements, and Russell put them in an envelope.

"I'll put these in the safe, Harry, and I hope we never have to use them."

DAVID ASH called me early the next week and brought me up to date on plans to seek court permission. He would need written statements from Jackie's doctors, David explained, and Leo Ottey would again represent Jackie. Leo would interview Christina once more, but this time it would be to get a statement about Jackie's wish "not to live this way" that she'd expressed on the morning of her stroke. David also said it would be important to have Dr. Pula testify at the hearing.

Dr. Pula had anticipated the request to testify from the moment I had told him that I'd decided to go to court. Now he found himself faced with a very difficult dilemma: the rights and desires of his patient seemed to be at odds with the laws of her society. Jackie had made her wishes known on numerous occasions, he knew. She had been emphatic and explicit in saying that she didn't want to be kept alive mechanically if she was going to be anything less than active and independent. And Dr. Pula knew that Jackie had made these statements based on firsthand experience with her own mother.

Dr. Pula had reflected on his own professional experience, discussed the case in detail with several colleagues, including three other neurologists and an intensive care specialist, and again reviewed the medical literature. The conclusion was clear: occasionally adults who are in a vegetative state following an intracerebral hemorrhage do regain consciousness after one month, but those who do are, at best, severely disabled. They have "overwhelming neurologic limitations as well as incapacitating mental impairments," as one recent medical journal article stated. He was also aware of the Maryland law that states: "It is the fundamental right of each competent adult to control his/her own medical care." Now, acting in Jackie's behalf as her legal guardian, I was determined that Jackie's treatment be discontinued, because the best outcome was far worse than what she would have deemed acceptable.

On the other hand, Dr. Pula realized, existing laws and legal precedents supported discontinuing medical care only for patients who were brain-dead, or for terminal patients with living wills who were near death, or for those who were in permanent vegetative states. Although unresponsive, Jackie was certainly not brain-dead. Even if she'd had a living will, it would not have been applicable, because Dr. Pula did not feel that her death was imminent; that is, she was not likely to die within two weeks, the usual definition of "imminent" death. Finally there was still the remote possibility that she would regain consciousness.

No, Dr. Pula would not stop Jackie's life support systems. But Jackie was his patient, and he felt that she did have the right to determine her own treatment — especially in circumstances where what was medically appropriate depended so much upon what constituted a meaningful existence for the individual. So, he decided, he would go to court with me, try to present the medical aspects of her case clearly, and testify that her plea seemed reasonable.

"Yes, Harry, I'll testify. I know you are trying to do what's best for Jackie. But I've got to tell you that I don't think there's a prayer of the petition's being granted. Not in this state," Dr. Pula said. "But who am I to tell *you* if there's a prayer."

Dr. Pula and the rest of the country's doctors didn't know the details yet, but that spring the American Medical Association's Council on Ethical and Judicial Affairs was hammering out guidelines, which would be published a few months later as *Current Opinions,** on social policy issues, including one of the most crucial: withholding or withdrawing life-prolonging medical treatment. Months later, when Dr. Pula would read it, he would find that it meshed with his views and fit Jackie's situation. The A.M.A. opinion states:

> The social commitment of the physician is to sustain life and relieve suffering. Where the performance of one duty conflicts with the other, the choice of the patient, or his family or legal representative if the patient is incompetent to act in his own behalf, should prevail. In the absence of the patient's choice or an authorized proxy, the physician must act in the best interest of the patient.
>
> For humane reasons, with informed consent, a physician may do what is medically necessary to alleviate severe pain, or cease or omit treatment to permit a terminally ill patient, whose death is imminent, to die. However, he should not intentionally cause death. In deciding whether the administration of potentially life-prolonging medical treatment is in the best interest of the patient who is incompetent to act in his

* See Resources, p. 273.

own behalf, the physician should determine what the possibility is for extending life under humane and comfortable conditions and what are the prior expressed wishes of the patient and attitudes of the family or those who have responsibility for the custody of the patient.

Even if death is not imminent, but a patient's coma is beyond doubt irreversible and there are adequate safeguards to confirm the accuracy of the diagnosis and with the concurrence of those who have responsibility for the care of the patient, it is not unethical to discontinue all means of life-prolonging medical treatment.

Life-prolonging medical treatment includes medication and artificial or technologically supplied respiration, nutrition or hydration. In treating a terminally ill or irreversibly comatose patient, the physician should determine whether the benefits of treatment outweigh its burdens. At all times, the dignity of the patient should be maintained.

AS the sixth week of Jackie's coma began, David prepared for the court hearing. He obtained letters from Dr. Pula and Dr. Michael G. Hayes, the head of the hospital's pulmonary division, who had also been treating Jackie. On May 6, Dr. Pula wrote:

> To Whom It May Concern: Jacqueline Cole has been under my care for over a month. During this time she has been continuously comatose. Despite vigorous therapeutic efforts in the ICU for the past month, her neurologic condition has shown no signs of improvement. She continues to be in a persistent vegetative state. Over the past month, she has had multiple medical problems. These have included bilateral staphylococcal pneumonia with a right side pneumothorax. Currently she is being treated with Vancomycin and a chest tube in the right thorax. She continues to be maintained on the respirator. She is being fed through a nasogastric tube. Despite these various efforts, she has had no sign of neurologic improvement. Her long term neurologic prognosis for any significant recovery is extremely poor.

On the same day, Dr. Hayes wrote:

To Whom It May Concern: I am the Pulmonary consultant of Jacqueline Cole. She presently has a Tracheostomy and is on a MA-1 ventilator (respirator) which is supporting her life. Her pulmonary status is markedly compromised by a condition called Adult Respiratory Distress Syndrome and complicated by an Empyema with a chronic chest tube.

Her prognosis is guarded. Her death is imminent and is being prolonged by the use of ventilatory support.

David submitted the doctors' letters as affidavits attached to a written "Petition for Court Approval to Withdraw Jacqueline Cole from Life Support Systems" and filed the papers with the Circuit Court for Baltimore on Tuesday, May 6. In the petition, David laid out five points:

• Judge Ward had appointed me as Jackie's legal guardian of person and property;

• Jackie remained comatose, "with no realistic hope or prognosis of recovery," as indicated by the doctors' affidavits;

• It is the policy of Maryland General Hospital and the treating physicians that the life support systems not be withdrawn without the court's approval;

• It is the agreed opinion of the children of Jacqueline Cole, after hours of heart-rending discussions, that this Petition be approved and, in fact, they believe their mother would want this matter to proceed in the requested fashion;

• The petitioner, Harry Cole, requests an emergency hearing to be held to hear the merits of this petition.

I HAD no doubt that the court would grant my request. Though Dr. Pula had said that he didn't think it had a chance, my ears heard the words but my mind rejected them. Paul Hoback cautioned me, too. One evening over supper at the Hobacks' house, Paul, the salty former newspaper reporter, told me, "Not in Maryland, Harry. Not in this state, where the law says you have to be brain-dead. Courts here aren't going to interpret that liberally." Again, I didn't process the words, because I believed that I was following Jackie's wishes and that I was acting as God would want me to act — to find a resolution that would allow redemption to emerge from Jackie's suffering.

During one of my evening visits to Jackie that sixth week, I was interrupted by a nurse who had to turn Jackie, toilet her, and check her IVs. I left Jackie's new room, 638, with its flowery vinyl wallpaper. The sixth floor was alien territory for me, a change neither welcome nor hostile, just different from the ICU floor that I'd come to know intimately. I felt strangely uncomfortable on the sixth floor. I didn't know where to walk, what to do, how long to wait for the nurse to finish. I jammed my hands into my pockets and walked down the empty corridor.

A door marked Supply Closet was ajar. I'll never know why, but I pushed the door open and switched on the light. The shelves were stacked with boxes and bottles of all sizes. My eyes fell immediately on one small packet on an otherwise bare section of shelving.

The label read Shroud Kit.

I picked it up. It contained a white plastic body bag. In the six weeks of visiting Jackie, I had seen several deceased people wheeled out, covered in these white plastic shrouds that fitted neatly over the body, drawn tightly head to foot, belted to a stretcher.

"This is for her. It's the last one here," I said aloud. "It's meant for Jackie. They'll wrap my Jacqueline in this shroud, place her on a gurney. They'll strap a belt across her stomach, and they'll take her from this place. A kind of final testament to whatever malevolent power in the world is taking her from me."

I placed the shroud kit back on the shelf. Tears stung my eyelids as I closed the supply closet door behind me. When I returned to 638, the nurse had finished, and Jackie lay as immobile, as far away and deathlike as she had been for weeks. "Please, God, grant her peace," I prayed.

"I love you, Jackie, but I have to say good-bye to you."

As David worked on scheduling the court hearing, I told Julie, the children, and Jackie's friends that I had decided to bring this tragedy to an end by going to court.

"That's what Jackie would want if she could speak for herself,

I'm sure, Harry," Julie said. "It's a shame you have to go to court, but if that is the only possible way to resolve this nightmare, to let her go with dignity and peace, then it must be done."

"It's the right decision, Dad," Thomas said. "It's what she'd want you to do." John agreed, as did Christina when I called her at college. "Yes, Dad. I'll tell the lawyers again what she said to me the morning she had the stroke. I hate all this legal stuff, but if that's the only way to go, we've got to do it. For Mom." And when I told Stephen, he didn't disagree with the decision, but he thought the timing was early. Our oldest son still believed that she was strong and might defeat all the medical odds.

"We've all hoped that from the beginning," I told Stephen, "but it's been one assault on her body after another from the start: the stroke, the pneumonia, the lung abscess, the cardiac arrest. There's no sign that she's going to get better, I'm afraid."

"I know, Dad, but, oh, I don't know . . . I just wish she'd wake up!"

When Maureen called the next day from a pay phone on a Los Angeles pier, I told her of my decision. We tried to talk about how difficult a decision it was to reach, but I could hardly hear Maureen's words through her tears. "You have to do what you think is right, what's best for Jackie," I heard her say. Maureen could barely hear me, too, because a flock of chatting Italian tourists were swirling around her on the pier. When they caught sight of their tour director, tears streaming down her face and nearly shouting into the phone, they stopped momentarily and stared. Then they went on with their tour and with their disparate lives.

And when I phoned Ron Bond, his reaction was similar to Stephen's.

"There hasn't been enough time, Harry. Are you sure this is what you want to do?" But as soon as the words left his throat, Ron knew the answer. From three decades of friendship, Ron knew how my mind worked: I thought a situation through from beginning to end, weighed various considerations, and finally reached a decision. Then I'd bounce my decision off others for reinforcement. That was just the way I worked, and Ron knew it.

Ron shared my agony. He had seen or spoken with me nearly every day and had visited Jackie daily in the early weeks and every other day since. But Ron knew that my mind was made up, that I had reached my decision after grave, lengthy deliberation, and it didn't matter what Ron might say now. Yet Ron felt obligated by the honesty that cements strong friendships to tell me, "Harry, I think you should take more time."

"I have, Ronnie. It's been six weeks. I've read the medical literature about what happens to patients who've been in coma over a month. Even the very few who survive are hopelessly dependent nursing home cases — exactly what Jackie said she'd never want to be. I've talked to Dr. Pula about all the possibilities, all the options we might have, and don't have. And I've got to do something to resolve this pointless suffering. All the medical machinery isn't saving her life. It's merely prolonging her death!" I said, with a note of finality in my voice, "and I've got David doing the legal things."

As soon as he hung up, Ron phoned David.

"Do you know what Harry is contemplating?"

"Yeah, he's already talked with me."

"Go slow on this thing, David. I think . . ."

"You know, Ron, I've talked with him a hell of a lot." David's usually soft voice grew louder. "Go slow? He's thought the whole thing out. This isn't some whim, you know. He's talked with the doctors, he's read the medical literature. He's prayed over it. He sees no value in prolonging Jackie's death for weeks or months more. What if we do wait another month, six months? A year? There's no medical indication that she'll improve, and there's certainly no evidence that after such a stroke she could ever return to an independent life. I've talked to doctors, read some articles, too. Even if she ever woke up — and there's virtually no chance of that happening — she'd be a vegetable. I hate to use that word, Ronnie. 'Severely disabled' might be a prettier term, but that's what she'd be, a vegetable. Someone would have to feed her, dress her, toilet her, bathe her. She probably wouldn't be able to talk or walk. Who knows what she could even understand? What's the point in buying more time? Harry's made a thoughtful, prayerful decision. God, you know him as well as anybody! He's doing what's best for Jackie, what she would want herself. The man's been in hell all these weeks. He's made a courageous decision, the greatest sacrifice a man can make. This is the right decision, and I think we should all support him. You know the agony he and those kids are going through . . ."

"I know? Sure, I know. I've been with him, David. You think I haven't felt it, too? But all I'm saying is to slow down," Ron said.

"No, Ronnie, he knows what he's doing. Harry really does. And the kids agree with him."

"Well, you can't count me among those who think this is a good decision right now. Maybe eventually, but not yet. I'm sorry." Ron hung up, feeling both frustration and relief at unloading on David what he couldn't unload on me.

Eight

In Court

TO: JCB   *Date: 5-8-86*

J. David Ash, att'y, called. His best friend's wife had a massive stroke in March and has been comatose since at Maryland General Hospital. On April 25, husband appointed guardian. Requests taking her off life support. Hearing needed. Was scheduled before Judge Ward today; but because of doctor's emergency, hearing had to be rescheduled. Would like to schedule for tomorrow after 1 p.m., as doctor said he could be here. Can you handle?

Carol Shay pulled the small ivory message sheet out of her typewriter and added it to the pile of messages for her boss, Baltimore Circuit Court judge John Carroll Byrnes. He would be the only judge in the courthouse tomorrow because all the other judges would be attending an out-of-town conference. One judge had to stay behind as the duty judge. Judge Byrnes had volunteered because he thought it would be a quiet day to finish writing a few opinions. But it didn't look that way to Carol Shay. Her phone never stopped ringing.

As he went through his messages later in the day, Judge Byrnes lifted his fountain pen and wrote at the top, "Yes. 1 P.M. 5/9/86."

FORTY-SIX years ago, John Carroll Byrnes's mother and his father, also a judge, had named their son after John Carroll, the founder of Georgetown University and the Jesuit who was selected in 1789 to be the first Roman Catholic bishop in the United States. John Carroll Byrnes never much liked the name "Carroll." But when he first ran for the Maryland State Senate in 1970, political rumor circulated in his district that another John C. Byrnes was planning to run. To distinguish himself from the other man, John Carroll Byrnes dusted off his middle name and began to use it publicly. John C. never ran. John Carroll was elected as a Democrat and served for twelve years before becoming a judge.

FRIDAY, May 9, was a glorious spring day, not a day most people would choose to sit in a hermetically sealed courtroom.

Early that morning, I went by my church office to drop off my "From the Pastor's Study" message to be printed in the weekly church bulletin. My message was one of God's saving power: "If we choose to believe the works of God — that he shares our lives' experiences and redeems our lives by showing us in his Resurrection that life is triumphant, powerful, and never-ending — then the quality of our lives will be immeasurably enhanced by God's saving power."

Then I drove to Maryland General to see Jackie before going to court. I felt certain of the outcome, that a judge would grant us permission to withdraw life support systems, and I was committed to the outcome of losing Jackie. This was the only fitting response I knew I could make to this situation. As I held her hand, I said simply, "Jackie, I'm going to help you today." Then I went to join David for a quick lunch before the 1 P.M. hearing.

David was thoroughly convinced that seeking permission to end Jackie's and my agony was the right thing to do. I found David reviewing his notes and "points and authorities," summaries of similar right-to-die cases, which he had already prepared for the judge:

> In Re Quinlan:
> 355 A2d 647   Court granted parents of comatose patient the authority to withdraw patient from life-sustaining systems. It was the opinion of treating physicians that the patient had very little possibility of recovery as commonly defined and that she would remain in a "vegetated" state.

> Matter of Conroy:
> 486 A2d 1209   Authority to terminate the use of life-

sustaining systems was granted even though this patient had the ability to physically move her arms, follow objects with her eyes and perform other such bodily functions. Patient was "semi-comatose" with no medical hope for recovery.

Severns v. Wilmington Medical Center, Inc.:
(1980 Del. Sup.) 421 A2d 1334   Husband who was acting as guardian was granted authority to discontinue the use of life-sustaining systems for his wife, who was in a comatose state, and it was medically unlikely that her condition would permit her to recall, speak or think.

John F. Kennedy Memorial Hospital, Inc. v. Bludworth:
(1983 Fla. App. D4) 423 So. 2d 611   Authority to withdraw patient from life-support system was granted when it was the known wish of the patient that this be done. Patient also had lost cognitive brain function and chances of recovery were extremely remote.

David hoped these four precedents would be sufficient. He knew little about John Carroll Byrnes. David had never appeared before him in court but knew his reputation to be that of a reflective, decent judge. David thought that the rightness of our appeal would prevail. Yet he was nervous when he walked into the old courthouse with Dr. Pula, Ron Bond, who had come along not to testify but to lend moral support, and me.

COURTROOM 404 would never be selected for a television drama. Carved out of space formerly used by the Baltimore branch of the FBI, the courtroom had an improvised look. The judge's bench was in a corner, in front of burgundy drapery. A heavy wooden desk for the court clerk dominated the central area in front of the bench. The low ceiling and fluorescent glare would have been more appropriate to a motel conference room than to a lofty hall of justice.

At 1:05 P.M., the hearing opened, as Judge Byrnes began: "I have read the file. I guess I should also note, for the record, I had an occasion in practice to represent a client who was in exactly this condition, so I have some personal familiarity with what is described in the medical evidence that I have seen in the file."

I heard that as a good omen. Perhaps the judge would sympathize with our pain.

Judge Byrnes didn't offer any details, but he was referring to a former client who had been severely injured by medical malpractice when she was in her forties. As her attorney, Byrnes had occasionally visited her in the hospital, where she lay in a fetal position. Judge Byrnes recalled how her family vehemently wanted her to receive every means of life support. From that experience, he also concluded that a patient in such a condition does not feel pain, though her family does. Greatly.

DAVID called Thaddeus Peter Pula, M.D., as the first witness. As he walked toward the stand, Dr. Pula later told me, he noticed a courtroom clerk working a crossword puzzle. Just another day for some people, he thought. Being in this courtroom felt so strange, so unreal, Dr. Pula thought. Who's grounded in reality here, anyway, that woman doing a crossword, or the rest of us?

After stating the routine information — his name, address, medical school, hospital residency, title, age (thirty-six), length of practice (ten years) — Dr. Pula was asked by David, "So you have had experience, extensive experience, with patients in this kind of condition?"

"Yes."

"How many patients?" asked the judge. A pattern was beginning. Unlike formal trials, this hearing would not be dominated by two adversarial attorneys arguing before a usually stone-silent judge. Rather, the judge would question as often as the lawyers.

"Oh, several dozen, I would say," Dr. Pula replied.

"When you say several dozen, you are speaking of patients exactly in the condition we are discussing in Mrs. Cole's case?" the judge inquired.

"Patients who are in a persistent coma or a persistent vegetative state, I think is the best term to use. Patients who have no deep response to pain but have intact brainstems."

"That is your description of her?"

When Dr. Pula said that was correct, Judge Byrnes questioned him more closely about how many times he had been involved as the "treating physician" with similar patients.

He replied, "The treating physician, probably about a dozen; a consulting physician for the rest."

I shifted my legs as I listened. Where the hell is this going? I wondered.

The judge pressed on: all these dozen were comatose? Yes, sir. And how many had life support systems withdrawn from them, resulting in their deaths?

"That's a difficult question in those terms," Dr. Pula said. He explained that all were on life support systems at one time. About half had died while on systems, and "the other half were subsequently weaned and ultimately died."

Judge Byrnes said, "The answer to my question is zero. That is to say, none were subjected to the respirator and had it withdrawn in the manner, under the court . . ."

"Currently that is correct." Dr. Pula replied.

"This would be your first patient of this sort?" Judge Byrnes asked.

"First patient of this sort of court order or this type of ruling involved."

The judge seemed satisfied and turned the questioning back to David, who asked Dr. Pula to describe Jackie's condition from the day of her arrival at the hospital up to her current condition. Judge Byrnes intervened several times for clarification. When Dr. Pula described posturing, the judge said, "Translate."

"When you would squeeze her and pinch her, give her a painful stimulation, she would respond in a characteristic way that would involve extension of the arms. That's decerebrate posturing. . . . It's a response that requires no cerebral cortex, or thought, or anything."

He went on to explain that the posturing ceased in the first couple of weeks, and since then Jackie had had "no response at all to deep painful stimulation and has continued to have intact brainstem."

"What?" Judge Byrnes looked up abruptly from the notes he was taking.

"Intact brainstem reflexes," Dr. Pula answered.

"Meaning what?"

"Meaning that when you shine a flashlight in her eyes, her

pupils constrict. When you touch her cornea with a cotton swab, she blinks."

"She does respond. That is what you call deep pain?" the judge asked.

"No, Your Honor. Those are brainstem reflexes. They require no cerebral input."

David stepped in quickly to get the testimony back on track. He felt that he was trying to drive a vehicle with a wobbly steering wheel. He asked Dr. Pula, "What type of life support system is Mrs. Cole on?"

"Currently she is on a respirator; she has a chest tube that's draining pus from her right lung, and she is on antibiotics, in addition to a nasogastric tube through which she is being fed," he replied, and went on to describe the history of her pneumonia in both lungs.

"If she were permitted to be withdrawn from the life support system, how would the [lung] infection react? How would she react to the infection?" David asked.

"I suspect she would react as someone else who was neurologically intact would, insofar as she would develop more rapid respirations because of the pneumonia damaging the lung itself. It's likely there is not enough normal lung functioning now, so that she would gradually develop less and less adequate oxygenation of her blood. And, finally, develop cardiac arrhythmia and die."

I shuddered. I had been listening to Dr. Pula's testimony with a conflicting detachment and an intimate interest. I felt as if I were watching a movie and were on the screen at the same moment. David's voice brought my mind back into focus: "One final question, and I know this is difficult to explain, but I have to ask you what you think of Mrs. Cole's chances of recovery, what kind of recovery it would be, and if you can put that, for simplicity's sake, into a percentage?"

"Sure," Dr. Pula answered quickly. "The term 'hopeless' is specifically used in current neurologic literature to refer to patients who are brain-dead. That is, when someone's brain has no cerebral functioning, no brainstem functioning. Mrs. Cole continues to have brainstem functioning, so she is not brain-dead, under the current definitions.

"So that one would say that — because of that — I would be reluctant to use the word 'hopeless.' However, if it's not hopeless, it's virtually hopeless. Chances of her having any reasonable, significant neurologic recovery are probably somewhere within one in a hundred thousand, one in a million."

David turned back toward his chair and said, "No further questions, Your Honor." But the judge broke in:

"Repeat the last sentence — chances of her having reasonable, significant neurological activity?"

"Having any significant functional recovery of her cerebrum, so that she would, quote, 'wake up' in any kind of sense, . . . is probably on the order of one in a hundred thousand or one in a million."

"That's a pretty big range." A tone of surprise crept into the judge's voice.

Dr. Pula spoke quietly: "When you are talking about cases like this, Your Honor, it's difficult to be more precise. Just to say, the numbers are very large and the chances are very small."

JUDGE BYRNES thanked Dr. Pula and asked Leo Ottey to begin questioning. Jackie's attorney led Dr. Pula through a description of a massive intracerebral hemorrhage. I felt as though I'd heard it before, all too often. When Leo asked what might cause the hemorrhage, Dr. Pula's answer washed over me. At this point, it simply was no longer important to me. I heard the doctor's words but they struck no chords:

"Usually it's caused by some sort of abnormality of the blood vessel itself, or there may be a congenital abnormality present from birth, such as a malformation or tumor that grows in the brain. As the tumor grows, the blood vessel becomes less normal and subsequently a rupture occurs."

In response to questions from both the judge and Leo, Dr. Pula painted a full picture of the damage caused by the rupture. I half-wished I could be anywhere else, yet I wanted desperately to be here, to help Jackie.

Leo questioned Dr. Pula about several aspects of coma and reached the crucial question: "She is not brain-dead?"

"That's correct. She is not brain-dead."

"Within a reasonable degree of medical certainty, Doctor, would you say that Mrs. Cole's condition is incurable?"

"Yes."

"And what is the basis for that opinion?"

"I think there is no reasonable chance of her recovering from the damage that has been done to her brain by the hemorrhage that occurred on March twenty-ninth," he replied.

"And within a reasonable degree of medical certainty, is it your opinion that Mrs. Cole's death is imminent?"

Dr. Pula turned toward Judge Byrnes and asked in a very respectful tone if he could answer that in a few sentences. "Sure." The judge nodded.

"If Mrs. Cole continued to have the most aggressive medical supportive care, she might be able to survive in this condition for months and months and months. If she had no care at all, she would surely die over, at most, a couple of days," he explained.

Again Judge Byrnes wanted to be certain. "So it would be your opinion that death is not imminent if she is maintained as she is now?"

"That is correct."

"You disagree with this physician, do you not?" the judge asked.

David squirmed in his chair. It sounded as if the judge was playing the role of opposing attorney, trying to trap his witness. David wished this were as easy as the guardianship hearing before Judge Ward.

"I'm sorry?" Dr. Pula wondered what physician the judge meant.

"Dr. Hayes. He is in your hospital, is he not?" the judge asked.

"He is head of pulmonary medicine."

"He has a different opinion. Does that surprise you?" Judge Byrnes inquired.

Dr. Pula's bafflement was apparent on his face. He and Mike Hayes had worked side by side on Jackie's case for six weeks. What would Mike have said in his affidavit that would differ from his prognosis?

"I think the difference of opinion . . . I talked with Dr. Hayes on many occasions over the course of the past couple of weeks. If there is a significant difference of opinion, I suspect it would be because of interpreting the question in a different way," Dr. Pula said quietly, trying to clarify the difference between pulmonary and neurologic approaches.

"That's what the heart of this matter is," Judge Byrnes said. "I should say this on the record: that Dr. Hayes's opinion, which is contained in a letter of May sixth, has this final paragraph of two sentences: 'Her prognosis is guarded. Her death is imminent and it is being prolonged by the use of ventilator support.' That concludes the letter. I don't know what that sentence means, 'her death is being prolonged by the use of ventilator . . .' "

Dr. Pula jumped in: "If I could comment on that?"

"There is not much you can say to it. I think it ought to be stated in the record. You can't speak for him. Let's go ahead," the judge said.

"Your Honor, for the record, I feel uncomfortable about that being a piece of evidence," Leo said. "I would like the court to make its decision —"

"I have to make a decision on all of the records in front of me," Judge Byrnes said firmly.

Leo and the judge jousted briefly over whether Dr. Hayes's letter would be a court exhibit. Judge Byrnes concluded that the whole file, including the Hayes letter, would be a court exhibit. I listened in anguish. It's going badly, I thought for the first time. This hearing is an intrusion on our lives. I know on a rational level that it is a legal formality that we must go through, but emotionally I can't understand or accept its necessity. I have reached an agonizing decision, one that I believe God wants me to make. I believe it is the most spiritually, morally, and medically fitting response to Jackie's situation. And I'm trying to do what Jackie said many times she would want done. I'm trying to help her, damn it! This is the most personal, private family matter, and here we sit in a public courtroom before a stranger who will decide Jackie's fate.

Leo turned the questioning to Jackie's chances of recovery.

"Doctor, within a reasonable degree of medical certainty, is there a reasonable possibility of Mrs. Cole ever emerging from her present comatose condition to a cognitive state?"

"No."

"And is it your medical opinion that the life support systems now being administered should be discontinued?"

"Yes," he answered.

"If Mrs. Cole were ever to recover from her comatose state, would you please describe what you think would be her general condition?"

Dr. Pula was uncomfortable about making such a long-shot prediction, but he plunged ahead: "If she . . . chances are so . . . if in some way she could possibly recover so that she would have some sort of awareness, then what would her neurologic condition be? I strongly suspect that she would be paralyzed bilaterally, that she would have significant difficulty moving either arm or either leg, that she would continue to need to be cared for completely in terms of complete scheduled nursing care, or at least complete nursing care, someone attending her, dressing her, washing her."

"Would she be able to speak?"

"It depends on the degree, even if you are talking about . . . most likely if that would occur, it would be severely slurred."

Then Leo turned the probability game to how long Jackie might survive if each component of the life support system were withdrawn one by one. How much more grisly can this get? I wondered. We're not choosing from the A or B side of a Chinese menu here. We're talking about my wife's life and death! About her dying more and more each day! About prolonging her inevitable death!

"If she is continuing to be fed but removed from the respirator and is no longer given antibiotics?" Leo asked.

"I would suspect she would die within a few days, a few hours. It's hard to be absolutely sure of that."

"Do the life-sustaining procedures currently in place, in your opinion, merely prolong Mrs. Cole's life without providing any benefit to her?" Leo asked.

Judge Byrnes leaned back in his chair. The question struck him as odd, coming from an attorney who was supposed to be representing Mrs. Cole.

"Yes," replied Dr. Pula.

"Do you know if any of the life-sustaining measures cause any pain?"

"No, I don't feel that in her current condition Mrs. Cole feels any pain."

Leo asked Dr. Pula a number of questions about how he judged her inability to experience pain, and the neurologist explained a number of clinical examinations and brainwave measurements that showed she didn't respond to painful stimuli, such as pressure and pinching the skin over her sternum and clavicular area.

Leo then asked if Jackie would feel any pain if her respirator or feeding tube were removed. No, Dr. Pula responded. Death by lack of oxygen or by dehydration and starvation would be painless in her comatose state.

Was this his opinion alone, or had he consulted with other physicians? Dr. Pula said he had consulted with other staff physicians, pulmonary consultants, infectious disease physicians, and residents on the house staff. "The opinions are, to the best of my knowledge, the same among all these physicians," he added.

"Is there an ethics committee at Maryland General or some other like body?" Leo asked.

"Currently a committee is considering issues of living wills, brain death, and orders not to resuscitate the patient."

"Have you consulted with that committee? Are they aware of this case?"

"Yes, as it turns out, I am a member," Dr. Pula replied.

Judge Byrnes asked, "Has it been placed before the committee as a community?"

It had not, Dr. Pula responded, but he had spoken with the committee chairman about Jackie's case, and "I discussed the situation with one of the hospital administrative vice presidents regarding what would be done . . . depending on what court orders you have."

"Let's once again assume the court provides the request and Mrs. Cole is removed from the respirator; will that be immediate or will she be weaned?" Leo asked.

"If that is what the court orders," interjected the judge.

"If I am allowed to just stop the respirator, that is what I would do," Dr. Pula said.

"Why wouldn't you wean Mrs. Cole from the respirator? What

are the factors that decide whether to terminate instantly, or to wean?" Leo asked.

"Because weaning is the normal process in which one removes a patient from the respirator with the expectation that the patient is going to survive the weaning process and go on to be normal."

Leo continued with more questions about the kinds of life support measures Jackie was receiving. Why is he going over this again? I wondered. We've been here more than a half hour and already heard about all the machines and tubes. I was anxious to begin my own testimony.

Finally Leo seemed to be winding down. "If Mrs. Cole continued to remain on the respirator, but she no longer received antibiotics for her infection, what is your opinion concerning what would happen to her, including a reasonable estimate as to how long she would survive?"

"I think she would probably die from a relapse of the pneumonia," Dr. Pula said slowly. "That is, I don't think that Mrs. Cole could rid herself of that infection without continued antibiotics. And so I think the pneumonia would flare up and, despite the respirator, the pneumonia would get to the point where she could no longer compensate for it. And she would die, probably in a couple of weeks, possibly sooner."

"Would that time be sooner if, in combination with stopping the antibiotics, she was removed also from the respirator?"

"That's my belief, yes."

Leo had finished. Dr. Pula was thanked by the judge and asked to take a seat. At last it was my turn.

DAVID opened gently. "Mr. Cole, you take as long as you wish to answer these questions. Your occupation, sir?"

"I am a Presbyterian minister."

"I suppose in the course of your ministry you have occasion to counsel people about life-and-death questions."

"Yes, I have."

"You, therefore, do not take life-and-death questions lightly when you counsel your parishioners?"

"I do not."

David asked how long Jackie and I had been married and "for the benefit of the court, describe your relationship during the course of your marriage with Mrs. Cole, briefly."

"We were very happy and we were happily married; that's as briefly as I can describe it," I said. As soon as the words were out of my mouth, I recognized how inadequate they were.

Judge Brynes asked, "Do you have children?" I told him that there were four, "all of whom we adopted."

"In infancy?" Judge Byrnes asked.

"No."

David began talking about the ages of the children, so the fact that I had adopted Jackie's children after marrying her was never made clear to the judge.

"Speaking of the children, Mr. Cole, for the court's benefit," David said, "describe the discussions you have had with your children."

"I discussed this matter with all of the children together at the hospital a number of weeks ago with Dr. Pula and Jacqueline's sister. We discussed the entire matter at length, and there was general agreement that if Jacqueline were not able to recover or survive this, then it would be our desire that she would simply be allowed to go on from here to somewhere else."

"When you say 'general agreement,' do you mean unanimous agreement or majority rule?" asked the judge.

"No, it was unanimous agreement," I answered. "We all came to the same understanding, and, just in terms of follow-up, I discussed it with them individually and their feelings are essentially the same and have continued to be the same since that initial discussion."

David asked me to relate the condition of Jackie's mother and how that affected Jackie's stated wish if she were ever in a similar position.

I described Helen's final illness and said, "These kinds of events in family lives often prompt reflection and discussion, which they did with Jacqueline and myself, and she did convey the definite feeling to me that if anything of a similar nature were ever to happen to her, she would simply not want to go on and be sustained in the way that her mother was."

David asked me to describe, "in just brief terms," how Jackie's situation had affected my life and the children's.

"'Brief terms.' I'm not sure I can do it in brief terms." I sighed.

"I am sure it's been traumatic. It couldn't be otherwise," Judge Byrnes said. David and I both felt an unexpected ray of hope.

"That is, in fact, the briefest term I could describe," I replied, grateful to the judge for the first time. Judge Byrnes then lowered the emotional thermostat and asked me to talk about the children and where they were in school. After I described each one, David turned the testimony back toward the heart of the hearing by asking why I believed the request to discontinue life support should be granted.

"I am convinced, from a medical point of view, having been sufficiently informed by Dr. Pula and other members of the treatment staff that there is no reasonable chance for her recovery. It should be done because I believe that she would not wish to continue to exist in this present state, and, given even the slightest chance of recovery, I do not believe that she would wish to live anything other than a full, rich, qualitative style of life such as she enjoyed."

David had no more questions, and Leo had only two others for me.

"Is it the family's desire to remove Mrs. Cole from the respirator and antibiotics?"

"I believe it's the desire of — yes, the children and myself."

"And not to remove the nasogastric tube at this time?"

"Not at this time . . . We talked about this, and we simply felt we wanted to retain perhaps even the slightest possibility, even if it's one in a million, that perhaps she could recover from this and, to give her the benefit of the doubt, simply to keep the feeding tube in. If you are going to ask me if that makes sense, perhaps it doesn't. But very little of this makes sense to begin with. We simply drew the line there. I would imagine that if she were to continue to exist on the feeding tube in a constant vegetative state, then I would be very anxious to likewise remove that support system," I concluded.

Leo had no further questions, and I returned to my seat next to David. As soon as I sat down, I wished I'd said something positive and lasting and redemptive, something that would have injected a profound theological moment into this legal morass. But I didn't. I couldn't. It was in my heart to say it and it was in my mind to know it. But I couldn't get the words out.

I wished I'd explained the theology of Jackie's situation, as I saw it. I was willing to make the ultimate sacrifice of letting her die and join God for eternity. Because I loved her so very much, I wanted her to have God's peace and wholeness and love that were now denied her by the machines and tubes postponing her death and perpetuating this medical purgatory. God's grace could finally be realized with her death, I wished I'd told the judge and lawyers.

Leo told the judge that he had spoken to several family members and wished to convey opinions from them.

"I won't accept that. Well, first of all, the family here is all way over the age of majority except for the one young son and for you to speak, . . . say that you have spoken to them," the judge said, then changed his mind: "But go ahead. I think you may want to say this for the record. Why don't you go ahead without interruption from me."

David, Leo, and I each felt a slight breeze of relief. Perhaps the judge wasn't going to be so rigid after all. Leo stated that he had spoken to Jackie's sister two days ago and that Julie had said that Jackie "very clearly expressed the wish that she would not want to be kept alive by machines, and this opinion of Mrs. Cole resulted from the condition of her mother."

Leo went on to explain that he had talked with Christina yesterday, and she had related what Jackie said on March 29 as she realized that she was suffering a stroke. Leo quoted Christina: "She raised her arm at one point and said, 'Christina, I am having a stroke. I can use my arm but I can't feel it. I am having a stroke,' and then she looked at me and said, 'Christina, you know I don't want to live this way.'"

Through his tortoise-shell glasses, Judge Byrnes shot Leo a look of amazement. "She said this during the course of a stroke?"

"Yes, Your Honor. It was the very stroke that rendered her in the condition she is in right now."

"All right."

"It was that stroke, as the doctor indicated, the symptoms started then . . ."

"But, I mean, this is a woman who is undergoing some medical distress that she understood to be, herself, a stroke?" Judge Byrnes's voice rose with incredulity. "Then she predicts ahead the consequences of the stroke and says she didn't — doesn't want to live like that?"

"Yes . . . It's extraordinary, and that is why I think it should be part of the record. I think it indicates how Mrs. Cole would feel if she were able to render an opinion right now or make some decision right now," Leo said.

The judge said he was reluctant to accept these statements as testimony. "That ought to be stated directly by the person; no question in my mind about that."

From his chair, David began, "I would like to say a couple of words, if it please the court. Your Honor, I think there is legal precedent . . ."

"It's also traditional to stand," Judge Byrnes scolded David gently.

"Excuse me, Your Honor." David rose and pleaded, "There is legal precedent for the court to approve this request. I am a personal friend of Mr. and Mrs. Cole's. I can tell you that each day has been a tragedy for the family. You were a little surprised when Mr. Ottey proffered the conversation between Mrs. Cole and her daughter. I submit to the court, if you had known Mrs. Cole, that would not surprise you at all. Your Honor, Mrs. Cole is vivacious, full of life. That's the way she wanted to live life. Your Honor, she is, as all the medical testimony that's been presented here confirmed, unable to do that. The recovery is one in one hundred thousand to one in a million. Your Honor, I submit the court should grant the petition and let Mrs. Cole pass with the dignity and respect with which she lived her life. Thank you, Your Honor."

Leo rose to summarize: "I believe that the issue before the court is really the issue of a disabled person's right to self-determination. I believe that right has legal grounding in what has come to be known as the right of privacy, a constitutionally protected fundamental right, the right to make important decisions concerning the person.

"I believe that my client has indicated, specifically on the morning of her stroke, her general desires. Unfortunately the court does not have before it any written document or any verbal statement from Mrs. Cole as to what she specifically wants done or does not want done. But I do think that the evidence in this case supports, generally speaking, the conclusion that Mrs. Cole should not remain on any life support systems that would artificially extend her life. And I believe that the evidence as presented shows that my client's right of self-determination will be protected if the court grants the requested relief. I should also point out that her right to self-determination should not be ignored or discarded solely because her present condition prohibits her from consciously exercising that right.

"The evidence is that she expressed an opinion concerning the artificial existence of life, her life in fact, over a long period of time, and during that time she was an adult, mature woman. I think that evidence is very important when it comes to determining what Mrs. Cole would have wanted. Thank you," Leo concluded.

"Suppose the stroke caused only partial paralysis, and she could not be as lively and vivacious as she was. Would she want that?" asked Judge Byrnes.

"Assuming that she is comatose?" Leo asked.

"No. I said if she were partially paralyzed."

"Then she would have the ability to speak for herself, I believe. Frankly, Your Honor, I don't know," Leo replied.

"I am going to take a few moments to review my notes, and I will have to ask you all to be good enough to be patient while I do so," Judge Byrnes said, as he stood to leave the bench.

# Nine

In Chambers

Judge Byrnes returned to 408A, his spacious, wood-paneled chambers, and pulled off his black robe. He walked around the desk and filled his pipe before bending his lean frame into the desk chair. His eyes caught the framed picture across the room. It was a handsome portrait of his all-American family. He, his wife, and three children had never had any serious health problems. He thought gratefully about that for a moment before opening the Cole case file.

The judge had carefully read the Quinlan decision an hour before the hearing. He scanned it again as he lit his pipe. A wonderful instrument, a beautifully crafted opinion, he thought, I just cannot agree with its conclusion. The judge's language is elegant. I admire it, but his legal logic just is not there. If you take out all the elegant language, and all the emotion, there's no legal basis for it. Under New Jersey law, Karen Ann Quinlan was alive. Just as Jacqueline Cole is alive under Maryland law. There is brainstem activity, so she is not brain-dead. She is alive, he said to himself.

The New Jersey Supreme Court's opinion was based on the right of privacy, which was "presumably broad enough," the opinion stated, "to encompass a patient's decision to decline medical treatment under certain circumstances, in much the same way as it is broad enough to encompass a woman's decision to terminate pregnancy under certain conditions." The court determined that Ms. Quinlan, if competent, would have the right to request that her respirator be removed. But to Judge Byrnes, the court made a crucial leap of illogic in deciding that "the only practical way to prevent destruction of that right was to permit the guardian (her father) and the family of Ms. Quinlan to render their best judgment as to whether Karen would exercise it in these circumstances."

A truly impossible task, Judge Byrnes thought. This was not a right-of-privacy issue to be carried out by family or guardian, he reasoned, but a question of life. Since Karen Ann Quinlan was determined to be legally and clinically alive, the reasoning of the New Jersey Supreme Court was unsound, Judge Byrnes thought as he reflected on its legal precedent, the landmark *Roe v. Wade* decision by the U.S. Supreme Court legalizing abortion under the right of privacy. As the Supreme Court ruled in that case, "The Constitution does not explicitly mention any right of privacy. In a line of decisions, however . . . the Court has recognized that a right of personal privacy, or a guarantee of certain areas or zones of privacy, does exist under the Constitution." Among the Constitutional origins of those guarantees: the First Amendment's protection of freedom to associate and privacy in those associations, the Fourth Amendment's protection of "the right of people to be secure in their persons, houses, papers, and effects, against unreasonable searches and seizures," and the due process clause of the Fourteenth Amendment, which protects liberties that are "so rooted in the tradition and conscience of our people as to be ranked as fundamental," in the words of the Supreme Court, which deemed marriage, procreation, contraception, family relationships, child rearing and education, and a woman's decision to terminate a pregnancy "fundamental" and worthy of privacy protection.

But to Judge Byrnes, there was no legal, recognized right in any of those intimate circumstances, for *someone else* to act as surrogate and exercise those rights except, arguably, in a medical situation where the decision is life giving rather than life taking. But there is no Constitutional right to life denial by a surrogate, Judge Byrnes believed.

God! Imagine the unlimited possibilities of fraudulent, even homicidal, intent, he thought — not-so-well-intentioned relations seeking to pull the plug if the death of a wealthy relative might benefit them financially.

We are a society of laws. The State has a legitimate, compelling interest in protecting life, he said to himself. No person, individually or by surrogate, may decide to place a life in unnecessary danger, no matter how meager its "quality" — whatever that may be.

No matter how many times he reread the opinion, Karen Ann Quinlan had been alive — medically and legally. For Judge Byrnes, that was the overriding fact. The traditions, moral values, and laws of this country dictate that individuals, the State, and particularly the courts do everything in their power to protect the most basic of all rights, the right to live, even in the face of family pain, expense, and despair, he reasoned. And yes, even in the face of the pained and despairing cry of the patients themselves. The right to live was the most fundamental of the unalienable rights in the Declaration of Independence, he concluded, and its absence made all other rights meaningless.

He looked over his bench notes, penned in black ballpoint on blue-lined notebook paper. He had written in his small, angular script, "Problems: issue is law, not family choice — even a choice born of love for the disabled."

Jacqueline Cole's family was suffering enormously, the judge recognized. They truly loved her and their motives were unquestionably above reproach. Even though her husband's testimony had struck him as rather emotionless for a man in these circumstances, the judge never doubted that this husband/father/minister was acting out of love. Yet a family's pain didn't give them the right to end her life, in his view. And there was no getting around the fact that she was still legally alive.

Under "problems," his bench notes referred also to "legal research — more extensive briefing of pertinent cases." The file was thin. David had presented him with only four cases, summarized briefly. This was not a deeply prepared pleading, Judge Byrnes thought. The level of preparation and expertise required for a case like this was markedly absent.

The judge knew that medical technology had outraced society's ability to resolve the medical, legal, and moral aspects of prolonging life when a patient is critically or terminally ill. And he knew that medical advances were a double-edged sword: while they prolonged life, they often failed to restore health. These medical advances were made nearly every day, much faster than society and the law could keep pace with them. More and more cases were being heard by courts across the country about not only disconnecting respirators but also discontinuing food, water, and medication. He wanted to know more about these court decisions, certainly more than this hastily prepared hearing offered him.

How soon would it be, the judge wondered, when an American court would be asked to rule on "active euthanasia" as practiced in the Netherlands, were physicians legally give 10,000 lethal injections each year to end the lives of terminally or critically ill patients. Well, that may come up in the future, but right now, Judge Byrnes said to himself, there isn't an adequate body of legal precedent presented by the attorneys in this case to convince me that the law allows Mrs. Cole's guardian to discontinue life support systems as long as she is legally alive.

As he reviewed the file and his notes, Judge Byrnes's brow furrowed. He was distressed about the lack of adversarial stance in this case. Instead of taking opposing viewpoints, both attorneys wanted the same result, though David wanted to end the family's suffering, while Leo argued that Jackie would have wanted to disconnect life support systems and that it was her right to determine her own fate. No one had argued for keeping her alive. She was legally alive, and no one was defending her right to live.

These two attorneys, it appeared to the judge, viewed this hearing as just another guardianship case. In such proceedings, a family comes to court with medical documentation that a relative is incompetent and requires a guardian. An attorney is appointed to represent the disabled patient's interests as part of the due process provision of the Constitution, among other points of law. But guardianship proceedings are rarely adversarial. The court-appointed attorney usually visits the patient and tries to communicate, if possible, what is happening. The attorney reports back to the judge, almost always concurs with the family's plea, and a guardian is appointed.

In five years on the bench, Judge Byrnes had handled many guardianship proceedings and couldn't recall a single case in which anyone contested the request for a guardian. But Jackie Cole's case was vastly different. The question was whether she would live or die, not who would handle her affairs. Yet the attorneys seemed to be treating it as a routine guardianship proceeding. Judge Byrnes knew Leo Ottey to be a fine young man who had often been appointed to represent a victim in a guardianship request, but the judge thought that the same nonadversarial attitudes that prevail in guardianship cases were spilling over into the Cole case.

I get the feeling, Judge Byrnes thought, that these attorneys have that mind-set: Here, Judge; sign here, Judge; (yawn) this is just another one of those. You know what these are like, Judge. We have them all the time. And I think they feel it's almost routine because the family supports the request, the doctors have signed off, and she expressed her preference before the stroke.

He reviewed the testimony about Jackie's stated wish "not to live this way." Just what did she mean by "this way"? Like "this" at the moment she was having a stroke? Disabled? To what degree? The law doesn't have a response to that, the judge thought. It's purely emotional.

The "quality of life" question greatly distressed Judge Byrnes. Should she ever come out of the coma and be disabled, what degree of disability would be acceptable? There seems to be a growing acceptance, he thought, of withdrawing life support systems based on this reduced "quality of life" standard. Many older people experience a reduced quality of life. Is the inability to play tennis or to attend cocktail parties, the loss of a limb or loss of hearing such a reduction in one's quality of life that it merits ending life? Can't people still enjoy life and love their families? Can't someone who has lost the ability to see enjoy the sounds of the world and the words of family and friends? he wondered. Should someone unable to hear not see and love what they see? How do we judge what someone in a comatose state may appreciate, love, or suffer?

The judge drew on his pipe and glanced across the room at the crammed shelves of tan-and-red law books. It's amazing, he thought, how many volumes have been written, how many lawsuits have gone on for years and years about matters like damages in an auto accident. We have all these fine nuances, definitions, law books, judges' interpretations. Yet there is a strange silence when it comes to this subject of rationalizing the termination of life support systems. Why is there such a thrust toward ending life? Who is benefiting from it? Is it purely economic? Is that what it's come to and no one wants to say it out loud — that we as a society cannot afford, or don't want to pay for, long-term care of comatose or terminally ill people in nursing homes for years?

Catastrophic health insurance was one major answer, he believed. When he served in the state senate, he had been one of the few legislators to push for a catastrophic health insurance bill to help families avoid financial ruin when a relative suffered a high-cost, long-running medical tragedy like Jackie's. He had joined a Republican to cosponsor such a bill, but it failed to pass.

JUDGE BYRNES looked at his calendar. The stroke had occurred forty-one days ago, six weeks tomorrow. He focused on his bench notes once more, before pulling a clean sheet of paper from the desk drawer. On this single sheet he wrote thirteen points of his decision. Each began with the word "No."

"No medical opinion that there is no hope of recovery . . .

"No express medical support for removal of life support systems . . .

"No mention that legal or medical definition of death pertain . . ."

When he finished writing his decision, he thrust his long arms into the black robe and returned to the courtroom.

David, Leo, Ron, and I had paced the fourth-floor corridors for nearly an hour, while Dr. Pula waited quietly on a courtroom bench. When we were finally called into the courtroom, I felt a rush of excitement. The petition would be granted — I just knew it — and Jackie would soon be united with God.

"Let me just say very simply that I am not going to reach a conclusion in this case today," Judge Byrnes began. "There's a very simple reason why. The focus of this hearing has been an ineffective preference of the family and stated preference of the disabled, Mrs. Cole. But that's not the test. The test that I am obliged to apply is a legal test, and the issue, therefore, is law and not the family's choice, even a choice that I am certain is made . . . for this unfortunate disabled person."

I was dumbstruck. I'm not hearing him correctly; he's not saying this, I thought, as I listened in disbelief for the full fifteen
minutes that the judge took to explain his decision not to decide —
at least today.

"There is no preferred or obvious answer in this matter. I have
been presented a case which has serious repercussions. Obviously,
first of all, for the disabled; second of all, in terms of legal precedent . . ." he said, before setting out his conclusions: "One of them
is that I will require much more extensive research and briefing of
pertinent cases . . . Secondly, I am troubled by the absence of
reference by the doctor to ethical standards that may pertain. It
does not seem to be of interest to many, but it is, I believe, of
serious interest because ethical standards and legal standards transcend and must transcend what the individual preference is. We
are a society that is governed by standards and law. It is obvious
that a judge is not free to permit the termination of life because
that is what is asked. That is not the standard. What is the standard is what we must investigate. I do not yet see a reference, other
than in the Quinlan case, to the applicability of various standards
which are under debate in this country . . . So that is the first
conclusion, that we must do far more legal research . . . And I
think further that counsel for Mrs. Cole will have to take a more
partisan posture in the case. This would have to be of its nature an
adversary proceeding; if there ever was one, it is this one. . . . This
is not a case where the issue is, Should a guardian be appointed
because the person has suffered from some serious disability.
. . . This is a question of whether a person lives or dies."

Judge Byrnes then commented that "too brief a time has
elapsed. This is May ninth and the stroke was March twenty-
ninth. . . . I would be surprised if one were to find any cases where
the time that elapsed between an onset of disability and decision of
a judge to permit termination of life support was within weeks.
I would be quite interested to see that, not disputing the possibility of it. But if there are such cases, I would like to know
about them."

I groaned silently. Too brief a time? God, doesn't he know it's
been an eternity? How does he measure sufficient time? I wondered. Does Jackie have to go on suffering like this for seventy

days? seven months? seven years? This is what she would have wanted! Why can't he give her what she wanted!

The judge continued by calling the medical statements in the case record "very imprecise and too brief in light of the seriousness of this situation. . . . There is virtually nothing in the record that I could rely upon by way of medical opinion. I am speaking now of the record in the court file, not including Dr. Pula's, to make this decision. There is insufficient commentary, including by Dr. Pula, of medical definitions and legal definitions of death. I gather and infer that Dr. Pula has a particular philosophy on the subject which makes him, I am sure in good conscience and medical, professional judgment, more likely to be liberal in these regards."

Judge Byrnes wouldn't accept Dr. Pula's "hearsay reference" that other physicians would agree with his medical conclusions. "I cannot accept — technically or, frankly, in conscience — a physician's stating, 'Well, other physicians agree with me.' I want to know what they are saying, and I want there to be a record of their saying it. . . . We have only one physician, among the several who have apparently had involvement with this case, who has expressed the opinion that the life support system should be removed."

In the judge's next several comments, he referred to the public's interest in this case: "Clearly the public has an interest in what a judge decides are the standards to be applied in withdrawing life support systems. To say that they don't have such an interest really defies common sense."

The public? I asked myself. Why? This is an intensely private matter between Jackie and me, our family, the doctors, and God. I couldn't comprehend a role for "the public."

Judge Byrnes referred to the state's attorney in the Quinlan case, who represented the public's interest "because there was great concern, of course, about the implications of those decisions in the criminal and other law context. . . . So I query whether or not the state's attorney ought to have some involvement here representing the public interest," Judge Byrnes explained.

David caught my eye. He looked as wounded as I felt. The judge went on to criticize the medical statements in the file as insufficiently explicit. He also said the order he was being asked to sign "does not expressly state what life support systems we are talking about. So if I sign it as it is, it would give the permission to withdraw all life support systems. . . . I think the order has to be, even if it were something I would sign . . . much more explicit, because life support systems are not defined by law, to my knowledge, in the statute."

Judge Byrnes closed the file folder on the bench and concluded, "This is my preliminary comment only, and it is not to suggest that I have reached any substantive conclusion. . . . I will ask counsel, if they wish to proceed with this matter, to propose a schedule that would anticipate responding to all that I have asked for."

As he arose to step down from the bench, Judge Byrnes turned to David and said, "And Counsel, no judge-shopping."

"Yes, Your Honor." The thought had already flashed across David's mind as he listened to the judge's comments. A hearing before another judge might gain our desired conclusion, but now Judge Byrnes had cut off that option. David knew the Baltimore Circuit Court brethren frowned mightily on attorneys who shopped around for judges who might be sympathetic to their cases. If he were to pursue this, David would have to reappear before Judge Byrnes with a pile of legal research and medical testimony. That could take weeks of work. At that moment, neither he nor I knew whether we wanted to follow this route.

# Ten

"What's Next?"

"That's it. It's hopeless. I'm not going to pursue this," I said to no one in particular as I walked out of the courtroom.

"We're all disappointed, Harry, but don't make up your mind right now. This has been a heavy afternoon," David cautioned. He thought I was incapable of making any decision so soon after the hearing. "Give me a little time to think about what possibilities we might have."

"My God, David. You sound like the judge! Don't make any decision . . . a little more time!" I exploded. As soon as I'd said it, I regretted it. "I'm sorry, David. But I'm so frustrated. In the middle of this tragedy, we have to go through this legal business — it's such an intrusion. And it almost makes me feel that I'm supposed to feel guilty, like some kind of criminal, at these hearings. Isn't everything bad enough? The children are losing their mother. I'm losing my wife. Then we have to expose our tragedy before a judge in a court of law, and get kicked back to square one! I'm just trying to do what Jackie wanted! Yes, I'm angry. I'm angry at this terrible loss — we're losing Jackie in the most cruel way. If *I* sound angry, think how angry Jackie herself would be if she were aware of this!

"And what's this business about the public's interest in our private family anguish? I don't understand that. Why does the world need to know that I'm asking permission to let my wife die? To give her what she said she would want in these circumstances? To bring a merciful end to this tragedy? To allow her the dignity she deserves?

"And why does the judge say 'too brief a time has elapsed'? Why must she suffer more? We must prolong her dying even longer? Who's to say arbitrarily how long is long enough? I honestly believe we're doing what's right here, what's right for Jackie. How is more time possibly going to benefit her?"

Dr. Pula had been silent as we waited for the elevator. But as we rode down to the lobby, he said, "I guess I just didn't get my point across. Even if she survives, she wouldn't be able to lead the kind of life she demanded."

"Well," David said, "I probably should have done more legal research, pulled in more doctors to testify. But, damn it, how many doctors does it take? You're the doctor, the medical expert. Why couldn't he take your recommendation? And maybe we should have had Julie and Christina come in and testify in person about Jackie's expressed wishes. But, I don't know. It might have turned out the same, regardless of how many witnesses we had. It's easy to play Monday morning quarterback now.

"You realize that we had law, medicine, and theology represented in that courtroom," David continued, shaking his head, "and we still couldn't get the right, the most humane, resolution. I suppose I was naive, thinking that it would turn out the way we wanted it to just because I believe so strongly that we are right."

I visited Jackie late that evening. I had never felt so helpless. Weeping, I told her, "I've failed you, my love. I cannot give you what you need, what you want. The judge didn't give us permission to end this nightmare. I am so very, very sorry." I held her hand and stared at her. Her expression, her muscles and limbs, everything about her was frozen, imprisoned in the coma.

As word of the judge's decision spread among family and friends, a dense cloud, thicker with despair than ever, seemed to hang in Jackie's room. Whenever visitors stopped by that weekend, they felt hollow. Friends and relatives had planned this visit as a final good-bye. Now everyone wondered how much longer this tragedy would continue. I sensed a great awkwardness in their silence. I knew the question on their minds: "What's next?" Yet no one spoke it aloud except Julie and the children.

"What can you do now, Dad?" John asked. I felt he wanted me

to give him a firm answer, as if I owned a bag of fix-it tools for every occasion.

"I don't know, John. I wish I did, but I just don't know yet."

THE Sunday after the court hearing was Mother's Day and I decided to bring Communion to Jackie. Trying as best I could through intense prayer to lift her soul to God, I began by reading some Scripture:

> "The eternal God is thy refuge, and underneath are the everlasting arms.
>
> Hast thou not known? Hast thou not heard, that the everlasting God, the Lord, the Creator of the ends of the earth, fainteth not, neither is weary? There is no searching for his understanding. He giveth power to the faint; and to them that have no might he increaseth strength.
>
> Fear thou not; for I am with thee; be not dismayed; for I am thy God: I will strengthen thee; yea, I will help thee; yea, I will uphold thee with the right hand of my righteousness."

Holding Jackie's hands in mine, I prayed:

> "Thou wilt keep him in perfect peace, whose mind is stayed on Thee: because he trusteth in Thee. Trust ye in the Lord for ever: for in the Lord Jehovah is everlasting strength.
>
> "Be careful for nothing; but in every thing by prayer and supplication with thanksgiving let your requests be made known unto God. And the peace of God, which passeth all understanding, shall keep your hearts and minds through Christ Jesus."

Then I took a wafer and dipped it into a small chalice which I use for hospital Communion, and I prayed:

> "Eternal God, you give life to all who wish to receive it. . . . Come and give life to Jacqueline now, so that she may see you and know all the secrets and see all of the splendid things that belong to her in your home for her in heaven. Come now, God, and take her home. She deserves to be with you."

I placed the wafer against her lips and then between my own. I made the sign of the cross, as I touched Jackie's forehead, shoulders, and heart, and said, "In the name of the Father, Son, and Holy Spirit. Amen."

When the children visited Jackie that Mother's Day, their remembrance of happier Mother's Days sharpened the poignancy of this one. When they were much younger, they drew pictures and made brightly colored cards for her. Jackie always hugged and kissed them, praised their handiwork, and displayed it on the mantel. And they were wonderful cards and pictures — we saved them all — because the children inherited Jackie's artistic talent. That talent was one more gift she would leave them, I thought, one that even her death could not steal from them.

When Stephen and Beth visited, Stephen brought a Mother's Day card and placed it among Jackie's many get-well greetings. When I returned to visit Jackie that evening, I noticed his card.

"Please wake up, Mom," he'd written inside the card. He truly believed that if anyone could beat those terrible odds, she could. As I held the card in my hand, I felt a conflict of impatience and empathy. My impatience said: Why won't he face reality? She's not going to wake up. Yet my empathy for him said: I feel your pain and sadness, Stephen.

For the next several days, I found myself impatient with almost everything. I knew it stemmed from my reaction to the judge's refusal to grant our petition. I talked with David on the phone several times in the days immediately following the hearing. My frustration needed a target, and it always seemed to be the judge's denial of our plea.

"Of all the objections he raised, the one that was worst was the one about 'not enough time.' That's a personal statement, David. How does he know what's enough time, or what's too much time, or what's the appropriate time? He made that statement within his own frame of reference, within his own sense of morality, David. I just don't see any legal basis for it.

"I'm trying to do what's best for Jackie, what she had always said she would want done if something like this happened to her, but now the court won't let me do that. I'm in a legal straitjacket: I'm helpless to help her. You know what it took for me to make the decision to let her go, David, and now I can't even act on that decision."

David had no answers. But he was a patient listener until I brought up a new development.

"We're going to have to move Jackie to a nursing home. A hospital social worker called me, and we're looking into possibilities where there might be an opening. The hospital thinks the acute care phase is over, and all Jackie needs now is maintenance, not hospitalization. A nursing home can give that kind of maintenance. God, can you believe it? Jackie in a nursing home?"

"Whoa, Harry. Under Judge Ward's guardianship order, we'll have to get court permission to move her," David said. "Remember the petition said that permission would be needed to change her 'place of abode'? That shouldn't be a problem, I expect, but don't do anything until I check into it."

"Yes, another court intrusion into our lives," I muttered.

I had talked with Dr. Pula, other staff doctors, and the hospital social worker right after Mother's Day. I was still uncertain whether we might pursue any other legal avenues, short of the lengthy, detailed one required if we went back to Judge Byrnes. But with that uncertainty and with Jackie's condition unchanged, we all agreed that she could soon be moved to a long-term facility. While Jackie's hospitalization coverage was excellent — 100 percent — I learned that it wouldn't cover nursing home expenses. So I called Herb Valentine, our Presbytery executive, to ask if my coverage included nursing home care. Herb was very sorry. "I don't think it does, Harry. But I'll check into it." Within the hour, he phoned me back. I didn't ask whether Herb had found a loophole or prevailed on the compassion of other decision makers within the church, but his answer was a comfort: Yes, Jackie's nursing home expenses would be covered for a while, at least until we might find some other financial arrangements.

On Tuesday I met with Dr. Pula again. I told him my only scrap of good news: that my benefit plan would cover nursing home care. Dr. Pula had a bit of good news for me, too.

"Jackie's pneumonia seems to be improving," Dr. Pula reported. "It looks like we're finally overcoming it."

In other circumstances that would have been good news, but at that moment it was only painful — a small skirmish won in the huge life-and-death battle that Jackie had no hope of winning. Even if the pneumonia were to be finally beaten back, that wouldn't restore her consciousness. Would she, I wondered, just go on and on, lying like a granite statue in a nursing home bed? The worst scenario in this entire episode of madness and pain! My beautiful, gifted Jacqueline, no longer human and not yet divine. No longer and not yet — the words rolled over and over in my thoughts. She was in some limbo, exiled from a family who deeply loved her and the God who created her.

THURSDAY morning, May 15, brought one of my regular twice-weekly meetings with Dr. Pula.

"The pneumonia is not as cured as we thought, Harry. In fact, there's a possibility that it's getting worse," he said solemnly.

"Maybe that's good news, Tad. I know that sounds upside down, but isn't everything about this situation? Maybe the pneumonia will take her, and she will finally find some peace."

"Well, I don't know, Harry. We're going to continue the antibiotics." Dr. Pula knew how strongly I clung to my belief that Jackie's death would unite her with God. But there was no question about it in the doctor's mind: all of Jackie's ongoing treatment would continue.

That afternoon I was to meet an old friend, John Gardiner Evans, who wanted to see Jackie for the last time. Since childhood, he'd been called Gardy to distinguish him from another John G. Evans, a cousin about the same age. Gardy and Jackie had dated before she and I met. Jackie later introduced Gardy to me, and we became good friends. He hadn't been on the "short list" of visitors when Jackie was in the ICU, so he had not seen her at all since the stroke. When she was moved to 638 and before the court hearing, I called Gardy and said, "Maybe you'd like to see her one final time." We'd planned to meet at the hospital the previous Friday, but the hearing ran later than expected, so we rescheduled the visit for the next Thursday afternoon.

When I met Gardy in front of Maryland General, he squeezed my hand with both of his.

"How are you and the children doing?"

"We're surviving," I told him. As we walked through the automatic doors and toward the elevator, I filled him in on the news that Jackie would probably be moved to a nursing home soon. Gardy couldn't envision that. To him and to all who knew her, the essence of Jackie was independence. How could this sparkling, bright woman become a total invalid, dependent on technology to stay "alive"? It was a complete distortion of her spirit, like bending a tree to grow away from the sun.

Suddenly I unburdened my thoughts on Gardy. "I hope so desperately that she understands how much I love her. I keep telling her that I love her, but in this coma, we don't know how much may be getting through, Gardy. Maybe none of it is, but I keep talking to her. I pray that something is being communicated. I'd give anything to know that she understands."

"Don't worry, Harry. I'm sure she knows and she'd respond if she could," he reassured me.

As we walked into 638, the low afternoon sunlight splashed across the bedsheet and onto the glossy linoleum floor. The whoosh of the respirator seemed louder, more intrusive than ever. The room seemed warmer and stuffier than usual, too. I walked over to the window and opened it a few inches.

Jackie looked like porcelain. Delicate, fragile, almost translucent. Yet, like a porcelain vase, she seemed hollow. What was inside? Was Jackie in there? I wondered how Gardy saw Jackie. I was accustomed by now to this sight, but I wondered and worried whenever someone saw her like this for the first time. How painful was it for him to see? What could I do to ease his pain?

"Do you want to be alone with her, Gardy?"

"No, that's okay." He didn't seem uncomfortable as he walked to the far side of Jackie's bed, while I stood at the foot. Reaching through the bed rail slowly, cautiously, as if not to disturb the tubes, Gardy took Jackie's left hand, lifted it up, and held it in both of his.

"Hello, Jackie. This is Gardy. How are you?"

How often we'd all asked that routine question, I thought, as if we really expected a response. A soft breeze stirred the window curtain.

Jackie suddenly opened her eyes!

She looked directly at me and smiled.

The world stopped dead. I could not move. My eyes and Jackie's locked. I was aware of nothing but her eyes. The respirator whoosh faded. The tubes melted away. The hands of the clock froze. Everything in that room evaporated except Jackie's glistening green eyes, those eyes I never thought I'd see sparkle again.

She was focusing on my face! This wasn't the blank, absent stare I'd seen two weeks ago. There was life in her eyes now. She was back! She was here among us. Oh, dear God, thank you! Suddenly, miraculously, a future opened up! A wondrous future had just burst into that room and exploded those past forty-seven death-shrouded days.

Jackie's lips moved, almost imperceptibly. That jolted me to speak.

"JACKIE! JACKIE! Are you awake?" Her head nodded slightly. YES! I rushed around the side of the bed and grabbed her right hand. Gardy still grasped her left. We were like two divers who had just reached a drowning woman. We didn't dare let go for fear she'd slip away from us again.

"I love you! I love you, Jacqueline!" I kissed her lips gently. Her lips moved.

"Oh, my God! You've kissed me back! Oh, Jackie, I love you so very much." I had never felt such a tremendous rush of emotion.

I glanced at Gardy, whose jaw had dropped. "I've got to get someone in here, a doctor, a nurse, somebody. Stay with her. Don't let go of her!" I rushed into the hallway.

Elizabeth Conner, the sixth-floor head nurse, was the first person I saw. She should have gone off duty at three-thirty, but it had been a hectic day, and now, at four-thirty, she had just finished reviewing patient reports with the evening staff and was getting ready to go home.

"My wife woke up!" I shouted to her. "Come and see her!"

Mrs. Conner put down her coat and purse. This was the last thing she expected. In twenty-eight years of nursing, she had seen so many facets of life and death that almost nothing surprised her. But when she walked into 638, she was awestruck.

"Mrs. Cole?" she asked quietly. Jackie's eyes focused on Mrs.

Conner's face. "She's clearly responsive," Mrs. Conner said. "This is intentional activity indicating brain function controlled by the patient, not the involuntary, nonpurposeful eye fluttering or grimace that she occasionally exhibits when turned."

Mrs. Conner had often seen stroke victims respond earlier and improve gradually, but she had never seen someone awaken from a coma this way. She turned to the door and called in Janice Budzynski, the young evening nurse assigned to Jackie's care. Recently graduated from nursing school, Janice was speechless. No one had ever told her in nursing school that something like this could happen.

Janice, Mrs. Conner, Gardy, and I stood like statues for a few moments until Mrs. Conner told Janice to call Dr. Pula and other doctors and to make notations on Jackie's chart.

I suddenly began to chatter like an overtrained parrot. I had to tell Jackie everything, to fill her in on all she'd missed: "This is a miracle! No one ever thought you'd wake up, Jackie. You had a terrible stroke. We thought we'd lost you. But God has brought you back to me, to the children. Oh, how thrilled they'll be to see you awake again. How they've missed you. How we all need you! And do you know what? You're retired — you'll never have to work again. What do you think of that?"

Jackie smiled. A small smile, to be sure, but a real one.

"I love you, Jacqueline! I love you so very, very much. Do you love me?"

Jackie nodded her head slightly. I kissed her face over and over again. Her eyes remained open, still fixed on my face. I've never felt such supreme joy. I knew I could never be happier. Never. God's absolute, inevitable presence had filled the room and had given us a gift of exquisite perfection and beauty, as beautiful as Jackie's open eyes. I had always believed that God performs miracles, but I hadn't seen one in person until that moment. I was in total awe of God's power — I could feel his power. Humble, amazed, and ecstatic all at once, I knew this was the kairotic moment I'd hoped for. I knew God *was!*

Within five or ten minutes, word of Jackie's awakening spread through the hospital. Doctors, nurses, orderlies, unit clerks were abuzz: "The lady in the coma woke up!"

"No way. You've got to be kidding," they said, until they came to her room to see for themselves. They filed in, crowded around Jackie's bed, and stared in silence, almost reverently, waiting for proof.

I couldn't contain myself; I had to show off this miracle, my wife. "I have something to show you," I proudly told the gathering. I looked at Jackie and said, "Sweetie, there are a dozen or so nurses and doctors here to see you. I want you to show them that you are really awake. Can you smile?"

Jackie smiled.

"I want you to nod your head."

She nodded.

"Can you blink your eyes?"

Jackie blinked.

I leaned over her head. "Can you kiss me?"

She kissed me.

These skeptical, professionally trained medical folks stood stunned and silent. Several moved closer to grip her hands, touch her face, look deep into her eyes, as if to prove to themselves that they weren't being deceived. Then they erupted. Some applauded. Someone near the door shouted, "Bravo!" Several wept. Some said, "Incredible . . ." "Unbelievable . . ." "Thank God . . ."

Mrs. Conner touched my sleeve. "We're trying to reach Dr. Pula and Dr. Hayes. Mrs. Cole is being moved back to ICU for closer monitoring," she explained. A sense of urgency suddenly filled Jackie's room. Instantly the wheels had been oiled, and a flurry of activity had burst forth from everyone's initial disbelief: The paperwork for the transfer had begun. An ICU bed would soon be assigned. A portable cardiac monitor and defibrillator, called Lifepak-6, would be hooked up for Jackie's transfer downstairs.

I looked at Gardy. "I need to call the children and Julie and her father and everyone! Let's go across the street to that restaurant, and I'll make the calls from there while Jackie is moved back to ICU."

"Great! And I'll buy you a drink to celebrate!" Gardy exclaimed.

I touched Jackie's cheek and said, "The doctors and nurses

have to work on you and take care of you, now, darling. They're going to move you to the ICU. Everything will be all right. Everything will be better now! I'm going to call the children and bring them back here to see you. I'll be back soon. Don't worry about anything. I love you!"

Jackie's eyelids were beginning to nod like a drowsy child's after a long, exciting day. That didn't bother me though. I knew she wasn't slipping back into the coma. She had reclaimed her life with God's good grace, and she wasn't going to leave us again.

Gardy and I bolted across Antique Row to the restaurant where I'd often eaten alone these past seven weeks. The hostess, the bartender, the waiters all recognized me by now, but for the first time they were startled to see me walk through the door with a beaming smile. As they stared at me, I realized that tears were streaking my face.

"She woke up! My wife woke up!" I boomed to the entire place. A waiter rushed toward me and pumped my hand. The hostess and the bartender bear-hugged me. The owner began crying as he poured drinks for Gardy, himself, and me. We toasted Jackie and laughed the first deep, freeflowing laughter in nearly seven weeks. After a stiff Scotch, Gardy and I headed for the pay phone. I dialed our home number. No answer. I dialed the restaurant where Thomas was working.

"Sit down, Thomas," I said when he came to the phone. "I've got incredible news: Mom woke up!"

Thomas was silent. "Did you hear me? Mom woke up! I'll be over to pick you up in a while and bring you back here to see her yourself."

I tried Julie, but her line was busy. "I'll call her and John later," I told Gardy. "Let's get back across the street and see if they've moved Jackie yet."

As I rushed down the sixth-floor corridor, I saw Dr. Hayes running toward Jackie's room. I had never seen him run before. He was incredulous when I caught up with him. Only nine days earlier, he had given an affidavit saying that her death was imminent. He was beaming at me. We shook hands heartily and slapped each other's shoulders like victorious jocks after the biggest game of the season.

"What are you going to do now, Mike?"

The pulmonary specialist was still very concerned about Jackie's pneumonia. Even if she had emerged from the coma, the pneumonia was nonetheless critical. Dr. Hayes told me that Jackie was headed back to the ICU for closer monitoring, and she would be continued on aggressive supportive therapy. As I thanked him, I felt an unspoken pact between us — we'd won her back and would never lose her again.

At 6:30 P.M., two hours after she opened her eyes, and forty-seven days after her stroke, Jackie was back in the ICU. I knew as I reentered the ICU that I would never again experience a day like this one. The woman whom I loved so much that I'd been willing to make the ultimate sacrifice of letting her die had been given life once more. And then it struck me — only six days earlier, I had asked a court to allow her to die. How close we had come to losing her forever! We had believed her recovery was hopeless, nothing better than a one-in-a-million shot. And here she was, eyes open and smiling. Jackie was that one in a million. Jackie was the miracle one!

Eleven

Untethered at Last

From the moment Jackie opened her eyes, I knew — absolutely knew — that she was back for good. She would recover. If she could beat incredible odds by awakening, she could return to her same, beautiful, full-of-life self. She would speak, walk, dance, take photographs, and paint again. I was soaring in the stratosphere, but Dr. Pula's feet were firmly grounded.

When word reached him, Dr. Pula rushed immediately to examine Jackie. She certainly had emerged from the coma, he discovered, but he feared the worst: what if this is the most she can do? That would be the tragedy — a life that she so explicitly did not want to lead, a paralyzed, dependent life. When he and I first met after Jackie woke up, Dr. Pula tried to bring me back down to earth gently.

"It's a miracle, Tad. It's a miracle!"

"It is really amazing that she has come out of the coma, Harry. But I've got to level with you. This could be a cruel hoax. She is still in extremely serious condition. The pneumonia remains a major concern. She may not be able to do much more than open her eyes and look at you. We don't really know the extent of damage the stroke has left. We'll have to watch her very, very carefully. We'll continue close evaluation, testing, and treatment. But we'll just have to take it one day at a time."

"But, Tad, she smiled! She kissed me!" My joy couldn't be smothered. Dr. Pula decided not to say much more at that point, but he feared that I would eventually crash-land.

Jackie was now settled and sleeping in the ICU, so Gardy and I left to round up the children and bring them back to see their miracle mother. On Gardy's cellular car phone, I became a modern, technological town crier. I first called Julie, who kept repeating, "I can't believe it. Really? I can't believe it. I'll come down right away. Really?" I called my mother and brother, Bonnie and Paul. All had the same I-can't-believe-it-that's-wonderful reaction.

Christina and John had returned home by the time Gardy and I arrived. Christina was standing by the stairs when I burst through the front door.

"Mom woke up!"

Christina said nothing. Her face was transfixed, blank. It wore an I-can't-process-this-information look. Before she could speak, I bounded up the stairs, two at a time, to tell John. He had heard me come in and was descending the stairs from the loft. When we collided in the middle room, I repeated, "Mom woke up!" John's face was contorted as if I'd told him a cruel joke.

"You mean it, Dad?"

"Absolutely. It's true, John. She did wake up. She opened her eyes and they sparkled. They were full of life! She looked right at me. She even smiled, and nodded when I asked her to, and she kissed me back when I kissed her!"

Christina had run upstairs. "She's really conscious? Really?" A slight smile crept across Christina's pale face as she slowly allowed herself to believe my words.

"Right! Really, truly awake! I saw her come awake with my own eyes. And the doctors and nurses have seen her awake, too."

"I guess I'm just afraid to believe you, Dad. I'm afraid of being let down," John said.

"Well, why are we standing here? Let's go see her!" Christina said.

"Yes! I phoned Thomas a few minutes ago and told him we'd go by the restaurant and pick him up. Then we'll all go see Mom, and you'll see for yourselves."

I ran downstairs and out to Gardy's car. Christina and John followed, still in a haze of half belief. Like a child with a new electronic toy, I jubilantly punched more numbers on the car phone. I called Stephen and Beth, Ron, and Jackie's father. John Lohsen didn't believe me, so he called Julie to be certain.

When we arrived at the restaurant, Thomas instantly ran across the room and leaped into my arms, nearly knocking me to the ground.

"Oh, Dad! Oh, Dad. This is too good to be true! This is terrific. Tremendous!" We laughed loudly, joyously, and held on to each other tightly.

When we arrived at the hospital, Jackie had dozed off. The children didn't see the wide-awake miracle I'd promised, but doctors and nurses reassured them that their mother's coma was over. The children wore expressions of dazed disappointment, but they were told that a gradual emergence from a coma was normal. No one springs out of a forty-seven-day coma and is instantly alert. These things are measured in inches, we were assured. The kids nodded, seeming to comprehend and to accept this explanation as medical fact, yet their emotions were in turmoil. Was she better or not? Was she going to recover, to be the same good old Mom, or was she going to be seriously disabled? No one could give them a clear answer.

Julie then arrived and saw nothing. She could elicit no response from Jackie at all. Because she had worked with stroke patients, Julie knew how devastating the effects could be. Her happiness that Jackie had awakened was intertwined with fear that Jackie's future could be just the one Jackie had dreaded, a pathetic future as an invalid.

At the end of this longest, most joyous day of my life, Gardy drove me home. "Thanks for chauffeuring me around, Gardy, and for letting me use your car phone to spread the great news."

"Don't thank me, Harry. It was my greatest pleasure to be part of this happiness."

I phoned David Ash as soon as I entered the house. David was lying in bed and watching television with his wife, Joyce, when the phone rang.

"David? This is Harry."

My God, David thought, there's only one reason he'd be calling me at this hour.

"She died, Harry?"

"No! No! She woke up!"

David could say nothing for two full minutes as tears filled his eyes and choked his throat. Finally he found some words: "That's great, Harry! That's unbelievable! Sure, it's a miracle! Hey, I've got to call the judge. How about you and I go see him tomorrow down at the courthouse? Okay?"

When he hung up, David bounced up and down on the bed like a kid as he told Joyce. She was a veteran nurse who'd seen patients without legs come into shock trauma units and leave walking. As she listened quietly to David, he grew annoyed with her because she didn't seem to share his excitement.

"Yes, it's great that she came out of the coma, David, but . . ."

"But what? Damn it! You're not giving this enough credit. I'm going to call the judge! Damn, I can't believe this!" David jumped off the bed and grabbed the phone book to look for Judge Byrnes's home number. When Mrs. Byrnes said the judge wasn't at home, David was crushed. He had wanted so much to relate this wonderful news himself. But he had to settle for a simple message: "Please, tell the judge that Mrs. Cole awakened from her coma today."

The next morning I called Louise Bailey, my church secretary, to say I'd be taking the next few days off to tell the world that Jackie was awake. I asked Louise to spread the good news to all our church members, to thank them for their prayers, and to ask them to continue praying for Jackie's recovery. Then I notified far-flung friends and relatives of Jackie's awakening. And I called several of my closest friends in the ministry. Each of them saw Jackie's emergence from the coma as an act of God's divine intervention. We ministers like to believe in miracles, but few of us ever actually witness one. As I told them that there was no apparent medical explanation for this, that the doctors couldn't explain her awakening forty-seven days after such a devastating stroke, they agreed it was truly a miracle. "Well, you've certainly made a believer out of me," Herb Valentine said.

I also sent a letter to the many ministers around the country who had been praying with their congregations for Jackie:

Dear Friends,
You have been so wonderful to Jackie and me and our family, and I am more thankful than you can imagine for all

of your expressions of concern for us. But most of all, I am especially thankful for your prayers.

Jackie has regained consciousness. This does not "compute" with the vast amount of medical information which indicated overwhelming odds to the contrary, but it is nonetheless real. I feel certain that the powerful and positive energy of your prayers has benefited Jackie, and I ask you and your congregations please to continue praying for her further improvement. I wish I could thank each of you and each member of your congregations individually and personally. Please share my message with them.

In Christ's love,
Harry Cole

Then I placed an overseas call to Maureen, who wept tears of joy and said she'd be home as soon as she could. I went to the Presbytery office and to the state education office to tell Jackie's colleagues. That afternoon I met David on the courthouse steps.

"Can you believe we were here exactly a week ago, Harry, and we went out of here bitching and moaning about the judge's finding! And here we are back again to tell him that she woke up! I didn't think his decision was right, but, oh, baby, what a wonderful way to be wrong!"

"It's a miracle, David. An incredibly beautiful miracle. God stepped in. God woke her up."

When we arrived at Judge Byrnes's chambers, Carol Shay said that the judge had just begun a new trial and wouldn't be available for a few more hours. David looked so disappointed — he reminded me of a kid peering into an empty Christmas stocking — but nothing could puncture my pure joy.

That Sunday I returned to my church with "tidings of great joy." I usually prepared my sermons pretty thoroughly, in advance, but this Sunday's was extemporaneous, unwritten, unedited, unabridged spontaneity:

"I want to share the most wonderful news with you. On Thursday, Jacqueline woke up!

"I left her just an hour ago. She opened one eye. She wiggled one set of toes. She squeezed both hands and kissed me several times. I told her that I was coming here to tell all of you about this." From the pulpit, I could see several handkerchiefs pulled out of pockets and purses to dab tears of joy.

I summarized the events of Thursday afternoon. "The doctors still cannot explain this. Perhaps they'll come to terms with it later in the week when we talk about what has happened, where Jackie is, and what faces us in the future. There is still cause for great concern. She has a serious case of pneumonia. It is still quite possible that Jackie will not survive. She may die. I do not believe, however, that she will. I believe that she will come back. I saw God's power at work when Jackie opened her eyes and smiled at me Thursday. I have seen God's grace and redemption. I have seen a miracle.

"I know that God is at work here, because Jackie is awake and I have told her that that particular combination, her own determination and God's Providence, is an unbeatable combination.

"There is a Greek word, *kairos,* that I have mentioned to you before. In Greek thought, there is a good deal of dualism. There are two forms of thought, two levels of history, two kinds of time. One is human time, chronological time, called *'chronos.'* The other time, *kairos,* is God's holy history, and the *kairos* occurs when God simply makes himself known in human time and space. That is God's inevitable moment. I never saw one of those moments before, but I saw one Thursday."

I recapped events from the morning of her stroke, through my decision to withdraw artificial life support, and the unsuccessful court petition. And I answered the unspoken question that must have been on many parishioners' minds:

"I have no guilt and I have absolutely no regret for the decision that I made to work toward ending Jackie's life. I want each of you to understand that very clearly," I said, "because I firmly believe that we have the right to determine whether or not we want our life prolonged by artificial means. As Jackie's guardian, I believe I had the right, if not the duty, to carry out her own expressed wishes. The miracle of her awakening does not change that basic belief in a patient's right to die. I acted for the sole purpose of bringing what I thought was the most fitting resolution to Jackie's situation. Medical people told us that she had only a one-in-a-million chance of recovery. Therefore, I reached my decision, because I love her and I saw no purpose in keeping her here, hooked to machines that weren't bringing her back to life but were merely postponing — we thought — her inevitable death. I acted to free her from that pointless situation so she could join our eternal Father in heaven. We believe that God sustains us in a truly endless eternity. And I believed that God, not respirators, IVs, or feeding tubes, would sustain Jackie for eternity.

"I am simply overwhelmed and I am at something of a loss, perhaps, to explain this in logical terms. The doctors can't explain it in medical terms. But I am absolutely certain of one thing: this is surely a miracle come from God. And I can now see over the last seven weeks, one day, three hours or so, how the Providence and the power and the grace of God have intervened in this entire ordeal. While we saw the artificial support systems only as means of postponing her death, they were helping to keep her alive until the moment when God would step in.

"You know how often I've said that the essence of God's grace is that it is at work even when we don't recognize it, when we least expect it. Grace is a no-strings-attached gift from God which we don't earn, which we don't deserve, but which he lavishes on us because he loves us as much as he does. And he keeps giving us his grace. It keeps on coming into our lives. It is the very substance of our lives. That is part of the joy, part of the miracle, of God's infinite love for us.

"I thank you for all your earnest prayers for Jackie, the children, and me over these past seven weeks. I am certain that your prayers have helped to bring her back, and I ask you please to continue praying for her improvement. Thank you. Each of you is very dear to me."

OVER the next fourteen weeks at Maryland General, before Jackie was transferred to a rehabilitation hospital, she would disappoint, delight, provoke, amaze, discourage, and occasionally bring laughter to us, to her friends, and to the nurses and doctors.

At first, many who had heard the dazzling news that she'd awakened were disheartened when they actually saw Jackie. She slept much of the time and was unresponsive.

Vanessa Ajayi had heard the news about Jackie even before coming on duty the next morning. Vanessa bounced into Jackie's ICU cubicle.

"Hi, Jackie! How're you doing?"

Nothing.

"Oh, Jackie! I wanted you to say 'Hello.'"

No response.

"They said you can open your eyes. Will you open your eyes for me?"

Vanessa saw no movement of her eyelids or anything else. Disappointed and angry, Vanessa left the cubicle and strode up to the nursing station.

"Who said she woke up?" Vanessa demanded.

By the end of the first week, Jackie gave small signs of movement and awareness. A slight smile. A blink of the eyes when asked to respond by blinking. Nodding of her head. But by the second and third week, her progress seemed to level off. Everyone was discouraged. Even I had to admit that she seemed to have plateaued. When I met with Dr. Pula, I expressed my pessimism for the first time since May 15. I could tell that he was trying to be supportive but realistic when he said, "Don't get your hopes up too much, Harry. Don't come as often. Don't invest so much of yourself in her recovery." I heard his words, but I knew I could not — would not — give up on Jackie. I couldn't cut back on the "marathon sessions," as Dr. Pula called my visits to Jackie. I was visiting her three times a day, morning, late afternoon, and night, just as I had when she was in the coma. But now that she was conscious, my visits were longer. There was more to do now: I held her and reassured her that she would get better. I moved her fingers, toes, and legs to stimulate her to a greater degree of awareness and response. But whenever I didn't see any, a sad disappointment crept in.

One evening I sat up long into the night. It was my first truly low point since Jackie had emerged from the coma, and it felt like an irritating, uncomfortable garment that I didn't know how to shed. I thought and prayed for some direction, some sense of what was appropriate to think, to feel, to do. But everything came up dry. Please, God, keep this miracle going, I prayed. Please bring

Jackie more and more improvement. I know you're at work here, but please give me some sign of encouragement. I am feeling so alone and helpless at times.

The next morning, when I walked into her ICU cubicle, Jackie's eyes were open. She seemed more aware. When I squeezed her hand once, she squeezed mine once. When I squeezed hers twice, she squeezed mine twice. I asked her to squeeze my hand twice and she did.

Whenever Julie visited during those first few weeks, she found her sister staring toward the foot of the bed, so Julie would crouch down at the end of the bed to come into Jackie's line of vision.

"Can you see me, Jackie? Are you looking at me? If you can see me, wiggle this foot," Julie asked as she touched one foot. After a few visits, Jackie slowly responded by wiggling one foot, and then toes.

One day I walked in just as Dr. Pula had finished examining Jackie. He was more optimistic than I'd ever seen him. As cautiously professional as he was, Dr. Pula couldn't hide his joy that Jackie was moving her fingers and wrists.

"Well, you can't deny it, Harry. She's moving things. She's active," Dr. Pula said, smiling. And the bonus was the defeat of her pneumonia. On June 3, nineteen days after she awoke, it was officially declared under control.

When Julie arrived one afternoon, she was shocked to find Jackie sitting in a chair — not really sitting but slumped like a rag doll, with pillows propping her up on each side. Jackie's head was sunk deep onto her chest, and she gazed out from the tops of her eyes. Julie was frightened by the pathetic sight. But a few visits later, after Jackie had gained more movement, Julie decided to gauge just what Jackie could do. Julie took a hairbrush from the drawer of the bedside table and put the handle in Jackie's palm. Not knowing what Jackie's mental state or physical capacity might be, Julie thought anything could happen. Jackie might stare at it without recognition, or drop it, or try to eat it.

Jackie's fingers closed around the brush handle. Her hand moved slightly. Her arm rose upward from the elbow. She couldn't raise the brush all the way to her head, but her hand and arm told Julie that Jackie knew what a hairbrush was, what it was for, and the direction it should go toward her hair. Julie was elated. Tears welled in her eyes. "Oh, Jackie! That's right. It's a hairbrush. Here, let me brush your hair for you."

For the first time, Julie was firmly convinced that her sister could function. "She's all there, I know it," she told her husband and son that evening.

Over the next several weeks, Jackie's ability to move increased. She could move her arms, toes, feet, legs, shoulders, and head. Whenever I watched her smile, make a fist, turn her head in response to a request, or even grimace, I excitedly thought I was watching Jackie's rebirth. She was coming back to life, becoming whole again.

On June 19, I asked Jackie to watch me as I moved around the room. She did so for the first time. The next day she repeated the feat and gave me an extended smile. For days I'd been asking her, "Do you love me?" and encouraging her to form the answer with her mouth. On June 20, she managed to answer my perpetual question for the first time. "Yes," her lips responded.

"Jacqueline, you are a miracle. You're God's very special gift. You have done a wonderful thing," I told her repeatedly.

Throughout her coma, I had hung on every physician's word and rarely challenged a medical statement. But by July, I began to question every doctor I met: "Where are we and where are we going?" No one was willing to make a firm prediction. It was as if Jackie were some just-discovered species. They hadn't seen a case like this before, so they had no background from which to predict.

I again contacted Dr. Howard Moses, the Johns Hopkins neurologist, who was amazed at Jackie's recovering status. Basically, all we could do was to wait and see, he told me. But that wasn't good enough for me. I needed more information and direction. I made a long-distance call to Tom Ducker, a neurosurgeon friend of ours whom I'd known from a previous parish. He, too, saw Jackie's recovery as a miracle. Yes, she was young and had a strong heart and strong lungs, thanks to her exercising them religiously, and those things no doubt contributed to her recovery. The fact that she was comprehending, moving spontaneously, and trying to speak only augured well, he told me. And, yes, the fact that the hemorrhage occurred in the right side of her brain meant that her language ability might rebound, since speech is controlled by the left side of the brain. How far her recovery would go was anyone's guess, but I believed that God would continue to bring progress.

BY early July, the blood from the hemorrhage in Jackie's head had been reabsorbed enough so that a CAT scan could reveal the actual cause of her stroke: an AVM, or arteriovenous malformation, a congenital abnormality of blood vessels in her head. Dr. Pula explained to me, "When you go from being a tiny embryo to a full baby, lots of cell divisions have to happen. Many organs and blood vessels are formed, and it's not uncommon, just as with aneurysms, that all of the billions of blood vessels won't form exactly right. It's a malformation, like a tangled cluster, that will sometimes rupture." He assured me that there was little chance of a recurrence. For one thing, the CAT scan showed no other AVMs in Jackie's brain, and, for another, the chances that a ruptured AVM would rerupture were relatively small, a 2 to 3 percent-per-year probability.

Adolphus Spain gave me a stack of articles to read about stroke victims' recoveries. I read them all and sometimes read the most encouraging parts to Jackie. I left the articles in her room for other visitors to read, too. In addition to the hospital staff's wonderful physical therapy work, family and friends became an informal therapy team to stimulate, exercise, and talk to Jackie constantly. As soon as they walked through her door, all her visitors seemed to be transformed into amateur therapists, prodding Jackie to smile, mouth a word, follow them around the room with her eyes, and squeeze their hands or wiggle their toes.

Word of her recovery was spreading from church to church. Prayers of thanks and prayers for her continuing improvement were offered. Each day the mail brought cheerier messages. I asked for a few moments at the May Presbytery meeting to thank everyone in all the churches for their prayers and to ask for their continued prayers for Jackie's full recovery.

Except for a few discouraging moments, I had been rocketing with hope and confidence for six weeks, from May 15 through June. But during the first week in July, I picked up a nursing manual in a bookstore. It was full of discouraging words like *ataxia* (loss of coordination and balance), *aphasia* (loss of language), *dysphagia* (loss of the ability to swallow). Seeing those words in black and white almost blinded me. For the first time, I consciously questioned my hopes for Jackie's full recovery. Perhaps she will never be able to stand up, to walk, to talk, I thought. That evening, when I visited Jackie, I realized that I was making great demands of her, asking her to make certain movements and try to speak. Suddenly in a great gush, my pent-up frustrations spilled out:

"I guess I'm just demanding things from you out of my own insecurity, out of my own need to see you get better as fast as you can, Jackie. I just believe so much in your ability to talk when you want to talk, to stand up when you want to stand up, to paint again."

Jackie grimaced.

"Am I upsetting you?"

She nodded her head. I felt that she wanted me to leave. A strange, new feeling, that one. Ever since she'd awakened from the coma, she'd seemed so intent on my being with her, so riveted to me whenever I was in the room. And whenever I had to leave, I felt that she was silently pleading with me to stay. Not now. For the first time I knew she would have kicked me out if she could.

On the drive home, I felt utterly helpless. Between deep sighs, I thought to myself, I'm so inadequate. Will I ever stop feeling so inadequate? But who's kidding whom here? Look at what you're up against, Harry. It's a miracle that she's come this far. The odds are still overwhelming that she may not get any better. Remember what Dr. Pula said that first evening after she woke up — that this could be a cruel hoax?

Back in the middle room of the empty house, I thumbed through the nursing manual again. Maybe miracles only go so far, I thought. This could be all there is! For weeks I had been delighting in all the positive progress Jackie was making, but I knew that I was avoiding a talk with doctors. If this was the extent of Jackie's recovery, how would I deal with it? What could I do next?

No one wanted to consider those alternatives it seemed. I'd been hanging on to every sign of progress, and I'd been totally swept up in it. My mood swings, my sense of well-being were attached to the simplest of Jackie's movements — or lack of movement. I knew I was either setting myself up for success with Jackie or setting myself up for bitter disappointment and failure if she should not recover any further. I was laying those demands at her feet to move her leg, straighten out her arm, follow me around the room with her eyes, say "yes" or "okay" and move her mouth, act like a normal Jackie. As if there was nothing wrong, as if she could overcome this in a wink of an eye or another day of miracles. But there was always the chance that Jackie had recovered as much as she could.

When miracles answer our prayers, I was learning, we can sometimes become naive. We set ourselves up for big disappointments if we cast our lot with making miracles all the time. Yet, once I'd had a taste of a miracle, I craved more . . . Faith, I told myself, have faith. God has done it before and he will do it again. Trust him. Wait for him to act. His love and grace will prevail.

Over the next several days, I kept busy with church work and visits to Jackie. But the same thoughts haunted me at the end of each long day. I felt very afraid, very alone. Walking toward the hospital one evening, I felt overcome with a sense of responsibility for Jackie's welfare. I wanted to take care of her. I wanted to make everything right again. Then a new thought occurred to me: God didn't act capriciously in letting Jackie continue to recover, slow as that recovery was. How could I be so arrogant as to worry or assume responsibility for her welfare? When would I learn to stop being everybody's father? When would I let God be God?

THEN Jackie began to rebound again. The doctors had been weaning her from the ventilator. Each day she could breathe without it for a few minutes more than she had the day before. By mid-July she was breathing completely on her own for the first time since March 29. She began to eat some solid food, especially if it was sweet, and she was more responsive than ever. With her new freedom to move her limbs, Jackie expressed her spunk and exasperation with hospital confinement by kicking sheets and pillows off the bed and pulling at tubes and IV lines. I teased her about becoming a brat again, and she smiled mischievously. But the brightest indication that she was progressing was her ability to mouth words. She could almost say them audibly, but the tracheostomy prevented it.

On July 8, I asked her what she used to do at work. Her lips clearly formed the word "certification." I was as thrilled as a young father hearing his baby's first word. Three days later, Lillie Crandall, an ICU clerk who had grown fond of Jackie and often kept her company and painted her fingernails, found Jackie in tears. When Lillie asked what was wrong, Jackie mouthed the words, "I want to go home." As soon as I walked in that evening, the nurses told me about the incident. I asked Jackie if it was true, and she nodded yes. I told her that I would take her home soon. Two days later, a friend, Lynne McCoy, and her husband, Bob, brought Jackie several daylilies from their garden. Jackie's eyes widened, and her lips formed the words, "Oh, they're beautiful." I thought that even the most perfect flower could never be as beautiful as Jackie silently uttering those words.

The phone rang in my office on Tuesday, July 15. When the caller identified himself as a staff physician, my first thought was that something had gone wrong. Every other call I'd received from a doctor had been one of distress.

"Don't worry. I'm calling about your wife, and she's doing fine. In fact, she's doing so well that we're transferring her out of ICU and back to the sixth floor today."

When I returned to Maryland General late that afternoon, Jackie was in room 652. Two months to the day earlier, she had awakened just down the hall in 638. I asked her if she realized the significance of the move out of ICU and back to the sixth floor.

"You've graduated from ICU, honey. You've been promoted upstairs!" But she didn't seem to care. I asked her if she wanted to go home, and she nodded yes.

I talked with Dr. Pula about planning Jackie's rehabilitation. In addition to the hospital's physical and occupational therapies, I looked into the possibility of enrolling her in a state vocational rehabilitation program. At the same time, I tried to explain everything to Jackie. I was convinced that she could comprehend what she heard, so I reviewed the circumstances of her stroke, why she was in the hospital, and what was being done to help her recover. I brought in a magazine article and read an excerpt to her: a woman about Jackie's age had had a stroke, and, over a three-year period, had come back to normal. "At this point, Jackie, you're very far ahead of where that woman was at a comparable time. I want you to understand that great things can come out of your situation. I want you to believe that you can become whole and happy and healthy. And you will be able to come home."

Jackie smiled and formed the unmistakable words, "I want to go home."

Twelve

Rehabilitation

Jackie's move to 652 opened a flood-gate of visitors. Dozens of friends and coworkers who'd waited months to see her filled her room with laughter and flowers and gifts. Her favorite gifts were sweets. She begged Stephen for ice cream and gummy bears. She devoured candy. Whenever a nurse discovered a food tray untouched, Jackie would get a gentle scolding: "You can't just eat candy, Jackie." Nurses began putting the candy out of sight. When someone brought her several small wrapped packages, Jackie asked, "Are they edible?"

I had watched her evolve from an infant opening her eyes and absorbing the sights around her, to a child craving candy, and eventually to a moody, provocative adolescent, swinging between dependence and independence. She'd yank out her feeding tube in the ICU. She'd convince visitors that she could walk. As she'd try to rise from the bed to walk to a nearby chair, she'd refuse help. A moment later, she would be flat on the floor.

Jackie flirted with doctors and made repeated overtures to me about climbing into bed with her. She insisted that I spend the night, as if she feared losing me if I left the room.

Until the tracheostomy tube could be removed, Jackie had difficulty speaking, so the occupational therapists introduced her to writing with a special pen. A note over her bed said, "This patient communicates by writing. Please encourage her to do so by using this adaptive pen." When I first saw the note, I crossed out "this patient" and printed "Jacqueline." The next day a new, hand-printed note went up: "Jacqueline communicates by writing. Please encourage her to do so by using this adaptive pen."

Her penmanship progressed over several weeks from scribbles to legible messages like "Don't install A/C. I'm freezing." Once she was weaned completely from the respirator, the hole at the base of her neck, where the tracheostomy tube had been, was plugged with a small metal plate, and the skin began to close over it. With the hole sealed, air could pass over her vocal chords once more, and her words at last became audible. A whisper at first. Like her overall recovery, her voice gradually grew stronger.

By July 29, exactly four months after her stroke, Jackie was free of all tubes. "No more feeding tube, no more oxygen tube! What a marvelous thing to see you finally untethered, free of those mechanical things," I told her.

But, for the children, Jackie's untethering would never be good enough. Christina, John, and Thomas struggled through the summer to understand their new mother. Each had a summer job, but between work and spending time with their friends, they still made time to visit Jackie every day. Sometimes their visits and mine would coincide, and other times I would meet them at home after a hospital visit. All summer long, they were quiet and introspective right after visiting Jackie. Their questions revealed their impatience and frustration with her rate of recovery:

"How long will she be in that wheelchair?"

"When's she going to walk by herself?"

"How much better is she going to get?"

"I don't know," I always replied. "I wish I could give you some encouraging, firm answers. The doctors and therapists say we have to take things one day at a time. But you know Mom — when she wants something, she'll go after it. Our job now is to give her all our support and encouragement. We've got to help her believe in her own recovery so she'll keep on fighting."

They nodded whenever I gave them this little pep talk. But I could see in their faces how badly they wanted Jackie to return quickly to her old self, racing around with them, laughing with them, listening to their concerns, going to the beach with them. To their one recurrent question, Would she ever do those things again? I could offer no promise. I believed that she would, but I had no hard evidence to back my belief. Each child needed time, perhaps a great deal of time, to grapple with this radically changed mother. I prayed that time would bring them healing and acceptance of Jackie's new condition, whatever it might turn out to be.

A few weeks earlier I had talked with the kids about how we could all use a little vacation. Jackie was well enough for me to take the kids to Cape Cod for a few days. But when I presented our plan to Jackie, she frowned. "Do you want me to go?" I asked. She shook her head with a decided no! So I postponed the trip. But by the first week of August, I saw such improvement in Jackie that I rescheduled the much-needed vacation. I tried to prepare Jackie by telling her over and over that I'd be away for only a week and would call her every day.

On the morning we were to leave, John and I stopped by 652 to say good-bye, but her room was empty. We found Jackie in the physical therapy department. When I spotted her, she was sitting in a wheelchair in the hallway. She looked so forlorn that I wanted to pick her up out of that wheelchair, hold her in my arms, take her home, and care for her myself — forever.

I asked the staff if I could wheel her back to her room. I was happy to be able to do even that. Seeing her unhooked from machines, sitting up and mobile, even if in a wheelchair, thrilled me. She can move around after all those months in bed, and I can be with her, I realized. I can go places with her, if it's only up three flights in an elevator and down a hospital corridor. Even that is good enough.

When we were back in 652, John and I lifted Jackie into bed. John kissed her good-bye and walked out to the hallway. I reminded her again that I was taking the kids on a short vacation and we'd be back soon. I kissed her good-bye over and over and told her I had to go, but I really didn't want to leave her. When I began to cry, she offered me a simple solution: "Well, don't go." I backed out of the room slowly, waving, and reassuring her that I would phone and would return in only a week.

The first time I called her from Cape Cod, she sounded sleepy and only responded with "yes" and "no." The next evening I stopped at a phone booth outside an ice-cream parlor. When she answered, I couldn't believe I was speaking with the same woman.

Jackie's voice was clear and strong! She spoke with perfect diction and vocabulary. It was almost as though this conversation had occurred before the stroke.

"My God!" I said, "here we are, having our first adult, intelligent, real conversation — and we're five hundred miles apart. I'm standing somewhere in the middle of Cape Cod with an ice-cream cone dribbling down my hand and tears dripping down my face! And you're talking so clearly, so fully, from a hospital bed in Baltimore!" As I told her repeatedly how much I loved her, what a miracle she was, how incredible the past four months had been, I found myself blubbering.

"Don't get upset, Harry. Everything will be okay," she reassured me.

JACKIE's new ability to speak revealed something not so welcome, though: it soon became clear that she had a major memory deficit. I understood that a stroke victim's memory usually takes longer to recover than other functions — perhaps a year or two or more — but throughout the summer, Jackie's inability to remember names and facts from moment to moment was everyone's greatest worry. Even Jackie's, as she became aware of it herself.

She always knew me when I walked into her room, but she often didn't recognize Julie. She didn't know one doctor or nurse from another and needed to be told repeatedly where she was and why she was there. After I explained once more that she was in the hospital, she asked, "Where will I be spending the night?"

Her memory loss caused Jackie anxiety and fear, disorientation, and sometimes panic, when she realized she couldn't grasp the context of the world around her. I continually tried to reassure her that I was by her side, that she was improving, and that she would recover and come home. But her dread of losing me whenever I stepped out the door only increased her fears. I was her anchor to reality.

"ICU-itis" was the term coined by hospital people to describe a patient's anxiety about being alone in a private room after a stay in ICU, where nurses, doctors, occasional visitors, and other patients are always in view. When transferred to a private room, where nurses come in less frequently and where a patient often cannot see activity in the corridor, patients often feel isolated and afraid. Dr. Pula mentioned this to the sixth-floor nurses and encouraged them to stick their heads in 652 whenever they could, just to say hello and to let Jackie know somebody was nearby. The nurses also turned on the radio or television to keep Jackie company and give her some stimulation when she was alone in 652.

Hospital therapists taught Jackie memory-retention skills such as writing names and events in a log book. Julie encouraged her to look for clues to conjure up a memory. If Jackie couldn't remember where she was, Julie suggested, "Look on the sheet or on your nightgown and see the hospital name stamped there." Occasionally Jackie would ask the time without realizing that she was wearing a watch. Julie would give her a one-word clue: watch.

In the early weeks, when Jackie didn't recognize her sister, Julie would stand in the doorway and wait a few moments so Jackie could simply look at her. Julie knew that Jackie needed time to absorb what she saw and heard. And Julie knew better than anyone that Jackie had always imposed a hurry-up, rush-rush timetable on herself. Now she tried to help Jackie relax: "You don't have to answer quickly, Jackie. If you don't remember, feel free to say, 'I don't remember' or 'if you'll give me a few moments, I think I'll remember.' Don't feel you have to give an answer instantly."

By mid-August, Jackie showed signs that her memory was improving. I told her on August 13, "When you get anxious, think about how I love you and you'll be okay." The next day she recalled my statement and added, "I know I have trouble remembering things." And the day after that, she could remember for the first time where she was: "Maryland General Hospital, and I was in a coma." That evening, she fed herself dinner for the first time.

I tried to help Jackie re-create a memory bank by telling her about our past. She repeatedly asked, "How did we meet?" Like a youngster begging papa for a favorite bedtime story, Jackie loved hearing the story retold and retold — and I never once minded retelling it. Each time the story was brand-new for Jackie. One August evening I taped our conversation so she could hear her own voice again.

H: Now I just told you how I met you and how you met me.

J: Yes.

H: You wore your pretty, short dresses. Black and gray, tight dresses. And how you smiled at me and how we met each other after watching each other for weeks.

J: Uh, huh.

H: I used to call you, too.

J: You did?

H: Yes, I used to call you from my extension to yours. Your was three-oh-three. Do you remember that?

J: Yes, okay.

H: And I used to call you and invite you to lunch.

J: You did?

H: Yes.

J: I don't remember that.

H: Do you remember our first luncheon engagement? Where it was?

J: Umm . . . at a restaurant across the . . . it's on . . . you know . . . I know it, but I just don't know.

H: It was in a hotel.

J: Yes. Was it the name of a duck or something? Mallard?

H: Well, they served duck. It was called, oh, I forget the name. It's not there anymore — William's Plum, that's it. We had our first lunch there, which consisted of a Jack Daniel's for me and you had, I think, a whiskey sour.

J: Did you need the Jack Daniel's?

H: Yes! I was nervous.

J: You were?

H: Yes.

J: You're so sweet.

H: Thank you. So are you. I love you.

J: I love you. I do.

Later she asked me when I fell in love with her.

H: I fell in love with you in stages, and the first stage was when I first saw you. And I thought you were absolutely beautiful. And then I fell in love with you a little bit more when we started going out, and a lot more when I saw you with the kids and I saw how you handled them and how much they loved you. I used to watch you work with the children and how they would mind you and listen to you, and kind of gather around you like little chickens around a mother hen.

J: These were my kids?

H: Yes.

J: Okay.

H: I just admired that, your devotion to them and their devotion to you.

J: It's genuine.

H: Yes, it's very genuine.

J: I know I'm devoted to them.

H: Yes, you are. Just as much today as you were then.

J: I do love you. I really do mean it.

H: I know you do. I love you and you really are a miracle.

J: No, you're the miracle.

H: Okay, we're the miracle together.

J: Okay.

WHEN I visited her another evening, she was dressed in a new blue nightgown, a welcome change from hospital garb. Someone had helped her skillfully apply makeup. When I called her a vision of loveliness, she said, "I didn't expect you to come . . . Can we eat now?" As I brought over the food tray, Jackie asked, "Can I have something more powerful, like a Jameson?"

"Irish whiskey? I don't think that's on the hospital menu, Jacqueline!"

At times she surprised us with an unusual word, the way a precocious child impresses adults with a "big" word. When I commented that I was so overwhelmed by the total experience of her stroke and miraculous recovery, Jackie pronounced, "You lack resilience."

Jackie occasionally expressed a poignant sense of pain about her memory loss. She told me in late summer that she thought her memory deficit limited our relationship and added sadly, "I'd like to forget it."

"You'd like to forget which, our relationship or your memory loss?"

"Oh, Harry, my memory loss!"

A moment later she rebounded and expressed a strong will to overcome it: "I don't believe what the doctors say. They were wrong about everything else they said about me, and they'll be wrong about this." Five days later she left Maryland General and entered a rehabilitation hospital.

I'D known that Jackie was ready for a change. For nearly five months, Maryland General had sustained her through a cerebral hemorrhage, coma, and gradual recovery. But I knew she was ready to move on. She was making progress in occupational and physical therapy sessions. Her muscle tone was improving. Despite her readiness to leave the general hospital for a rehabilitation one, I was a bit ambivalent about the change. Maryland General had become something of a home to Jackie and to me. She had received excellent care and nurturing, and I had received kind support from doctors, nurses, therapists, and even the security and maintenance personnel who always had a cheery greeting for Jackie. Moving Jackie was like sending a child away to college — something a parent does with mixed feelings of trying to hold on and trying to push toward independence.

Sometimes those ambivalent feelings need the gentle shove of a single moment that crystalizes conflicting emotions and creates action. It took one significant moment to show me that the time for a change had come for Jackie. On an August day, when I accompanied her to an occupational therapy session, I watched Jackie breeze through exercises that had been difficult for her only a few weeks earlier. Now they seemed childlike for her. These were exercises to build cognitive skills: recognizing shapes, matching objects. She was bored and asked for drawing paper. She began to sketch other people in the therapy room. Recognizable facial features appeared on the sketch pad. There was no doubt about which person she was drawing. The portraits didn't reveal all the skill and talent she'd shown before the stroke, but they clearly showed that Jackie could do more than recognize circles and squares.

I consulted with Dr. Pula, other physicians, the hospital's therapists and social worker about finding a rehabilitation hospital that could accelerate Jackie's recovery. I visited one facility that struck me as sterile and cold. Then I toured Montebello Rehabilitation Hospital. It had a more well-worn appearance, but its work was apparent wherever I looked. Patients at every stage of rehabilitation were involved in a purposeful activity, either as part of a group or one-to-one with a therapist. I saw stroke patients of varying ages receiving physical, occupational, and recreational therapy. On another floor, I watched young head-injury patients, many of whom had been in motorcycle accidents, tooling around in wheelchairs as they had on their cycles. They were talking, occasionally joking, with each other on their way to the next activity. They reminded me of high school or college kids changing classes. Everyone seemed to have a full, challenging program from nine to five. As I watched one patient struggle to use disabled limbs on the parallel bars, I realized that these patients worked even harder than their therapists.

I spoke with nurses, members of the stroke unit staff, and Dr. Susan McCartney, the physician in charge. I told her that I saw Jackie's recovery from the coma as a miracle and that I wanted the miracle to continue, to rehabilitate Jackie to the greatest possible extent. Dr. McCartney had read Jackie's background and talked with her therapists at Maryland General. She agreed with me that Jackie's was a most extraordinary case and said that she was confident that Jackie could be helped at Montebello. She could begin in four days if I wished. Based on the impression of my tour and on my conversation with Dr. McCartney, I did something I ordinarily don't do: I made an intuitive decision. Jackie would enter Montebello on the following Tuesday.

As word spread through Maryland General that she was leaving, nurses, doctors, clerks, everyone who'd come to know her over the past five months had mixed feelings. She had become something of a star patient — "the coma lady who woke up." Everyone was sad to see her leave but happy that her recovery would be pushed more intensively at a rehab hospital. On the morning of her discharge, August 29, several people stopped by to wish her well. Dr. Pula's partner, Dr. Mike Sellman, called her "Pumpkin" three times and kissed her good-bye. A young intern, whom I knew only as Jack, joined me for coffee in the cafeteria while the nurses dressed Jackie for discharge. I remembered him from the afternoon Jackie awoke. His was one of the amazed faces staring at Jackie just minutes after she opened her eyes and smiled.

"The day your wife awoke was the most inspired moment in medicine that I've ever witnessed," Jack told me.

Jackie's speech therapist, Lisa Mienert, came to say good-bye and told me that, with proper, extensive therapy, great progress could be made on Jackie's memory. I was buoyed and grateful to hear that.

I'd told Jackie about Montebello several times over the past few days, but she didn't seem to grasp or remember the significance of the move. And when Dr. Pula stopped by 652 the day of her discharge, he had to reintroduce himself to her all over again. In more than three months since she'd emerged from the coma, he had examined Jackie dozens of times. Yet she could never recall his name. On her discharge report, Dr. Pula noted a "profound recent-memory loss," as well as a quadriparesis, or weakness in both arms and legs, leaving her unable to stand or walk.

When Jackie was dressed to leave, we stopped at the second floor. I wheeled her into the ICU for one last good-bye with the nurses who'd cared for her so long and so well. They were proud of Jackie and rightly proud of themselves. She had received excellent nursing care. When she left the ICU she had no bedsores, contractures, or broken areas on her skin. That's a testament to fine nurses when someone has been in a hospital bed for so long. And beyond the physical aspects of nursing, Jackie had received their friendship and genuine concern. As the nurses marveled at Jackie, I stood back with tears in my eyes and basked in the shadow of their affection for her.

"Come back and see us, Jackie . . . Send us pictures, Jackie . . . We know you'll do so well . . . You'll knock their socks off, Jackie!" I thanked them for all the care and love they had showered on Jackie, and she beamed a brilliant smile at each of them.

Some of the staff had suggested that she be transferred to Montebello in an ambulance or at least in a wheelchair van. But I was adamant. I would drive Jackie there in my own car. I wanted to demonstrate to myself and to the whole world the great contrast with the way she had entered the hospital. No coma, no ambulance, no emergency room entrance this time! Jackie was leaving wide-awake, out the front door, and into the car I'd parked at the main entrance.

Outside in the warm August sunlight, Stephen, Thomas, Christina, and John were beaming as I wheeled Jackie through the doorway. They had brought Charlie.

"Look who came to see you, Mom!" Charlie bounded from the car door and sprang into Jackie's lap. Five months had been a long time for faithful old Charlie, but he hadn't forgotten her. They had a grand reunion in that wheelchair. Whether it was the sight of Charlie slobbering all over her or whether it was the beautiful sight of their mother hospital-free at last, Stephen, Thomas, Christina, and John couldn't contain their excitement.

"It's so good to have you out of there, Mom . . ." "You look terrific! . . ." "You're really getting better!" they exclaimed at once. For the last five months, I had longed to see them smile like that again. And when I saw that picture, the shutter of my mind's eye snapped it and preserved it forever.

As I drove Jackie away from Maryland General, she remarked about how strangely noisy the city sounded all around her. I realized what a time capsule she'd been in.

"Do you recognize this street we're on?" I asked her.

"North Avenue."

"That's right!" I was grateful for every small recognition that Jackie could pull out of the past.

I almost felt as though I were driving her to camp. Her toothbrush, her underwear, all her things were packed. Like a kid going to summer camp, she would learn things, grow, develop, become strong. I remembered how she and I had driven the children to their first overnight camp near the Chesapeake Bay years ago. I remembered our reluctance about leaving them in the care of others. Would they be okay? Would they be well cared for and safe?

Though every rational cell in my body told me that this transfer was right for Jackie, I was still hesitant about taking her to Montebello. I momentarily fantasized about driving right on by. I thought, I've taken her out of the hospital on my own, and for these few minutes she is completely mine. In my world. I'm solely in control of her life. She belongs to me exclusively.

As we approached Montebello, I felt a pang of anxiety. Giving her up again to other people who would care for her was far more painful than I'd expected. Thomas had followed us to Montebello, and he stayed with Jackie to help her settle into her new room while I worked through the maze of institutional paperwork. I talked with a "financial adviser," who wanted to be sure this high-cost care would be paid, and with admissions people, social workers, dietary staff, her head nurse, and her physician, Dr. McCartney. I think I spoke with everyone but the chaplain. Probably redundant, I thought to myself.

When I returned to Jackie's room, she was in bed and wearing a hospital gown again. After seeing her dressed and outdoors only an hour earlier, I was instantly depressed. These moments of regression do come, I realized, like the times she makes progress for two days and then slips backward on the third. I knew I couldn't do anything about that. I'd simply have to live with the ambiguity of this experience.

# Thirteen

As Long As We Both
Shall Live

For the next two months, Jackie was put through her rehabilitation paces at Montebello. Physical therapy sessions strengthened her lax muscles and loosened her limbs. She learned to use a walker. She underwent speech therapy and memory training. She had to relearn how to toilet and dress herself. When she entered Montebello, Jackie was incontinent and unaware of the difference between continence and incontinence. Her short-term memory was so poor that she couldn't recall whether she had been to the bathroom five minutes or five hours earlier. The hospital's normal routine was to toilet patients every two hours around the clock. Within a month, Jackie was toilet trained. She was also able to come home on a Saturday–Sunday overnight visit.

As she grew stronger physically, her personality also began to reemerge. Especially her sense of humor. Asked where she put her memory log, she'd smile and say, "I forgot." One Monday morning, a nurse asked her, "How was your weekend at home?"

"Oh, it was great. Harry and I had sex . . . I think. I think I remember that." Jackie laughed.

When Jean Sorrentino visited and apologized for not coming to see her in a while, Jackie teased, "If you hadn't apologized, I wouldn't have known you hadn't been here."

Jackie asked Jean if her friends at the office missed her and wondered if her old job would be waiting for her. Jean knew of Jackie's disability retirement but was uncertain if Jackie was fully aware of that fact and its significance. So Jean turned the conversation in another direction.

"Oh, Jackie, why would you want to come back to the office? This is a great chance for you to begin something new. Why don't you think about changing careers when you get out of here? I've always told you that you should be using more of your creative talents. Why don't you go into fashion design, be a clothing consultant, or something like that? You've always been so artistic and fashionable."

Jackie looked down at the drab gray sweatsuit she was wearing and gestured with a sweep of her hand. "Oh, right. Me, a fashion consultant," she deadpanned.

IN mid-September I received a telephone call from Rafael Alvarez, a Baltimore *Sun* reporter. He had received an anonymous tip to read the transcript of our court hearing, he said, and he would like to write a human-interest story about us. Why not? I thought. Word of Jackie's miraculous recovery was already spreading among our acquaintances and far-away churches. Who'd want to keep this good news private? Mr. Alvarez came to the house and talked with me at length. He interviewed Jackie when she was on a home visit from Montebello. His story, headlined "Woman's Awakening from Coma Fuels Ethical Debate," ran on the front page of the Sunday *Sun* with a color photo of a smiling Jackie, sitting in a wing chair in our living room and surrounded by Christina, Thomas, John, and me.

The story was immediately picked up by wire services, and a national media invasion began. During the week of September 18, Jackie's story appeared in newspapers across the country, from the New York *Post* to the San Francisco *Examiner*. *Time*, *People*, *USA Today*, Phil Donahue, Oprah Winfrey, the "Today" show, even the foreign media from Canada, Europe, and Australia, all wanted Jackie's story. Montebello was besieged with phone calls from the press. The next afternoon, reporters trooped into the Montebello dining room, and Jackie held a press conference.

"How do you feel, Mrs. Cole?"

"Wonderful."

"Are you glad to be alive?"

"Very glad to be alive."

"How do you feel that your husband was about to pull the plug?"

"He was trying to do the right thing. I love him, and I'm happy I woke up and we're together again."

I was beside Jackie and smiling proudly at her when I was surprised to hear my own name.

"And Reverend Cole, how do you feel now about your decision to pull the plug?"

"I don't regret or feel guilty about my decision because, given the best available medical information, we thought Jackie had no chance of any real recovery. So I made that decision because I thought it was the right, fitting thing to do at the time, given all the facts we had. I do believe now that Jackie's awakening and her continuing recovery are miracles from God. But I still believe that a patient has the right to determine her own treatment, or withdrawal of treatment. As Jackie's guardian, I was acting on her behalf, doing what she had often said she'd want in such a situation."

Talk-show producers began imploring us to come on their programs. I put them off, saying, "We'll see, after Jackie gets out of Montebello." We'd been living in our own little circumscribed world for six months — we couldn't believe this media attention was focused on us.

One Sunday morning, I picked up the phone to hear the clipped voice of a BBC reporter in Belfast, Northern Ireland. "The world is often dark here. That's why I called. We need to hear your story of hope."

That call made me realize that we should go public with our story and appear on television when we were asked to let the world know that there is hope, that God loves us and hears our prayers and performs miracles. That would become our mission, a way of showing God our gratitude, of paying him back, so to speak.

Much of the media coverage was brief and pegged more to "the miracle" than the right-to-die question. Other coverage, like Connie Chung's for the magazine-format program "1986," was deep and detailed. In early October, Ms. Chung and her crew spent the better part of a week interviewing and taping Jackie, Dr. Pula, Judge Byrnes, David Ash, Stephen, Thomas, Christina, John, and me.

Sitting around the dining room table, the children were completely frank with Ms. Chung, exactly as Jackie had always encouraged them to be. Stephen said, yes, he had thought it was too soon to disconnect artificial life support after only six weeks. "She's a very strong woman. She's very stubborn," he said. "I was just going on feelings, but I thought, She's going to pull through."

How did they feel about the judge's decision? "I was pretty shocked and I was angry," Christina told Ms. Chung, who responded, "Shocked and angry? That surprises me."

"Really? I didn't see that it was his decision. We knew my mother. We knew what she always wanted."

Now that she's survived, did they feel guilty about trying to pull the plug? No, Thomas explained, "We were all very conscious of what her feelings were, and so we cannot feel guilty because we were just obeying her."

The children's distress about Jackie's disabilities was spread across the lace-covered table for a nation of viewers to witness. "Although happy to have her alive," Ms. Chung concluded, "the children don't believe she's living what she had always described as a quality life."

"I don't see, for her, there's all that much to live for right now," John said, "if everyone's doing everything for her, which is exactly the opposite of what it used to be."

"But she's alive," Ms. Chung interjected quietly.

"Just because she's alive, what can you do if you can't help yourself?" John replied.

"It's one thing," Thomas added, "if a person can't be a productive part of society. But it's another thing if you can't be a productive part of yourself."

"Are you saying, she's living exactly the life that she didn't want to live?" Ms. Chung asked.

"I believe so," Christina said.

The children's statements were more controversial, perhaps because they were broadcast on national television, than they would have been if spoken privately. Several of our friends were disturbed and saddened to hear them. But, as one old family friend noted, the kids were repeating precisely what Jackie herself had said before the stroke: that a less-than-optimal life was not worth living for someone who'd always lived life full tilt, as Jackie had.

The youngest three in particular clung to a memory of the only mother they'd known. Stephen, older, married, and out on his own, was more ready to accept Jackie's new limitations. But Thomas, Christina, and John weren't prepared for the abruptness with which Jackie's stroke ripped her from the fabric of their lives. Jackie and I were both somewhat surprised by their remarks to Connie Chung, but we realized that they'd been through a tremendous shock of nearly losing the mother to whom they had been extremely close, and they were having difficulty adjusting to the loss of the Jackie they'd known.

At their stage in life, our children faced the usual decisions: Shall I go to college or get a job? What do I want in life? Where do I want to live? How independent can I be from my parents? When will I ask them for money? How can I earn and save on my own? Whom shall I live with? Whom shall I love? Who loves me? If these typical, early-twenties decisions weren't tumultuous enough for any young adult, they were loaded for our children. Their single most vital relationship — the lifelong one with their mother — was radically changed by her stroke. It set Thomas, Christina, and John adrift. They were anchorless and far from a secure port when they spoke with Connie Chung that October, only seven months after Jackie's stroke. At that point in her recovery, their "new" mother had difficulty remembering things; her cutting wit had softened; she was no longer svelte and always on-the-go but now needed help walking. The stroke left the children frozen in time. They wanted Jackie back exactly as she had been. It would take months for them to accept their recast mother.

WHEN Jackie was discharged from Montebello in November, 1986, she walked out on her own and returned home for good. That was the best Thanksgiving we could ever have. At Christmas, I took over Jackie's tradition of trimming the tree as she gave me armchair advice. I filled the bay window with the tallest, widest tree I could find and decked it with a thousand tiny white lights.

For the first time since her stroke, Jackie danced — by herself, then with Thomas, and with me to the strains of Christmas music. That first poststroke Christmas reverberated with symbolism: Christ was born. Christ came to Earth. Jackie had been reborn. Jackie could walk among us again.

That Christmas Eve, when our congregation gathered for its annual candlelight service, I read, as I do each year, the beautiful story of Christ's birth from the Gospel of Luke. When I came to the passage proclaiming the angel's announcement to the shepherds: "Be not afraid . . . I bring you tidings of great joy . . . for unto you is born this day . . . a Savior, who is Christ the Lord. . . ." I looked out at Jackie from the pulpit and thought of our own great, personal rejoicing. God had given the world his son, and he had given me back my wife.

In the two years after her discharge from Montebello, family and friends were continually amazed by Jackie's progress. She became able to walk unaided, stumbling or becoming off-balance with less and less frequency. She had operations on both her elbow and fingers to correct stiffness caused by lack of use during the coma. The hole at the base of her neck, where the tracheostomy had been, had closed long ago but left a deep indentation. Plastic surgery took care of that. And she resumed videotape exercising to trim some of the weight she'd gained. The combination of steroids, which help to shrink swelling in the brain but also increase the appetite, and general inactivity while hospitalized had given her too many unwanted pounds.

Jackie also took a painting course at the Maryland Institute of Art. She proudly showed a vibrant still life to Bertha Butler, who visited us nearly two years after she had carried Jackie downstairs and into the ambulance. "I can't believe it," Mrs. Butler kept repeating. "When we took you out of here, I never thought you'd see the inside of this house again. Now, look at you! You look wonderful, a picture of health!"

"And I owe you a lot of thanks for my health," Jackie told Mrs. Butler. "I don't remember a single thing about that day I had the stroke, but I've been told how quickly and well you responded. I am very, very grateful."

Jackie also had an opportunity to meet and thank another key player in her life, another whose action while she was comatose was vitally important: Judge Byrnes. Several months after Jackie was discharged from Montebello, she and I visited Judge Byrnes in his chambers, where he graciously invited us to sit down and chat, have a cup of coffee, and tell him about Jackie's continuing recovery.

JACKIE'S memory improved, thanks to tricks learned at Montebello and at Sinai Hospital's "Return" program, which she attended on a day basis after leaving Montebello. In the early days of her recovery, Jackie learned to write things down in order to remember them. She still does that but to a lesser extent. She also learned to lock a fact in her memory by repeating it a few times. For instance, we were planning to visit our friends Richard and Mary Preston in New York one weekend. Richard called to say they wouldn't be home when we arrived, but he told Jackie that he would leave his apartment key with the doorman. During their phone conversation, Jackie repeated twice, "I'll tell Harry the key's with the doorman." When I arrived home about an hour later, the first thing Jackie told me was, "The key will be with the doorman."

Jackie resumed her old hobby of photography as we took the train across the country in January 1988. We had been invited to appear on some television shows in California, and I'd been asked to address several college ethics and theology classes about our experience. Jackie and I both love the stimulation of travel. With camera in hand, Jackie captured parts of the country we'd never seen and viewed familiar places in a fresh way. I loved looking at her snap pictures. It was like looking into a series of mirrors and seeing an image reflecting itself over and over again. My beautiful Jacqueline photographing beautiful scenes — I was seeing beauty mirroring beauty. I watched Jackie enjoy a second chance to relish the world, and I thought how fortunate I am to have been given a second chance to be with her and to love her.

Sometimes I've been asked, "How back-to-normal is Jackie? How many of her capacities has she recovered?" I don't think there's an accurate, scientific way to measure that. She walks with a slight stiffness, but otherwise her physical abilities are near normal. Her speech and her sense of humor couldn't be better. Along with relearning to walk, toilet, and dress herself, Jackie has also relearned to apply makeup. The result is lovely. And after two posthospital years as a natural brunette, she has had her hair frosted again. A stranger meeting Jackie for the first time would be incredulous to learn that she had suffered a near-fatal stroke and a forty-seven-day coma.

Jackie's memory is the main, lingering deficit. Her memory bank can sometimes resemble a hunk of Swiss cheese. She can easily recall details from years ago: "Did you know John's first word was not a single word but a whole sentence? He said, 'Shotzie [our old dog] ate my cookie.'" Yet she has trouble recalling anything about Stephen and Beth's wedding just six months before her stroke. It seems that the stroke erased events about a year before it and impaired some of her ability to recall recent events. For instance, she now enjoys telling everyone she meets about our new, first grandchild:

"Did you know Stephen and Beth had a baby boy? And they named him Vincent," she'll say. Then a half hour later, she'll ask, "Did I tell you I'm a grandmother now?"

So, when I'm asked questions about "how much" Jackie has returned to normal, I can only take a guess: Maybe she's 70 percent back-to-normal. But I'd take 70 percent of the "old" Jacqueline any day over 200 percent of any other woman. Not only did Jackie emerge from her coma, but her recovery has been a continuing process, and for me this is continuing evidence of the miracle God wrought. Each day I have been able to sense, almost touch, her return to life.

JACKIE occasionally has been distressed by her limitations. On one of the many notecards that she used as an informal journal for a while, she wrote, "All my life I've wanted to paint and draw. As a child and young adult, I stole moments from a busy day to paint and draw. Now I have the time, the money, the talent, but no pleasure — it's work!!! And I don't enjoy it one whit. How can this be?!?! Well, be it is, at least for the moment. Maybe this too shall pass. Good God, I hope so. All I want to do is clean and organize things! Good grief. It's really come to that!"

In a February 1987 journal entry, Jackie wrote, "Since my stroke, I have difficulty integrating people and experiences. They just don't seem to fit one into the other. Their objectives, goals, and motives lack continuity and vision — maybe that's my problem, not theirs. I really do not understand why people do what they do, and do they realize there is no consistency, continuity or logic in their actions. I hope I don't sound superior — I'm just puzzled. My brain is still not working correctly, and I am aware enough now to feel the confusion and bewilderment. As I've said before, you're a long time in waking up and I sense I have a long, long way to go."

In the same month, she wrote, "Recovering from a stroke is not unlike climbing out of ooze — very slowly you emerge into the sunshine. And fresh air abounds. You breathe deeply and feel the warmth of the sun on your bones and you are immediately happy and content because the sun is out and you're very much alive."

And eight months later, she wrote, "Here I sit thinking things that are neither honorable nor profound. My observations are still basically naive, and I suppose that my awareness of their naïveté is positive and noteworthy. Everywhere I am surrounded by people who are lively, enthusiastic, and above all else, young! Well, by God, I am still young — sort of — and very much alive, definitely. I just wish I were busier and people weren't so damned nice to me. Everyone treats me with kid gloves, like a prized piece of Meissen ware or Waterford crystal."

Her wish to be busier has been realized as we patched together several activities to break her cabin fever and get her out among people. She has been volunteering one day a week with Meals-On-Wheels. With Betsy Toland, a lovely woman who does the driving, Jackie takes hot meals to isolated, lonely older people. They love Jackie, and she loves to talk with them, though she doesn't have as much time to chat as she'd like, because the meals must be delivered to the next person's home quickly. Another day she works in the Planned Parenthood thrift shop — close to becoming a fashion consultant, as Jean Sorrentino suggested.

These activities do more than fill her time. They also fill her need to be around people, converse, feel useful, and give of herself. For several months, she also worked one day a week as a receptionist at a church in our neighborhood, but she gave that up in the second year after the stroke, when she took a paying, two-day job at our church day-care center. Jackie has always had a wonderful way with children, and this work has been fulfilling for her. I love to steal a few moments from my church work, walk over to the day-care room, and watch her with the children. She wipes their runny noses, tousles their hair gently, teaches them to zip their jackets, reads them stories. It reminds me of the days when I first met Jackie, surrounded by Stephen, Thomas, Christina, and John.

MAUREEN, Bonnie, Adolphus, and Carol have stood by throughout Jackie's recovery and remain the most dear and loyal friends. Whenever she is home on a leave from the cruise ship, Maureen spends hours with Jackie. Bonnie sees Jackie nearly every day. Because Jackie no longer works with Adolphus and Carol, they see her far less often, but Jackie talks with them on the phone frequently. Adolphus still invites us to his beach house. When we visited him in the summer of 1987, seventeen months after her stroke, Jackie announced that she was going to take a long stroll along the sand. Adolphus jumped up to accompany her.

"Let me go with you, Jackie."

"I can go by myself."

"Well, let me come along. What if you go too far and aren't sure how to get back?"

"Oh, all right. Come on along."

On their long walk, Jackie confided to him that she wished she could take a beach stroll alone, drive a car, be independent again. She cried at her loss of independence. "I can do those things, Adolphus, but Harry won't let me." Just as she had unburdened her concerns on Adolphus all those years before the stroke, Jackie did so once more. And just as he always had, he offered her comfort mixed with honesty and good sense: "But Jackie, you can't do all those things by yourself now. You've got a good life with Harry. He's devoted to you, and you're a very lucky woman to have a man who loves and cares for you so much."

"I know, and I do love Harry very much, much more than I ever did. It's funny, isn't it? When I first met Harry, first started dating him, I responded to his love for me. When he asked me to marry him, I was bowled over by the fact that a man could have such a loving, generous spirit. Nobody ever loved me like that before Harry. He not only loved me, but he wanted to take on a woman and her four kids! How could any woman say no to love like that?

"Oh, we used to have our fights but now look how our love has grown — he's cared for me through all of this, and I love and appreciate him so much more than I ever did before I had the stroke."

As they turned around, Adolphus and Jackie began to jog slowly toward home. Adolphus held Jackie's hand because, at that point, her balance was still somewhat unsteady. The heart-to-heart with Adolphus had comforted Jackie and the jog invigorated her — "God, it feels good to be able to do this again!" she exclaimed as the wind swept her hair off her face and the August sun warmed her skin.

Carol has taken Jackie clothes shopping several times — quite a role reversal from the early days of their friendship, when Carol looked to Jackie for fashion advice. Now, when Jackie selects clothes that Carol doesn't think look right, Carol is just as blunt with Jackie as Jackie had been with her.

"Jackie, you're not a size seven anymore, girl! Why are you trying to squeeze into that?"

"Sure I can. And I'm going to!"

In Macy's, once, they had a good, loud, sisterly argument that left other shoppers gawking. Jackie and Carol laughed all the way home about the stares they'd received.

Julie and Jackie are far closer than they had ever been. Julie has discovered a softer, more loving sister, whose caustic wit has grown gentler. As Jackie has recovered these past few years, Julie has been delighted to find all of Jackie's old defensiveness gone. Jackie doesn't always have the quick, often biting, comeback answer. She doesn't seem to need it. Julie finds her sister more patient, more tolerant, and no longer in the rush she had always been in.

Ron Bond finds Jackie to be essentially the same person, but he describes her as a jigsaw puzzle fallen to the floor. "The pieces are all there. Many are still together. But others are scattered and need to be refitted together," Ronnie says.

JACKIE herself realizes a change in her personality. "Sometimes I think I've had a lobotomy," she has often commented. "I am more patient now. I used to be *sooooo* impatient. Maybe that's one of the things my kids don't accept about me now. I'm not on them as much as before. I'm more patient, and that may confuse them. They may see that as a weakness." The stroke may have punched holes in her memory, but it has stolen little of her insight.

Ever since Jackie's stroke, Thomas, Christina, and John have been somewhat adrift. I often recall Maureen's comforting words, when she was home to visit Jackie in the ICU: The children would be separating, moving away from me and Jackie at this point in their lives anyway, Maureen had said. And indeed they were.

Thomas lived at home and worked at various restaurant jobs for the first year after the stroke. But by March 1987, he concluded that his year of mourning should end.

"It's time to start living my life again," he told us, and we agreed. A minister friend of ours in Scotland had told Thomas, "If you ever need a place to escape to, come and visit us in Scotland." Thomas took up the offer and reserved a plane ticket for March 29, 1987, exactly a year after Jackie's stroke.

The very same day, my father's long battle with Alzheimer's disease and prostate cancer came to a merciful end. He died peacefully in his sleep that afternoon with my mother at his side. My father's death, on the first anniversary of Jackie's stroke, rounded out a year of tremendous pain and loss and change in our lives. Jackie's father, too, had died rather suddenly on Christmas Day, 1986. It was as though God was bringing everything to closure, I thought.

Thomas offered to change his flight plan for that day but I told him there was no need to do so. As I drove him to the airport, he talked of how sorry he was to be leaving on the day my dad had died.

"Our family seems to have a penchant for anniversaries and

holidays, don't we?" I said. Jackie's mother had died on her fortieth wedding anniversary. Her father died on Christmas Day. And
now Thomas was leaving and my father had died on the anniversary of Jackie's stroke.

Thomas stayed in Scotland through the summer, when John
joined him to travel through Europe. When he returned, Thomas
resumed working in restaurants again and then found an apartment where he could live and work as the building superintendent.
His responsibilities grew until he was managing six buildings with
107 apartments. He is writing a novel and doing some directing
and acting with a local theater group. Thomas also had a bit part
— as a corpse — in a Tom Selleck movie, *Her Alibi,* which was
shot in Baltimore.

If his mother had never had the stroke, Thomas says, "I probably would have finished college with an electrical engineering degree and would be working in some company and hating every
minute of it." Thomas has continued to be the big brother to
Christina and John. He has tried to guide Christina in her love and
school lives, and he shared his apartment with John for a while.
Thomas wears Jackie's scarab around his neck to this day. He
seems to have accepted the changes in Jackie. He now says,
"Things happen that are beyond our control, and you can only
accept them as best you can." But at times I see in his face the quiet
pain of losing the mother he used to have.

The autumn after Jackie's stroke, Christina returned to Philadelphia but not to classes. She took a year off from college and
worked in a gourmet food store. In the fall of 1988, she resumed
her courses and took a part-time job. John made it through his
senior year of high school but decided against attending college.
He sketched and painted, tried some acting and modeling — a
limited opportunity in Baltimore — and worked briefly at a job I
found for him at the University of Baltimore. In late 1988, John
left for California with some friends to try his hand at acting and
modeling there.

While the miracle for our family is that Jackie has come back to
life, the sadness is that the children miss the mother they'd always
known. It hasn't been easy for the children to accept the realign-

ment that the stroke forced upon us: before the stroke, the children were dependent on Jackie; now Jackie is dependent on me, and they are more dependent upon themselves than on us.

JACKIE has grown emotionally in classic leaps and bounds. Her total dependency on me immediately after the coma eventually began to chafe and she yearned for greater autonomy. She has told me that she wants to drive again, but I know she is not ready or able. She could easily become lost because of her short-term memory problems and her poor sense of direction.

Jackie loves to take walks around our neighborhood, but she occasionally becomes disoriented. If we're lucky, a neighbor helps her find her way home. More than once I've had to call the police for help in finding her. This is no small concern, as we live in an urban area where street crime is no stranger. By the second year after her stroke, Jackie was better able to find her way around the neighborhood, yet I still worry. Late one afternoon, when I expected her to be at home, there was no answer when I phoned from my church office. I thought she might have walked down the street to visit Bonnie. I waited about ten minutes and called home again. No answer. I called Bonnie. No, Jackie wasn't there. I waited a few more minutes. Again, no answer. Should I panic and drive home to look for her? After thirty minutes of no answer, I did rush home. Jackie was there, blithely eating rice cakes at the kitchen table.

"Where were you when I called at four o'clock, at four-fifteen, at four-thirty?"

"I just walked to the A & P for these rice cakes."

There have been too many moments like this. Each time I'm torn between panic and letting her have more freedom. We now have a system: If she's going out, she is to call Bonnie or Julie, if she can't reach me, to say where she'll be and when she expects to be back. Not too overprotective, am I?

Jackie has also asked me, sometimes seriously, sometimes lightly, when she'll get her own credit card and her driver's license again. She reminds me of a teenager, testing me, challenging me to let her grow up. When we were once visiting David Ash, she teased, "How can Harry's guardianship of me be revoked, David?"

The three of us laughed about it. Neither David nor I gave Jackie an answer, and she didn't pursue it. I suppose someday the guardianship could be legally erased, but that is a far horizon. I wish I could allow her the old freedoms, but for her own safety and protection, I cannot. At least not yet. Jackie's poor memory, her penchant for getting lost, her lack of sharp critical judgment, her emotional and financial dependency on me all add up to a continuing need for my guardianship of her. While I earnestly believe she will eventually regain her independence, that day has not yet arrived. Every time I see her get confused while cooking dinner, or not complete a task, or forget to turn off the stove or iron, I am reminded of her limitations and the need she still has for me to take care of her.

The stroke ripped our lives apart like a tornado, and, in its wake, left our relationship dramatically changed. Before the stroke, Jackie and I were close to separating, possibly divorcing. The pull and tug of Jackie's desire to be more independent conflicted with her dependence on me and on our wholeness as a family. My intolerance of things like Jackie's credit card use and our differences about raising the kids were real then, but they seem so trivial now. I was not fully aware of it then, but those problems were masking my love for Jackie. We were two stubborn, impatient individuals, who matured through this ordeal to become a strong, loving, interdependent couple.

I never realized the depth and strength of my love for Jackie until I nearly lost her. Once God stepped in and she awoke, I knew what a fragile, precious gift I had received. Not only had Jackie's life been restored, but she now depended on me and loved me in a totally new way. Our love for each other and an abundance of God's grace have helped carry us through her gradual, often demanding, recovery period and still maintains us today. And I fully believe it will forever.

Jackie's stroke and rehabilitation forced our marriage to take a new direction. In the beginning of her recovery, Jackie was heavily dependent on me. I was her emotional anchor to a world she had to rediscover when she awoke. But I've also had to be her practical, daily anchor: I had to help her dress, toilet, and bathe until she could do these tasks for herself. She is now far less dependent on me for physical things, but to a great extent she is still dependent in emotional ways. She sometimes asks me what she should wear, if her makeup looks all right — questions that were inconceivable before the stroke. And I am the one who continues to drive her places, arrange for her medical check-ups, take her shopping, check on her whereabouts, plan most of our social and church-related engagements. I love protecting Jackie, taking care of her, possessing her. Some of our friends have said that I always wanted all of Jackie and now I have 100 percent of her. Perhaps so. But the imbalance in our relationship is one neither of us would choose if given the option. We would each prefer an equal partnership of shared responsibilities. But, while Jackie and I both wish she could have more independence, autonomy, freedom to come and go, and less dependency on me, her limitations still do not permit it.

About a year after she left Montebello, when she was taking a painting course at the Maryland Institute of Art, Jackie told me one day not to pick her up outside the classroom. She wanted to walk to the campus store and buy some art supplies after class.

"You've got to let me go, Harry," she told me flatly.

I worried about her safety. Would she be able to find the store without getting disoriented? Cross the street safely? I knew I was fretting about her as I would a little child, but I recognized that Jackie needed to make this trek to prove to herself — and perhaps to me — that she still had some independence left. I reluctantly agreed. She went to the store and bought the supplies without any problem. I thought: Part of me loves her the way she is. I don't want her to grow up. I love taking care of her. I know I'm terribly possessive, but it's similar to my feelings about the ministry. We human beings are made to reach out, to protect and care for each other. And I love to do that.

As Jackie and I both acknowledged that she needed more independence, our relationship began to move from protector–protectee toward a more equal partnership. When we occasionally clashed over what I was willing to let her do or not do, we'd throw words at each other but without the intensity of our old prestroke fights. Now an argument was even refreshing, a sign for both of us that things were moving closer toward normal.

"My 'fight' with Harry was a relief," Jackie wrote in her journal. "He said such wonderfully ugly things to me that it made me feel very human and very real. I wouldn't want to do it on a daily basis or even weekly basis. Once in a while it's a good thing to do — sort of clears the air and makes me feel more human, more alive, more intact. No, I never want to fight the way we used to — just every so often. It's refreshing. A real shot in the arm. . . . Our relationship has taken a new dimension, more adult, not so much the father–daughter relationship. Much more the husband–wife relationship. Thank you, God."

AND God has become a greater part of Jackie's life than before the stroke. She prays each night, attends church regularly and attentively, takes an interest in my sermons, says a blessing before meals. As she learned the details of her coma and awakening, she concluded that her survival was indeed a miracle, that God woke her up. To my great joy, Jackie has become a woman of substantial faith. For years before her stroke, I knew that Jackie had a spiritual potential that she hadn't reached. Now my belief has been confirmed. God is much more part of her consciousness now. Having lived this miracle, Jackie and I both know and feel God's love. Every day.

When we were asked to appear on Oprah Winfrey's program, Oprah opened the show by saying that Jackie "has been called a modern-day Lazarus." She asked Jackie, "How do you explain this?"

"I think I'm here to give hope to the world. There's a God, and he loves us all," Jackie replied.

Had she been a religious person before this experience? Oprah wondered.

"No, not at all. It was a fight to get me to church, and I'm a minister's wife!" Jackie said and laughed, a bit to my embarrassment, before millions of viewers.

ON November 25, 1987, Jackie and I renewed our wedding vows at 6:00 P.M. at the First and Franklin Presbyterian Church, where we'd been married exactly ten years earlier. This time I wasn't late. Well, actually I was. Jackie and I arrived at the church in plenty of time, but we realized that we'd left our rings on the coffee table, so I rushed home to get them.

The worship service was framed by Bach, just as it had been a decade ago. The organist and trumpeter played "Jesu, Joy of Man's Desiring" for the prelude and "Now Thank We All Our God" for the recessional. While we wanted to re-create as closely as possible this marriage service to the original, we couldn't have the same minister, Bill Bearden, because he had moved away. This time we were married by the Reverend Harry Holfelter.

Jacqueline Victoria Cole and I, Harry Alexander Cole, exchanged anniversary rings inscribed with our initials and date; hers a diamond and sapphire and mine a gold signet. We repeated our vows: "Jacqueline, it is you whom I love and cherish, and I renew my promise and covenant before God and these witnesses, to be thy loving and faithful husband in plenty and in want, in joy and in sorrow, in sickness and in health, as long as we both shall live."

"Harry, I love you and rejoice in you, and I renew my promise and covenant before God and these witnesses, to be thy loving and faithful wife in plenty and in want, in joy and in sorrow, in sickness and in health, as long as we both shall live."

After the service, a small reception was given for us by our friends Jim and Barbara Judd, whom I had just married a month before. In a lovely ice-blue dress, Jackie danced ever so gracefully, so full of life. As long as we both shall live, I thought. The words rang joyously in my ears . . . As long as we both shall live . . .

# Fourteen
Reflections

Jackie's amazing recovery confronts and confounds one of the most agonizing issues of our time: When, and in what circumstances, do we allow a hopelessly ill patient to die? What is "hopeless"? What do we do with modern medical technology that can prolong a patient's life far beyond the point of cure? Because the technology is available, must we always use it? When do artificial life support treatments cease to aid recovery and merely postpone death? Who decides if and when artificial life support may be withheld or withdrawn? The patient? The family? The doctors? The hospital or nursing home? A court? All of the above? None of the above?

When I reached my decision to end Jackie's artificial life supports, I never thought of myself as a player in a cosmic right-to-die debate. I was caught up in an intensely personal family tragedy — we were losing a wife and mother. From every reasonable perspective, she had left us. Her awareness of everything was gone. She could no longer interact with us or the world around her. Jackie was tethered by mechanical means, not to "life" but to an artificial existence. Over those six weeks following Jackie's stroke, I became convinced that medically there was no reasonable hope of recovery. But, as long as machines were breathing for her and nourishing her lifeless body, Jackie could vegetate for months, even years. (I'd heard a coma expert quoted as saying the record for length of time in a coma was thirty-seven years!) Even if, by the most remote chance, she would regain consciousness, there was no likelihood that she could resume any semblance of a meaningful life. I knew that such an empty existence was exactly what Jackie would not have wanted. I saw no point in allowing this suffering to continue indefinitely.

My goal was to replace pain and suffering with mercy. Out of my deep love for Jackie, I did what I thought was in her best interest and what would have been her own wish. But her completely unexpected recovery has thrust us into the right-to-die debate. As our story received increased public attention, I was often asked, "How could you, a minister, a man of God, decide to end your wife's life?" or "After she awoke, did you feel guilty about your decision to end her life?"

I realize that we have muddied the waters surrounding a person's right to die. But the fact that Jackie recovered so miraculously does not change my basic belief that an individual has the right to determine his or her medical treatment, including the choice to terminate artificial life supports that do not heal but only postpone death. I also believe that a person's surrogate has the right to make that decision when the patient is unable to do so. I still hold those beliefs firmly. In fact, even after Jackie's recovery, I was prepared to make the same decision all over again — this time on behalf of my father. When he was in his final days of suffering from prostate cancer and Alzheimer's disease, my mother, my brother, and I consulted with his urologist and our family doctor. If need be, we were ready to make the decision: No heroic measures; do not resuscitate; no artificial life supports. But Dad died naturally before we had to make that decision.

And what does Jackie think? Even in the face of her miraculous recovery, Jackie believes that a decision to withdraw artificial measures is a humane and just decision when a patient is hopelessly ill. When she has been asked, "Do you hold anything against your family for trying to disconnect life support?" Jackie has replied, "Absolutely not. They didn't want to see me miserable, just existing and just vegetating. I support what they did one hundred percent. I would have done the same thing if I were they."

IN the old days, before mechanical ventilators, nasogastric tubes, jejunostomy tubes, antibiotics, and defibrillators that restart hearts which have ceased to beat, families had fewer choices. Fewer decisions. If Grandpa lay dying in his own bed — and most people did die at home, surrounded by family, until recent years — the family doctor was called. Doc drove to the house in his Model A to examine Grandpa. If the diagnosis were cancer, massive stroke, pneumonia, "hardening of the arteries," or something else that he could not cure, Doc would try to relieve Grandpa's discomfort. And sometimes, as death could be heard entering the room, he may have eased death with a shot of morphine.

No one questioned his judgment. No one went to court.

Modern medical technology has forever changed all that. By 1986, when our family faced the decision to withdraw artificial support, a new landscape had been painted as a backdrop to our decision. That landscape had fuzzy areas, but several details were sharp: a handful of widely publicized court decisions had allowed other families to discontinue artificial life support and public acceptance was growing that doing so was not ethically wrong, but acceptable and compassionate. In a very short time, contemporary society was coming to affirm two relatively new principles:

First, individuals have the right to accept or reject medical treatment. We may spell out in advance our wish not to be maintained by extraordinary or artificial means, and we may designate a surrogate to make that decision if and when we become incapable of making it.

Second, although machines are now available to sustain a terminally ill person or one who is permanently unconscious, they don't have to be used simply because they are there.

But the paint on the landscape wasn't completely dry. Medical advances were forcing us to make new, complex, and difficult choices. Medical technology exploded in the second half of the twentieth century with new means to support life artificially. Medicine far outraced society's ability to deal with the ethical and legal ramifications of the new life-supporting technology. As soon as we grappled with one dilemma, another seemed to present itself almost the next day.

Fraught with concern for civil rights, the 1960s focused great attention on an individual's right to vote, to live in integrated neighborhoods, and to attend desegregated schools, but less attention on an individual's right to determine his or her health care. Yet all of these individual rights were linked together. Though overshadowed by other civil rights decisions, several court decisions in the 1960s established the right to refuse treatment and the right of informed consent. Courts ruled, for example, that prisoners' rights had been violated when they were given experimental medications without their knowledge or consent.

The concept of a living will evolved in the 1960s, too. In 1967, a Chicago attorney, Louis Kutner, who was president of World Habeas Corpus, proposed the idea of a living will to the Euthanasia Society of America, the predecessor of today's Society for the Right to Die. A living will would allow individuals the opportunity to spell out — in advance — their wishes about refusing particular medical treatments (artificial, life-sustaining, "heroic" means) if they became hopelessly ill and unable to voice their wishes at that time. A year after Kutner's proposal, a Florida legislator, Dr. Walter Sackett, introduced the first bill in the country to make the living will a legally binding document. But sixteen years would pass before the Florida state legislature would pass its Life Prolonging Procedure Act.

As the 1970s opened, several significant developments occurred. The American Hospital Association in 1973 approved a "Patient's Bill of Rights," which specified the right of informed consent and the right to refuse treatment. Hospitals around the country now gave patients, usually upon admission, a statement informing them of their right to know what treatments and procedures would be given them and asking their permission to provide such treatment. A patient could refuse to grant permission for certain treatments.

The concept of the living will began to catch hold in the 1970s through the mass media, particularly when Abigail Van Buren wrote about living wills in her "Dear Abby" column. Public pressure increased on state legislators to enact living will statutes, and by 1977, Arkansas, Idaho, Nevada, New Mexico, North Carolina, Oregon, and Texas had enacted living will laws. By the time of Jackie's stroke in 1986, thirty-eight states and the District of Columbia had enacted living will legislation.

But it wasn't until the second half of the 1970s that the right-to-die debate burst on the public stage as Karen Ann Quinlan's serene, sweet face, with her long, straight hair parted down the middle, appeared on front pages across the country and in millions of homes on the evening news. Karen Ann Quinlan became a household name in 1976, when the New Jersey Supreme Court upheld her right to die. The very next year a total of sixty-one living will bills were introduced in forty-two states. Many proponents of the right to die, including the Society for the Right to Die, found significant flaws, inconsistencies, and limitations in these bills. In 1978 a model bill was drafted in a legislative services project at Yale University Law School in cooperation with the Society.

In states where living will laws had not been enacted, courts provided the only recourse when an individual or family's decision to discontinue artificial life support conflicted with hospitals', physicians', or nursing homes' determination to continue those supports. One year after the Quinlan decision, the Massachusetts Supreme Judicial Court ruled that a patient has the right to privacy "against unwanted infringements of bodily integrity in appropriate circumstances." The case involved a sixty-seven-year-old patient, Joseph Saikewicz,who reportedly had an IQ of 10, could not communicate verbally, and resided at a state mental institution. When Mr. Saikewicz was diagnosed as having an incurable type of leukemia, a court-appointed guardian and two doctors testified in probate court against treating him with chemotherapy, because the treatments would cause painful side effects and he would be incapable of understanding the procedures. The probate court accepted the recommendation against treatment and found that any favorable gains would be outweighed by his age, inability to cooperate with the treatment, his suffering, and the improbability of remission. The case was appealed to the Massachusetts Supreme Judicial Court, which affirmed the lower court's decision. Mr. Saikewicz died before the state's high court could issue its full opinion, but when it did, the Supreme Judicial Court stated, "The constitutional right to privacy . . . is an expression of the sanctity of individual free choice and self-determination as fundamental constituents of life. The value of life as so perceived is lessened not by a decision to refuse treatment, but by the failure to allow a competent human being the right of choice." The court went on to say that "the substantive rights of the competent and incompetent person are the same in regard to the right to decline potential life-prolonging treatment." When the person is incompetent, the court reasoned, the doctrine of "substituted judgment" could be applied to determine the patient's wants and needs. That is what I felt we were doing in Jackie's case — offering our substituted judgment in telling the court of Jackie's previously expressed wishes.

The Saikewicz decision was not as widely heralded by right-to-die advocates as might have been expected, however, because the Massachusetts Supreme Judicial Court also ruled that future cases involving an incompetent patient would have to be brought before the probate court. In this regard, the Massachusetts' justices departed from their New Jersey brethren in the Quinlan case.

"We take a dim view of any attempt to shift the ultimate decision making responsibility away from the duly established courts of proper jurisdiction to any committee, panel or group, ad hoc or permanent," the Massachusetts high court wrote. "Thus, we reject the approach adopted by the New Jersey Supreme Court in the Quinlan case of entrusting the decision whether to continue artificial life supports to the party's guardian, family, attending doctors, and hospital ethics committee." Many physicians and right-to-die proponents greeted this ruling with a collectively heavy sigh as they envisioned lengthy, burdensome litigation each time terminally ill patients or their families sought discontinuation of treatment. They dreaded the idea of spending more time in courtrooms than in hospitals, and they feared liability for withholding or withdrawing treatment unless judicial approval had been obtained. But two years later, the Massachusetts Court of Appeals clarified the question of prolonged judicial proceedings in the case of Shirley Dinnerstein.

At sixty-seven years of age, Mrs. Dinnerstein had suffered a stroke, had a coronary condition, and was in the advanced stages of Alzheimer's disease when her adult son and daughter and her doctor asked the court to determine that a "no code" order (one that instructed doctors and nurses not to resuscitate her if she suffered cardiopulmonary arrest) could legally be entered on her medical chart. Her adult children and doctor specifically asked whether court approval of a "no code" would be required in view of the Saikewicz decision. A probate court passed the question up to the Massachusetts Court of Appeals, which determined that these medical circumstances differed from Mr. Saikewicz's. Resuscitation procedures, the Court of Appeals said, are often intrusive, violent, and painful, and in Mrs. Dinnerstein's circumstances would only serve to prolong her dying. The Dinnerstein decision was significant because it was the first to uphold the validity of "no code" orders in the case of an irreversibly, terminally ill, incompetent patient. And it cleared up the matter of seeking judicial approval. The Saikewicz requirement of judicial proceedings applied only when treatment offered a "reasonable expectation of effecting a permanent or temporary cure of or relief from the illness," the appeals court ruled. This time, most physicians breathed a sigh of relief when they read the court's decision: "This case does not offer a life-saving or life-prolonging treatment alternative within the meaning of the Saikewicz case. It presents a question peculiarly within the competence of the medical profession of what measures are appropriate to ease the imminent passing of an irreversibly terminally ill patient in light of the patient's history and conditions and the wishes of her family. That question is not one of judicial decision." The Dinnerstein ruling placed decision making for an incompetent patient, in the terminal stages of an "unremitting, incurable, mortal illness," clearly with the physician in accordance with the family's wishes.

In 1980, courts in Florida and Delaware joined those of New Jersey and Massachusetts in upholding an individual's right to die. The Florida case was the first to involve a competent patient, Abe Perlmutter, who suffered from Lou Gehrig's disease (amyotrophic lateral sclerosis). At age seventy-three, Mr. Perlmutter was dependent on a respirator and bedridden in a Florida hospital, where he not only told his family of his intense suffering but he also tried to remove the respirator himself. When he asked a court to authorize removal of the respirator, a bedside hearing was held, and the judge authorized the respirator's removal. But the state attorney general appealed, claiming that anyone who helped remove the respirator would be guilty of assisting in a suicide. The District Court of Appeal ruled that Mr. Perlmutter should be allowed "to make his choice to die with dignity. . . . It is all very convenient to insist on continuing Mr. Perlmutter's life so that there can be no question of foul play, no resulting civil liability, and no possible trespass on medical ethics. However, it is quite another matter to do so at the patient's sole expense and against his competent will, thus inflicting never ending physical torture on his body until the inevitable, but artificially suspended, moment of death. Such a course of conduct invades the patient's constitutional right of privacy, removes his freedom of choice, and invades his right to self-determination." With his family at his bedside, Mr. Perlmutter's respirator was removed, and, after forty hours, he died. The Florida Supreme Court affirmed unanimously the District Court's decision fifteen months later. It limited its opinion to the facts of the Perlmutter case and did not set forth guidelines for future cases, but the Florida Supreme Court did suggest the need for legislative resolution, as the issue "is not one which is well suited for resolution in an adversary judicial proceeding. It is the type which is more suitably addressed in the legislative forum." The Delaware case also addressed the need for legislative guidance. In that case, Mary Severns became comatose and suffered irreversible brain damage after an automobile accident in 1979. Her husband asked the court to appoint him her guardian, to allow discontinuation of a respirator and of "certain life-sustaining" supports, and to grant an order precluding civil and criminal liability for these actions. The Delaware Supreme Court deliberated for five months and then held that Mr. Severns could be appointed the guardian of her person. But it bounced his request to discontinue life support back to a Chancery Court. That court approved Mr. Severns's request in 1981, more than a year after Mr. Severns began legal proceedings. Mrs. Severns continued to live, despite discontinuation of all authorized measures, until 1984, when she died of a cerebral hemorrhage.

In appointing Mr. Severns guardian, the Delaware Supreme Court also noted the need for legislative guidance: "We earnestly invite the prompt attention of the General Assembly . . . with the hope that it will enact a comprehensive state policy governing these matters which are, in the words of *Quinlan,* of 'transcendent importance.' " Indeed, justices across the country, becoming concerned about the courts' growing role in the right-to-die arena, began turning to state legislatures to enact legal guidelines. In

1979, Kansas and Washington joined the original seven states that had enacted legislation in 1977; between 1981 and 1984, thirteen more states enacted such laws. During the same period, the highest courts in Georgia, New Mexico, New York, and Washington ruled in right-to-die cases.

The beginning of a new decade was also marked by a significant statement from the Vatican. Dying needn't be prolonged by "burdensome" procedures, the Vatican Declaration on Euthanasia affirmed in 1980. The Roman Catholic Church had long and vigorously opposed euthanasia — and still does. But the 1980 statement served to guide many Catholics — state legislators, doctors, hospital administrators, and attorneys — who were intimately involved in right-to-die decision making. In other words, the church was reassuring them that this was not euthanasia.

As early as 1954, Pope Pius XII, speaking to the Eighth Assembly of the World Medical Association, said that a person cannot be merely an object of medical experiments, a thing upon which new medical methods and techniques might be tested. In 1957, he distinguished between "extraordinary" and "ordinary" medical measures when he addressed a group of Italian anesthesiologists. The ordinary–extraordinary distinction was made within a general theological belief that human life is a gift from God the Creator and should not be deliberately destroyed by man. Yet the distinction clarified that the obligation to sustain life was extended to ordinary, beneficial medical therapies, but did not require extraordinary ones. The ordinary–extraordinary distinction goes back several centuries and has special meaning in Catholic moral theology, but the distinction's prominence in the right-to-die question originated from its use by Pope Pius XII in 1957: ". . . normally one is held to use only ordinary means — according to circumstances of persons, places, times, and culture — means that do not involve any grave burden for oneself or another."

As a clergyman, I found the Pope's 1957 statement very relevant to Jackie's situation. He drew a distinction between suffering that has a significance to salvation (Christ's bearing the Cross and his suffering on it, as well as the early Christian martyrs who suffered rather than deny their faith) and suffering that is pointlessly without significance to salvation. He said, "The Christian

. . . is never obligated to desire suffering for its own sake." In explaining why a Christian needn't accept all pointless suffering, he used the example of a woman in childbirth. She may certainly accept some relief from pain, Pope Pius XII said, even though Scripture says, "In sorrow shalt thou bring forth children" (Genesis 3:16). And to his anesthesiologist audience, he said that an anesthesiologist (and by extension, we may assume, any physician) "is seeking according to the Creator's ordinance . . . to bring suffering under man's control."

In 1957 the Pope may never have imagined how many people would soon ask relief from pain and suffering in the face of hopeless illness. But I found his words pertinent to circumstances like Jackie's: "The acceptance of unrelieved suffering is in no way obligatory and corresponds to no rule of perfection. Cases regularly occur in which there are serious reasons for not accepting unrelieved pain and in which circumstances do not require such acceptance. It is then possible to avoid pain without putting oneself in opposition to the teachings of the Gospel."

AS state legislators debated right-to-die legislation, the number of cases that sought resolution through the courts mounted. Between the 1976 Quinlan decision and 1988, approximately ninety right-to-die dilemmas were resolved in courtrooms from California to Maine. This may seem a small number when contrasted with the total number of deaths that occur in the United States each year — some two million. But these agonized families found themselves in courtrooms because their loved one's situation didn't fit neatly into their state's legal guidelines on a patient's right to determine his or her treatment. Courts in twenty-four states and several federal district courts have recognized a patient's right to refuse life-sustaining treatments. Yet the Society for the Right to Die, which among its many other functions tracks court cases and advises attorneys, has concluded that "right-to-die law is not widely known or understood by many lawyers, let alone health care providers, physicians, and patients or their families."

Certainly David Ash and I would second that. David is a good friend, whose primary concern was helping me find relief for

Jackie's lingering agony. Like many people in a critical situation, I turned to my "lawyer friend," even though he was not a specialist in this emerging area of law. I never even considered shopping for "expert" legal counsel. In retrospect, David and I were too hasty and ill-prepared when we went to court. Perhaps the very real necessity to speed the legal process of obtaining guardianship had spilled over and kept us in a fast-forward mode. But we didn't think we had the luxury of time-consuming legal research. Had we had that luxury, David could have prepared a more thorough, detailed case based on other right-to-die court decisions. But our eyes were focused on what we knew Jackie would want us to do — end this pointless suffering.

By 1988, thirty-eight states and the District of Columbia had enacted living will laws. Each state's is slightly different. Some states have amended earlier laws. Some laws specify that only certain artificial means may be withdrawn (a respirator, for instance, but not feeding tubes). As living wills evolved differently from state to state, a number of attorneys, physicians, and right-to-die advocates became somewhat disenchanted with living wills and viewed them as limited in scope. Instead, they turned to the "durable power of attorney" as a more flexible alternative. An ordinary power of attorney is a means of authorizing someone else to make decisions for you, usually financial decisions, if you are on a trip or temporarily in the hospital, but the ordinary power of attorney lapses if you become incompetent. The advantage of the durable power of attorney is the fact that it remains in effect if you become incapacitated and unable to make your own decisions. All fifty states and the District of Columbia recognize the durable power of attorney. Some states allow a durable power of attorney to pertain specifically to health care.

While courts and state legislatures weighed the issues, the medical profession did the same. In 1983, the President's Commission for the Study of Ethical Problems in Medicine and Biomedical and Behavioral Research published a report, "Deciding to Forego Life-Sustaining Treatment." The commission recognized that physicians' dual goals of prolonging life and alleviating suffering can conflict, and, in some circumstances, alleviating suffering may take precedence over prolonging life. But the commission also warned that shortening a patient's life should never be the primary goal of medical treatment.

Exactly two weeks before Jackie's stroke, on March 15, 1986, the American Medical Association issued its opinion that "it is not unethical to discontinue all means of life-prolonging medical treatment" if a patient's coma is "beyond doubt irreversible and there are adequate safeguards to confirm the accuracy of the diagnosis and with the concurrence of those who have responsibility for the care of the patient." The A.M.A. opinion maintained that a physician may "cease or omit treatment to permit a terminally ill patient whose death is imminent to die. However, he should not intentionally cause death." And it recognized "the choice of the patient, or his family or legal representative if the patient is incompetent to act in his own behalf." While acknowledging that an individual's preference "should prevail when determining whether extraordinary life-prolonging measures should be undertaken in the event of a terminal illness," the A.M.A. also stated, "Unless it is clearly established that the patient is terminally ill or irreversibly comatose, a physician should not be deterred from appropriately aggressive treatment of a patient." The A.M.A. polled its membership during the summer of 1986 and found that 73 percent of the respondents favored "withdrawing life support systems, including food and water, from hopelessly ill or irreversibly comatose patients if they or their families request it."

When the Quinlan case publicly opened the right-to-die debate, most people understood "pulling the plug" to mean turning off a respirator. No sooner had some courts granted permission to disconnect a respirator than requests began to be made to withdraw feeding tubes. Many permanently unconscious patients can breathe on their own without a respirator but are sustained by artificial feeding tubes because they are unable to swallow. An estimated 10,000 permanently unconscious patients are maintained by tubal feedings on any given day in the United States, and some right-to-die advocates say that is a low estimate.

The feeding tube question has opened another chapter in right-to-die history. Many doctors and right-to-die advocates see the feeding tube (either nasogastric, through the nose and esophagus to the stomach, or the jejunostomal, through the abdominal wall directly into the small intestine), or intravenous feeding as artificial mechanisms like the respirator — a machine that performs a function which the patient cannot. But the question of withdrawing food and water carries an emotional overlay for many people. By 1988, judicial opinions in thirteen states found that a patient has the same right to refuse artificial feeding as he or she does to refuse any other treatment. The New Jersey Supreme Court wrote in the 1985 case of eighty-four-year-old Claire Conroy: "Once one enters the realm of complex, high-technology medical care, it is hard to shed the 'emotional symbolism' of food. However, artificial feedings such as nasogastric tubes, gastrostomies, and intravenous infusions are significantly different from bottle-feeding or spoon-feeding — they are medical procedures with inherent risks and possible side effects, instituted by skilled health-care providers to compensate for impaired physical functioning. Analytically, artificial feeding by means of a nasogastric tube or intravenous infusion can be seen as equivalent to artificial breathing by means of a respirator. Both prolong life through mechanical means when the body is no longer able to perform a vital bodily function of its own."

Despite doctors' and judges' opinions that feeding tube withdrawal is equivalent to withdrawing a respirator, the "emotional symbolism" remains. Some people view the withdrawal of artificial feeding as a step closer to active euthanasia, as practiced in the Netherlands, where each year doctors give an estimated 10,000 hopelessly ill patients lethal injections to hasten death. (Some anecdotal evidence indicates that active euthanasia is practiced by a small number of doctors in France and Scandinavian countries, but the Netherlands is the only country where active euthanasia is openly practiced.)

If right-to-die cases had been limited to the question of withdrawing respirators, the issue might have leveled off as the body of case law increased and the number of living wills and durable powers of attorney burgeoned. But the withdrawal of feeding tubes has kept the debate alive, particularly within the Catholic community. Cardinal Joseph Bernardin of Chicago, chairman of the United States bishops' Committee for Pro-Life Activities, has warned that acceptance of withholding or withdrawing nutrition and hydration could lead toward the acceptance of euthanasia. He has called for "a nuanced public policy" that would neither "open the door to euthanasia" nor keep alive terminally ill patients who "should be allowed a natural death." He told a University of Chicago Center for Clinical Medical Ethics conference in 1988, "I am convinced from a moral point of view that the essential bond between food, water and life argues convincingly for the presumption that nutrition and hydration should always be provided. But I am also convinced that we are not morally obliged to do everything that is technically possible."

Bishop Louis Gelineau of Providence made headlines early in 1988 when he issued a statement in the case of Marcia Gray, a forty-nine-year-old Rhode Island woman who had been in a coma for two years. Mrs. Gray's husband had sought a theological opinion when he went to court to discontinue feeding tubes after eight operations produced no improvement in Mrs. Gray's condition. Bishop Gelineau asked Father Robert McManus, the diocese's vicar for education, who holds a doctorate in moral theology, to research and write an opinion. The bishop approved Father McManus's opinion, which held that the primary intent in removing Marcia Gray's feeding tube would be "to alleviate the burden and suffering of the patient and not to cause her death." The opinion said that artificial feeding was an "extraordinary" means of care and could be removed without violating church teaching. Mrs. Gray, in a persistent vegetative state, had no reasonable hope of recovery, and the opinion stated that "This lack of reasonable hope or benefit renders the artificially invasive medical treatments futile and thus extraordinary, disproportionate and unduly burdensome. In issuing Father McManus's opinion, the bishop said that the opinion "does not contradict Catholic moral theology and in no way supports or condones the practice of euthanasia."

Yet Bishop Gelineau's statement about the Gray case was seen by many as out of the Catholic mainstream. Ten months later, after a federal judge decided that Marcia Gray's feeding tubes could be disconnected, the bishop issued another statement, saying that Father McManus's opinion "was presented for this particular case and was not issued to set a precedent or be considered as the only interpretation of the official teaching of the church in this matter." He reiterated that the church's magisterium had not issued a definitive statement on "the moral necessity to provide nutrition and hydration to the permanently unconscious patient." Mrs. Gray died November 30, 1988.

JACKIE'S case was quite different from the majority of cases that have reached courtrooms across the country — and the many more private cases that never reach beyond a hospital room or nursing home. Jackie did not have a "terminal illness," which usually is accepted to mean an incurable or irreversible condition that most probably will cause death in a short period of time with or without treatment. Terminal illness may have one advantage: it usually comes on gradually, giving patients and their families some time to think about and discuss death and whether the patient wants to accept or reject certain life-support mechanisms. Older people and those with a terminal illness are more likely to confront their own mortality and perhaps to write a living will or grant a durable power of attorney than a vigorous forty-three-year-old wife/mother/career woman. Jackie had done neither, though she had expressed many times her wish never to have her life prolonged artificially.

Yet in her youth and in the sudden onset of her stroke and coma, Jackie's situation was similar to several significant, well-publicized cases that took months, even years, to resolve through the courts. Like Jackie and Karen Ann Quinlan, these were people who were stricken in the prime of life:

Nancy Jobes was twenty-five and pregnant when a 1980 automobile accident caused a severe loss of oxygen to her brain, resulting in massive, irreversible brain damage. The fetus did not survive. Nancy Jobes was fed through feeding tubes, breathed through a tracheostomy, received antibiotics and antiseizure medication, all of which maintained her in a persistently unconscious state. Five years and two months after her accident, her husband and parents requested that the feeding tube be removed. The nursing home refused and her husband asked the New Jersey Superior Court to authorize removal of the tube. Nearly a year later, and after a bedside visit and seven-day trial, the court determined that she was in a persistent vegetative state and that, if competent, she would not want to have her life artificially prolonged in that condition. It approved removal of the feeding tube. But the nursing home appealed to the state Supreme Court, which, over a year later, authorized the termination of tubal feeding. The nursing home appealed again, to federal trial and appeals courts and to the U.S. Supreme Court, all of which denied its request to postpone the tube removal, pending further review. Ms. Jobes was moved to a hospital, and, after the appellate route was completed, all life support was withdrawn. She died several days later — more than seven years after the automobile accident.

Paul Brophy, a forty-five-year-old Massachusetts firefighter, suffered a brain hemorrhage caused by an aneurysm in March 1983. Surgery was performed to correct the condition, but he never regained consciousness. He was in a persistent vegetative state and was fed artificially because he could not swallow. His wife, Patricia, a nurse, asked the hospital to withdraw the artificial feeding mechanism in December 1984, twenty-one months after her husband's aneurysm. The hospital refused to disconnect it but did agree to enter an order not to resuscitate him and another order to implement a "nonaggressive treatment plan." Mrs. Brophy sought court authorization to withdraw or withhold all medical treatment, including artificially provided nutrition and hydration. A Massachusetts probate judge acknowledged that Mr. Brophy would not have wanted to receive artificial sustenance, as his wife, seven brothers and sisters, and five adult children all agreed. In his career as a firefighter and rescuer, he had seen many debilitated victims and had on numerous occasions expressed his wish not to be sustained artificially. But the probate judge concluded that the state's interest in preserving life outweighed Mr. Brophy's right to choose his own treatment. Mrs. Brophy appealed to the Massachusetts Supreme Judicial Court, which, in a four-to-three decision in September 1986, concluded that the substituted judgment of close family members to refuse artificial feeding of an incompetent person in a persistent vegetative state must be honored. The hospital asked the court to reconsider its ruling. The court refused. The hospital appealed to U.S. Supreme Court Justices Rehnquist, Brennan, and White, who refused to block the

Massachusetts Supreme Judicial Court's ruling. Mr. Brophy was then transferred to another hospital, where the feeding tube was removed. With his wife by his side around the clock, Paul Brophy died peacefully eight days later from pneumonia, three and a half years after his aneurysm occurred.

The Brophy ruling was significant because it was the first written state supreme court opinion authorizing artificial feeding removal to be issued while the patient was still alive. It held that a person in a persistent vegetative state doesn't feel pain and that the removal of the feeding tube from someone in that state does not cause death — rather, the underlying condition, which prevents swallowing, is the cause of death.

Compared to Nancy Jobes and Paul Brophy, Jackie was in a coma a very short time when I decided to seek court authorization to remove life supports. Did I decide too soon? Should I have delayed the decision? Jackie might well have remained in that coma for years, like Nancy Jobes or Karen Ann Quinlan or Paul Brophy. At the time I reached my decision, I believed, based on the best available medical evidence, that Jackie was in a persistent vegetative state, because her coma had lasted over a month. If she were to go on that way, our family faced not only the incredible pain of watching her vegetate, but we also faced harsh practical realities. As generous as the Presbyterian Church might be, I couldn't realistically expect it to pay the full cost of maintaining her for years in a nursing home — an average of at least $30,000 annually. How could I continue to send three kids to college with that additional financial strain? I undoubtedly couldn't without going deeply into debt and/or selling the house. And one of the worst parts of that prospect was the thought of Jackie's reaction — if she knew about it, she would utterly despise the fact that the cost of maintaining her indefinitely in a nursing home placed a burden on her family.

Perhaps my decision to go to court was more premature than others, but at the time I saw no reason to prolong our tragedy. However, two years after Jackie's stroke-induced coma, the American Academy of Neurology took a position on "certain aspects of the care and management of the persistent vegetative state patient," in which the Academy addressed the question of timing:

"A certain amount of time is required before the diagnosis of PVS can be made with a high degree of medical certainty. It is not until the patient's complete unconsciousness has lasted a prolonged period — usually one to three months — that the condition can be reliably considered permanent."

My decision was clearly on the early side of the one-to-three month span, though I had no way of knowing that, of course, in 1986. Had the Academy's position been made before Jackie's stroke and coma, I undoubtedly would have waited the full three months. And her awakening would have made the question of withdrawal moot! But again, at the time, and given the information available then, I saw Jackie's month-long coma, especially a coma brought on by such a massive stroke, as a hopeless and pointless eternity. Believing that her coma was most likely irreversible and that the damage caused by the stroke was so enormous, even on the remote chance that she might awaken, I saw no point in postponing death — particularly because of Jackie's own expressed wish.

After Jackie proved that her coma wasn't permanent, when she opened her eyes and smiled on May 15, forty-seven days after her stroke, I often wondered about timing. Upon reflection, I've concluded that I wanted to bring that kairotic moment to pass. My mistake was pushing for that moment. God was going to step in and wake Jackie at his kairotic moment, and his timetable and mine weren't synchronized.

Whether my timing was premature or not, the route toward my decision to withdraw life supports was the same one that all families must take when a loved one is terminally ill or permanently comatose. We all want to do what is "best," what is morally right and compassionate. We all seek to choose good over evil, the least harm for the most potential good. And facing tremendous emotional, and usually financial, costs, we decide that living takes precedence over dying. We were living; Jackie was dying. She would never have wanted us to suffer because she lay indefinitely in a coma. She would have told us, "Get on with your lives. Live them fully, as I did mine. And let me go."

As a minister, I could only reach my decision based on my ethical training and theological roots. I have come to believe that there are no absolute truths in life, except that God *was* in the beginning of things and that, among other things, God created us. To keep ourselves organized and honest, we created ethics. When God forbade Adam to eat from the tree of knowledge — and he did it anyway — Adam made the first ethical decision. While it may have been the "wrong" one, the point of the biblical story is that all moral action is made in response to some previous action or initiative toward us by others. As mentioned earlier, I was heavily influenced, not only at the critical time of Jackie's coma but also at other points in my life, by the late ethicist, H. Richard Niebuhr of Yale University. Niebuhr's basic assertions were that we have the ability to respond to various ethical dilemmas and that everyone is responsible for his or her own behavior. We are free to make different decisions, which may not always reflect what we were taught was "right" or "wrong," "good" or "bad." Our moral responses, Niebuhr stressed, are made on the basis of what we believe to be both good and right in a given situation, a situation in which everyone's welfare will be affected by our action. Niebuhr attached a certain measure of personal integrity to our moral conduct, integrity based on our relationship with an initial source of moral authority — God.

With Niebuhr, I believe that God initiates a relationship with us that is intended for our own good. We choose to be responsible to God in making ethical decisions. When we ask ourselves, "What is going on here? How is God working in my life? What shall my response be, and how will it affect everyone else?" we respond to God's goodness by making a "fitting response," as Niebuhr called it. We make a fitting response to a God who establishes a relationship with us on very personal terms. God is our Creator, who is revealed to us in our hearts and minds, our Sustainer and Judge who gives order to our lives, and our Redeemer who shows us love and mercy in all aspects of our relationship with him. As God's character unfolds in the course of this relationship, we begin to understand how God is involved in the various ethical situations arising in the course of our relationships with others in our lives. We begin to discover what God's creative, governing, and loving intentions are in a given moral situation, and we then try to determine what our appropriate response shall be. This fitting response provides maximum resolution to the ethical issue at hand, while it also answers the individual needs of those affected by our decision. A fitting response not only assures God's full intentions to give insight and support to our moral deliberations, but it also holds us accountable for our actions. It sustains our continued dependence on God to live together with one another in relationships in which God continues to create, sustain, and redeem us, and it calls on us to act in a responsible, loving way to seek relief for the suffering of others.

In the crucible of ethical decision making, we weigh benefits against burdens. How did the benefit of mechanical life support weigh against the burden of Jackie's prolonged vegetative condition? It seems we have a basic choice: we can blindly follow a rule (It is wrong to kill, therefore we must never do anything to bring about death) or we can evaluate each moral dilemma and respond to it with compassion and an attempt to bring forth the most good and do the least harm. Yes, it is wrong to kill, but isn't it also wrong to lose our humanity in blind obedience to rules? By "rules" I mean any ethical standards employed to make an ethical decision. Many ethical systems have a degree of absoluteness about them. Our challenge is to make the fitting response based on where we see ourselves in relation to God and other people in the circumstance. If we mindlessly obeyed all absolute rules, there would be no room for abortion or for not resuscitating a terminally, hopelessly ill person.

I was convinced in the awful spring of 1986, and remain convinced today, that my decision to seek removal of Jackie's life support systems was the best, most fitting choice, given the best medical evidence available to me at the time. Jackie's miraculous recovery hasn't changed that belief. Though I knew her deep coma prevented her from experiencing physical pain, I saw her ordeal as a growing insult to her dignity and her spirit as well as to her body. I knew that her suffering would be intolerable to her if she were actually aware of her condition. I considered and reconsidered her wish "not to live this way." I wanted to honor her wish, and I wanted to make the most fitting response to our anguish. My decision was the only way to carry out Jackie's own intent and to bring relief to our suffering. I knew from the children's faces how they were suffering. I could see it, feel it, practically touch it, each time I watched them by her bedside. The situation became increasingly intolerable for me as well. I had to take action. I had to make a fitting response to bring our pointless suffering to an end. It was the only way I saw to give a tragic situation meaning and grace and mercy. I sincerely believed that keeping Jackie tethered to artificial life support meant keeping her from a state of grace. As great a loss as I would suffer by her death, I would be able to free her to join God, and I would be able to let our family move through the grieving process and begin to live again. I knew this is what Jackie would want, and I believed it is what God would want.

Niebuhr's ethics provided a significant personal insight into being able to justify my decision to disconnect Jackie's life support systems. He gave me the necessary awareness of my freedom and responsibility to act in a way that fit the situation of my beloved wife's massive stroke and extended coma.

Yet the question nagged: how could I decide to let my wife die when she was technically alive? I have since been asked, "How could you do such a thing? It seems so cold and heartless." For me, it was quite the reverse. I wanted what was best for Jackie. I loved her deeply, but I knew I must make a fitting — though heartbreaking — moral choice in response to the worst of all possible life-and-death situations. I felt a profound sense of loss over my decision to let her go, yet I had no reservations about it once I made up my mind. The crucial matter for me has never been "how could I do such a thing as let my wife die" or "how I felt when she woke up" but how I could justify my decision through the medical and legal consequences of my actions and in the practice of my own personal beliefs.

From the medical standpoint, there was never any question that Jackie was alive. She was in a deep coma and couldn't breathe on her own. There was no response to deep pain stimulation. No muscle tone. No reflex activity in her arms or legs. But the results of two EEGs indicated some electrical activity; her brainstem wasn't dead. I was encouraged by this fact at the beginning of our ordeal, because I've always believed that the practice of medicine involves a moral obligation to try to cure illness even if predictably fatal. Yet I also believe that our obligation to cure or even to support life in the face of an incurable illness ceases when we can no longer contribute to a patient's ability to live a purposeful life, a life striving toward wholeness and personal fulfillment. And to the question, "But what constitutes a purposeful life?" only the family, those who know and love the patient, can offer an individual answer, I believe. A "purposeful life" for one person may not have the same definition as it would for another. If the patient is incapable of answering for himself or herself, closest relatives must determine that answer based on their knowledge of the patient.

Jackie's life no longer demonstrated a purposeful quality. She was not living a meaningful life — for anyone — especially herself. When I decided to go to court, she was imprisoned in a coma, losing a battle with pneumonia, lying motionless in a persistent vegetative state with no apparent chance of recovery. In reaching my decision, I researched a number of authorities on the eventual outcome of stroke and coma patients. In Drs. Plum and Posner's *The Diagnosis of Stupor and Coma,* which I borrowed from Dr. Pula, I learned that the prognosis for patients who remain in a persistent vegetative state after two weeks was "uniformly poor." Plum and Posner cited a study in which only four of 110 chronically vegetative patients survived after three years and none were even able to resume their lives as independent human beings with any type of normal social behavior.

I also knew that physicians and families of patients in extended comas must acknowledge the possibility, however remote, that these patients can return from coma. Throughout our ordeal, I asked Dr. Pula and other members of the medical staff if there was any possibility of Jackie's surviving her stroke and its complications. I was told that anything was possible, but no one associated with her case had any knowledge of anyone ever living through what had happened to Jackie. We were initially encouraged by the news that her neurological condition had stabilized — we wanted to believe in the smallest possibility that she would recover. But with time, I began to realize that the chances of ensuring her survival — let alone her returning to any semblance of a purposeful life — were overwhelmingly against her. I came to the conclusion that the moral obligation to treat her illness had declined in proportion to her overall condition. I could no longer accept the premise that Jackie was not clinically dead because she was clinically alive and therefore should be treated as if purposeful life were possible. Based on all the medical information relevant to her case over those first five weeks, I reached a point at which my sole response was to seek court permission to remove her life support systems.

Prayer has long been my natural coping response. From the earliest moments of Jackie's stroke and coma, my thoughts and actions were sustained by prayer. I believe that prayer need not be a formal exercise, in which we can expect direct answers to our questions of God, but it is often an intuitive and contemplative experience, an awareness of a spiritual presence and direction in our lives, an awareness of God's presence. Prayer became an invaluable source of consolation and inspiration in making my decision to give up my wife.

That first afternoon after her stroke, as I broke the news to friends, I asked God aloud, "What is going on here?" That first night, in the depths of my despair, I demanded of God, "Why did this happen to her, to us?" And as the days wore on, with no improvement in her condition, I realized that I needed to ask a different set of questions: What was God revealing to me here? What evidence of God's love and best intentions did I have in this experience? How could I respond, and what could I learn from the experience itself?

Niebuhr made the point, in *The Responsible Self,* that the characters of people are often formed by the sufferings that pass through their lives — not only the events themselves but our interpretation and response to them. Because suffering is something we naturally want to avoid, but often cannot, our coping response is also a measure of our integrity. It helps to define our character and shape our personal beliefs. To me, a person has integrity if he or she doesn't avoid suffering just for the sake of avoiding it. Something can be learned from suffering: we can become more insightful, more sensitive to others' suffering and more responsible because we suffer ourselves. That is a measure of our increasing integrity, which is our sense of responsibility to care for the needs of others, to be kind and loving in the face of suffering.

Niebuhr's observation leads to the question inherent in our suffering experience: What is the fitting thing to do to relieve the suffering and what is to be learned from it?

Through prayer I came to believe what God was revealing to me — God was providing the means of grace by which our suffering could be relieved. In the midst of our suffering, my personal relationship with God could be sensed, but I saw no evidence of God's intention to preserve the circumstances of Jackie's illness. She was incapable of leading the kind of life she desired; she continued to languish in a vegetative state with the pointless likelihood of a prolonged death months, even years, away.

There was nothing redemptive, nothing creative, in this experience. My unerring belief in a life after death led me to interpret God's initiative here as an indication that Jackie's earthly life was to end for some greater moral good, one that transcended our present circumstances, which we had yet to understand. To make a fitting response, I needed to be open and trusting in God's redemptive, merciful intention to reclaim her life — that would be the greater good for all of us who loved her.

When I reached the point of deciding to remove Jackie's life supports, I had come far enough in the process of my own moral deliberations to take the risk of losing Jackie and to be held accountable for my actions. I realized that continued efforts to prolong her life were wrong for her as well as for us. I wanted to stop her suffering and to bring relief to each of us who witnessed it. I wanted God's will to be done in Jackie's life, and I wanted God's peace in all of ours.

The fact that Jackie woke up just six days after I took my decision to court has never caused me to doubt the veracity of my intention to allow her life to end mercifully. I bear no guilt for what I did. Jackie has understood and supported my decision. Just as I believe I made a caring, informed, moral decision, I also believe that her one-in-a-million recovery is the exception, a true miracle.

THE events of Jackie's illness and those forty-seven days of intense anguish, climaxed by her dramatic awakening, have had a profound effect on me, on what I believe, and on how I live in relation to God and to others. This experience has put my life into a new, sometimes joyous, perspective. I have gained a deeper awareness of the meaning of human suffering and a new respect for creative human potential. Suffering is basic to being human and an integral part of our Judeo-Christian heritage. Witness the suffering of Job, the cries of anguish in the Psalms of David, and the church's historic reliance on confession and absolution from sin as a means of relief from suffering. But I am not convinced that suffering is the only part of the human condition, nor is its condition chronic. It is one experience among many, and, as in our case, it does have a purpose: that it can be relieved and lead to joy and wholeness in life.

Like Job, whose friends tried to give comfort and reason to his suffering, I had some well-meaning friends who told me that Jackie's stroke and coma were God's way of testing my faith. But as I lived through the ordeal, I could never believe it was a test. And I did not see it as God's "fault," because I refused to accept the notion that God caused Jackie's illness. I believe in a gracious, loving God, not one who causes bad things to happen to good, innocent people. Rather, it was that "intelligent power of evil," which I discussed earlier, that caused Jackie's stroke. I believe that because the events fit the pattern of what evil means to me. Evil is the worst that happens to us — the loss of knowledge, of hope, of joy in life, the loss of someone you love, the loss of a future together where your love can flourish. All of these qualities of life, so crucial to me, were lost when I faced losing Jackie.

As I struggled to understand the meaning behind our suffering, I reread a book titled *Should Treatment Be Terminated?* by Thomas Oden, professor of theology and ethics at Drew University. Oden says that the Christian faith teaches that life is God's gift, immeasurably valuable and always meaningful, even in the midst of suffering. Oden questions whether it is possible to reach a point where relief from suffering could be greater than the meaning of life itself. He answered his own question by reaffirming his belief that life has meaning even in the worst circumstances and that there is no point where relief from suffering exceeds the value of life, even if and when we fail to grasp its meaning.

I've always believed in the sanctity of life and its significance, even in the worst-case scenarios. Over and over in my prayers and deliberations, though, I came to the conclusion that, as important as her life was, I had to let Jackie go because this suffering was pointless and unredemptive. When suffering reaches the point of meaninglessness, it separates itself from life and obscures life's meaning altogether. Then suffering must cease in order to discover the true meaning of life's experiences. But I agreed with Oden on another point: great suffering like Jackie's can be a profound experience for learning. I learned that I could give up the person I loved the most in this world and trust God to use my decision for good. That would be the ultimate grace.

In the Old Testament story of Abraham and Isaac, Abraham responds to God's call by taking his son up to a mountain to be sacrificed. Heartbroken, Abraham feels compelled to respond to God's initiative. He is willing to give up what he loves more than himself because he believes it is the fitting thing to do. Yet, at the moment when Abraham is about to strike, God intervenes by providing a lamb for the sacrifice and gives Isaac back unharmed. This story is a lesson in faith, not so much a test of faith, but an act of faith on Abraham's part. He makes a fitting response to God's action and thus learns that God's providential care is sufficient for relief from his suffering.

The New Testament account of Jesus' crucifixion conveys a similar message, though here it is God who acts on faith. God responds to human suffering by going beyond Abraham and actually giving up his son to die, in the hope that humanity will learn that, when suffering ends, new life begins once again.

From Jackie's illness, I have also learned that it is God's willful intent to answer prayer. Speaking through the Old Testament prophet Isaiah, God assures those seeking God in prayer that "Before they call I will answer, while they are speaking I will hear" (Isaiah 65:24). The task is to know how to speak and what to pray for. I have learned that prayer is not a means by which we can make demands on God to relieve suffering, or bring peace and prosperity into our lives, and realistically expect that to happen. Prayer is above all else an affirmation of faith, a statement of our belief. In prayer we acknowledge God's existence and influence over the events of our lives. We express our confidence that God will provide us with the means to cope with those events. Jesus makes this point clear when he tells the disciples that before praying, they should have faith in God. For me, that is the essence of the power of prayer — to respond to God in faith by being open to God's will in our lives.

I have learned that the power of prayer is seen in its ability to help us to wait for God to act. Our act of faith is waiting for God. I don't mean that we sit back and do nothing while we wait for God to respond to our prayers. Rather, we wait for God to act with anticipation and expectation that our prayers will be answered in God's own time and way. In that way, we will have understanding and peace. The Psalmist reflects this attitude: "My soul is waiting for the Lord. I count on his word. . . . Because with the Lord there is mercy and fullness of redemption" (Psalm 130, verses 5 and 7). Henri Nouwen, the noted Roman Catholic spiritual leader, refers to this as an attitude of "active waiting": we are open and present to the moment at hand when something that we want to happen will happen.

I believe that God answered my prayers during the course of Jackie's illness, although it is clear to me now that they were not answered in the way that I'd expected. I was asking God to resolve our situation on my terms and in my own time. I learned, however, that relief from our suffering could only come on God's terms and in God's time. As Jackie's coma dragged on and I began to pray and wait for the moment when God would act, I came to believe that he would act if and when we "pulled the plug." Jackie would either survive or die, but either way it would be God's answer to my prayers. What I failed to understand was that, while I was actively waiting for God's intention to be revealed, it was the wrong time to expect anything. The *kairos,* God's saving moment, had yet to arrive, and I had yet to discover the right moment, when God's purpose would be disclosed.

Perhaps I should have listened to the words of the prophet Isaiah: "The Lord waits to be gracious to you . . . blessed are all those who wait for him" (Isaiah 30:18).

The fact that God didn't chose to be revealed until the forty-seventh day of Jackie's illness did not mean that he was not involved during the first forty-six. Here was another discovery I made as a result of Jackie's stroke: God is always present and at work in every circumstance of our lives, no matter how obscure or how terrible, no matter whether God's effect is apparent or not.

In an essay I later wrote for *Second Opinion,* a quarterly journal addressing health, faith, and ethical issues, I explained that, in reaching my decision to remove Jackie's artificial life support, the time came when I realized that everyone and everything working to prolong Jackie's life — doctors, nurses, therapists, machines, even myself — needed to be cleared out of the way so that God's creative, redemptive work could be done.

My former ethics professor caught up with me. When Dr. Donald W. Shriver, Jr., now president of the faculty at Union Theological Seminary in New York, read my article, he responded by claiming that God was present and accounted for in all the efforts to preserve Jackie's life. If we were to acknowledge God's role on day forty-seven, we had to acknowledge his involvement in the whole struggle from day one. Dr. Shriver's points were two: that God acts in all situations of our lives, not just the ones we might want to select; and that we are all partners in God's actions — doctors, nurses, the judge, paramedics, and not just myself.

In retrospect I look at the crucial moments when I decided to let Jackie go, and I realize that it was part of God's initiative to bring this experience not to a merciful end but to a joyous conclusion. I did try to force God's hand, only to find that it was guiding each of us along a path to a new beginning in Jackie's life.

Dr. Shriver also suggested that I claimed to know too much, not about God's initiative in our lives, but about what I would be permitted to know about God's intentions. I assumed in a time of utter darkness and despair over Jackie's condition that God was absent. I now realize that the fact that God was hidden in the darkness did not mean he was not trying to initiate contact with us. God is at work in all situations of darkness and despair. He creates light out of darkness. He sustains us in times of confusion and doubt and redeems our suffering. Redeeming suffering is taking it upon oneself to change it, to make it better and to give back new possibilities to the sufferer for further change and growth. I believe this is what God did in the course of Jackie's illness. God turned the worst of all possible life-and-death situations into one of a victorious new life.

This was the miracle of grace for us. I believe that within all the experience of emptiness and defeat in our lives, God comes to each of us with a gift. The gift is a victory for us. We have not earned the victory. We really don't deserve it. Yet we cannot ultimately refuse it, because God is forever reaching out to give the victory to us. This is the state of grace into which God calls us all. It is not unlike what the theologian Paul Tillich meant by "being struck by grace" in his book *The Shaking of the Foundations:* ". . . at that moment a wave of light breaks into our darkness and it is as if a voice was saying, 'You are accepted. YOU ARE ACCEPTED, accepted by that which is greater than you, and the name of which you do not know. Do not ask for the name now; perhaps later you will do much. Do not seek for anything; do not perform anything; do not intend anything. Simply accept the fact that you are accepted.' If that happens to us, we experience grace . . . and nothing is demanded of the experience . . . but acceptance."

JACKIE's illness and her extraordinary awakening and recovery were for me a true demonstration of our acceptability to God. And as I accept the reality of her return, I am compelled to respond to God's graciousness by acting on my own potential for creativity and change. To be given another chance, to envision the possibilities for change and personal growth is a rare opportunity for anyone. Our lives become a partnership with God, who creates, sustains, and redeems life itself. Our friend, Dr. Robert Schuller, pastor of the Crystal Cathedral Congregation in southern California, speaks of the possibilities that are ours to achieve because of the reality of grace in our lives. In his theology of self-esteem, he maintains that those who have experienced God's graciousness have an inherent sense of self-worth about them that is rooted in God's call. They interpret this call to be one of commitment to serve others. They seek out human needs and are challenged to meet them. And the underlying assumption about their actions is that they will be successful because of their partnership with God. They know that they are acceptable and they know they will not fail.

Through the experience of Jackie's stroke, I have come to believe that it is possible for us to reach ever-increasing levels of creative human potential. I believe that the process of life is one of achieving new levels of knowledge and growth. In witnessing Jackie's near-death and her recovery, I have seen the quality of her life rise dramatically as she has achieved higher levels of accomplishment — from the depths of stroke and coma, to barely being able to move her lips, to recovering her speech, her wit, and her mobility, to greater independence each day.

Determining the quality of our lives is an elusive task because it is so subjective. We measure ourselves in comparison with others about whom we actually know very little. But it is helpful, even vital, to test our mettle if we really want to learn from our experiences of suffering and of joy. From the experience of Jackie's stroke and recovery, I have felt a full range of emotion, from the deepest despair to the height of ecstasy and joy in God's presence. I have certainly grown in this experience: I have gained a deeper level of spirituality and faith; I take life more seriously. I am more peaceful and confident about God's ability to work things out and my ability to make difficult decisions. I've gained a greater insight into human experience, which, I believe, has made me more sensitive to the suffering of others. I know their stories because I have lived one myself.

I recall when Jackie and I appeared on a television talk program with the family of William Schroeder, the world's first artificial heart recipient. Mel Schroeder remarked that even though his father had gone through a terrible ordeal, he was grateful to be alive and felt that he had achieved a quality of life that he hadn't known before. William Schroeder maintained that attitude throughout the remaining months of his life until he died. His disposition reflected the medieval concept of *ars moriende,* the art of dying well. In dying well, we also live well; there was a unity and wholeness to his life.

In Hebrew, *"shalam,"* or wholeness, refers to healing and salvation and is considered in both the Old and New Testaments a gift of God. In the course of Jackie's illness and in the act of awakening, I believe that God has brought a wholeness and new life to each of us. Her return was a true act of deliverance for me and an answer to my most private prayer that her life be spared. I celebrate her life and rejoice in the vast creative and redemptive power of God. Jackie's awakening has prompted me to tell our story as an affirmation of God's healing power. It has been called a miracle by almost everyone who has heard about it. I know of no other category in which to place it. Miracles are often consigned to ancient history and faraway places. But even one such as John Calvin, the staunch fifteenth-century Protestant reformer, believed in miracles, because they showed the love of God. As a twentieth-century man, I, too, happily confess that miracles can happen. I know. I saw one with my own eyes when Jacqueline opened hers. Within the literal twinkling of an eye, I saw evidence of God's eternal power to re-create, to redeem, and to bring healing into our lives, and I joyously accepted it as God's gift to Jackie and to me. I now have a new sense of calling: To repay God for this miracle, I have told Jackie's story as evidence of God's grace and love. I have counseled people across the country who have heard of Jackie's recovery. I have listened and felt their suffering as I have tried to give them guidance and hope. Jackie and I are both spending time with groups of stroke victims and their support groups for the same reason. We believe God didn't bring about Jackie's miracle just for the Cole family, but to give others hope and faith as well.

H. Richard Niebuhr once remarked in a class on Christian ethics that "every recovery from illness is a little Resurrection." This was his testament to hope in God's healing power over our every suffering moment. It is testimony to my belief that God is a part of every aspect and every relationship in our lives and affirms what Calvin liked to tell his followers, that "during our whole life, we have to do with God."

Yet, I must stress that, even in the face of Jackie's miraculous recovery, we both still reaffirm the decision to disconnect artificial life supports. I can say it no more clearly: given what we knew of Jackie's condition at the time, I made what I believed was the best moral decision, one that honored her wishes and one that sought to bring redemption out of pointless suffering. I believe that Jackie's "one-in-a-million" recovery doesn't weaken the right-to-die position — it strengthens it.

When we appeared on "Donahue" right after Jackie was released from Montebello, Phil Donahue summarized Jackie's story and commented, "Stories like these make you never want to pull the plug." No, Phil, I don't believe that. Jackie and I both strongly believe that there are circumstances in which patients and families may decide to disconnect artificial life supports. They have the legal, moral right to do so for the terminally ill and those who are in permanent comas. The difference is that Jackie and God proved that Jackie's coma was not permanent. For those families who must make such a decision, I would reaffirm that their decision will lead to freedom from suffering for their loved one and for the grieving family, and it will bring about a state of grace born of making a caring, informed, moral decision.

Jackie and I continue to learn from our experience. But all that we have learned so far affirms the simple religious truth of our childhood: God is love. He hears all our prayers and comes in the fullness of time to deliver us from despair and the dark nights of our souls. This has been a continuing journey of faith and discovery of new life for us. From this journey comes the brightest message of hope, one we happily share with others. Jackie and I feel privileged and blessed to have the opportunity to tell our story and to affirm that even in the most dire of circumstances, there is an eternal hope for renewed life in us all.

Guidelines

Jackie's story has stimulated a variety of interests in the medical circumstances of her illness, the legal and ethical implications of my decision, and the inspirational nature of the whole experience. I do not want the story to end, however, without some reference to its practical considerations — without something coming out of it that can be used by others who may be faced with a similar life-and-death decision on behalf of a loved one for whom they are responsible.

The late American psychologist Carl Rogers, whose work I admire greatly, often spoke about what he termed the "significant learnings" that had helped shape his life. He felt that a personal accounting of what he had learned through the critical events of his life would be helpful to others who found themselves in similar situations.

We do learn from our experiences, and they often lend themselves to practical applications. What follows are the applications that I have learned from Jackie's illness. They are included here in a series of seven guidelines for those who may be faced with having to respond to a situation similar to my own. These guidelines are neither authoritative nor exhaustive. They are a result of my personal experience and reflections on conversations with those involved in the fields of bioethics and health care. I offer them simply for what they are, a source of guidance and support for someone who is confronted wih the painful and awesome task of deciding whether a person they love should remain on artificial life support systems against overwhelming odds of any recovery from a critical illness resulting in coma or a persistent vegetative state.

1 — The first and foremost issue to be considered in disconnecting life supports is the physical condition of the pa-

tient. What is the overall medical status of your loved one? Is the disease considered terminal? Have various complications set in, such as pneumonia or low blood pressure, that could further weaken the chances of recovery? Have all possible medical procedures to effect recovery been exhausted? Ask these and other questions of the attending physician. Have him or her answer you in terms that you readily understand. Learn to recognize the difference between routine and heroic measures in your loved one's treatment plan, and be aware of the point when "aggressive" treatment procedures designed to sustain life only serve to prolong the process of dying. Don't be intimidated by medical personnel or procedures. The only intimidating factor here is the action you may have to take and you need to be as medically well informed as possible in making your decision. Certainly seek a second opinion, or even a third, if you feel it is necessary or helpful in reaching your decision.

2 – When you are faced with making a decision that could mortally affect the life of another person, you should, insofar as possible, respect the wishes of that person in your deliberations. If he or she stressed, prior to the illness, a desire not to be kept alive by artificial or heroic means, then you have an obligation to respect that judgment in reaching your decision. If the person requested to be kept alive under any circumstances no matter how dire, then you need to respect that right, even if physicians advise you that the situation is hopeless. I believe that the patient's right to self-determination should take precedence here — at least until there is an informed consensus among the treatment team and other family members that further action should be taken in the best interest of your loved one, based on his or her improving or deteriorating condition.

3 – Think through your own feelings on the right to live or die. How do you feel about "pulling the plug," apart from this particular instance? Rely on your own personal values and religious beliefs as you have always known them. Seek out competent advice from a member of the clergy, or, if

possible, the ethics committee of the hospital. Your feelings should be consistent with your actions to continue or to forego life support measures for your loved one. Don't feel that because you are in an extraordinary situation of responsibility you need to call upon a whole different set of moral standards to justify your decision. Accept the fact that you already possess the fundamental intellectual and moral capacity to come to a fitting decision. If this were not the case, it is highly unlikely that you, even as a parent, child, or spouse of the stricken patient, would be given the responsibility to decide whether or not life-sustaining measures should be taken in the first place.

4 — Try to avoid formal legal proceedings in making your decision. I say this not out of any sense of animosity over my own experience in court, but rather from what I learned from it. The judge in our case had what I now see as an impossible task. He was forced to make an arbitrary decision in a situation that, in my opinion, defied the legal categories of right versus wrong. Although I was sensitive to the judge's compassion in our case, I am now more aware of the court's inherent tendency to simplify conflicts for the purpose of making a legal decision. Court action is appropriate in settling a conflict among family members over a loved one's right to die. However, in most noncontroversial circumstances I believe the courts should support the autonomy of the patient — even when that right to decide extends to members of the family.

Try to confine your legal contact to receiving advice on what your rights are as the responsible party. What are your legal options? What are the legal definitions of terms such as "imminent death," "terminal condition," "brain death" in your state? What are your loved one's rights if he or she has, or does not have, a living will? Legal counsel is vital in helping you make your decision. Seek it out in any circumstance, but remember that the ultimate decision to act one way or the other should remain with you.

5 — If it is difficult to make a medical or legal decision to

remove a loved one's life support system, then it is all the more challenging to make the correct moral decision. When it is finally left up to you, what is the fitting thing to do?

A guideline which I have come to feel is morally acceptable to follow is this: If the medical condition and prognosis of your loved one is so poor that continuation of life by artificial means is of no conceivable benefit to that loved one, then it is fitting and appropriate to take the needed steps to allow him or her to die with mercy and dignity. In the final analysis, it is not your relationship to your loved one, or his place in the family, or her use to her community that determines the future course. It is the patient's inherent ability to recapture a lost identity and self-worth. When your loved one lacks strength and resolve to do that for himself or herself and return to a purposeful life, it is morally right to see his or her life come to a fitting and timely end.

6 — Practice active waiting. As I mentioned in the previous chapter, active waiting means that we become open and aware of that moment when the change or healing that we're waiting for is about to happen. In a crisis event this means that we anticipate that time when the crisis will be resolved. In making the decision to remove your loved one from life support, you anticipate that your action will bring resolution and peace to what you see as a tragic and hopeless situation and that the anguish and turmoil that everyone experienced throughout the ordeal will be ended.

Expect a resolution of your decision. Don't necessarily expect miracles, but be confident that your decision is the fitting thing to do. Don't be pressured by physicians or other family members into making a decision before you are ready and able. Wait for the moment when everything — the medical and legal advice and all the moral issues — comes intuitively together for you and you are ready to act.

7 — When you have at last made your decision to remove or not remove artificial life supports, be at peace with yourself and what you have done. Don't feel guilty about your choice and don't try to second-guess yourself. Be ready to

live with the consequences of your action by realizing that
you were given an almost impossible job to do and you did it
as well as you could.

When I finally decided to seek permission to remove Jackie's life
support systems, I felt for the first time in weeks a sense of calm
and peace and resolve in my life. I realized that I had done the right
and fitting thing in Jackie's life and in my own as well. I looked
forward to what was to come with confidence that God would
provide. And God did provide — in a way that I never could have
imagined. Providence is not as kind to all of us, but through my
experience with Jackie's illness I am convinced that there is meaning and purpose in all the events of our lives. I recall a comment
that Dr. Pula made sometime after Jackie woke up from her coma:
"Life does not lend itself to logical analysis." I agree. But to what
does life lend itself then? I believe, more than anything else, that it
lends itself to an indefatigable hope — hope in the inherent
goodness of life, in the human spirit and the will to conquer adver-
sity, and in the knowledge that good can and will come out of evil.

When we react to God's involvement in our lives, when we
make what we truly believe is a fitting response to God's presence
within us, we are empowered by God's grace to pursue good and
avoid evil. God does give us his grace freely. When we decide to do
what is good and right in a given situation, we are responding to
God's graciousness. We continue to respond to God by maintaining and enriching our relationship with him.

We are never forsaken by God. He never lets us go. The only
way to separate ourselves from God is to forsake that relationship
ourselves, to say "no" to God by denying his grace and embracing
evil. That is the one unpardonable sin. In *Creation in Christ*,
George MacDonald "quotes" God, as it were, by saying: "I forgive you everything . . . [but] the one thing that cannot be forgiven
is the sin of choosing evil, of refusing deliverance. It is impossible
to forgive that sin. It would be to take part in it . . ."

God cannot conspire with evil, because God is good. God cannot be a party to it, because God would no longer be God. If we
choose to pursue evil, we willingly remove ourselves from our

state of grace. We have no further contact with God. We are incapable of making responsible moral decisions. We have no hope of being good.

In accepting God's grace, we become totally acceptable to God. We become God's children, and we are good. God loves us more than we can possibly imagine. He is continually and forever saying "Yes" to us as we say "Yes" in return.

In our very private moments together, I have told Jackie that she is God's eternal "Yes" to me. She is proof of God's presence and love in my life. Her life affirms that God says "Yes" to each of us, that we are accepted and forgiven, and the good that we do does conquer evil. We need only to respond to God by living in his grace and choosing good. George MacDonald speaks of God's grace in this way: "He passes by and forgets a thousand sins, yea tens of thousands, forgiving them all — only we must begin to be good, begin to do evil no more."

It is my hope that our story will help each of us to begin.

Resources

The following organizations and publications have been helpful in offering valuable information about medical, legal, and ethical aspects of the right-to-die issue:

THE AMERICAN MEDICAL ASSOCIATION'S *Current Opinions of the Council on Ethical and Judicial Affairs,* 1986, offers history and principles of medical ethics, terminology, and opinions on nineteen social policy issues (withholding or withdrawing life-prolonging medical treatment, and other subjects such as organ donation, fetal research, genetic engineering) and opinions on physicians' inter-professional relations, hospital relations, confidentiality, advertising and media relations, fees, records, practice matters, professional rights and responsibilities. This 52-page booklet may be purchased for $15 from A.M.A., Order Dept. OP-122-9, P.O. Box 10946, Chicago, IL 60610.

CONCERN FOR DYING, An Educational Council, 250 West 57th Street, New York, NY 10107 (212-246-6962), distributes living wills and durable power of attorney forms upon request. It also published, and sells for $5.00, *Deciding to Forego Life-Sustaining Treatment,* the 1983 report of the President's Commission for the Study of Ethical Problems in Medicine and Biomedical and Behavioral Research.

THE HASTINGS CENTER'S *Guidelines on the Termination of Life-Sustaining Treatment and the Care of the Dying* was published in 1987, after more than two years of research and discussion by leaders in medicine, nursing, health care administration, law, and ethics. It offers comprehensive ethical guidelines for decisions about foregoing life-sustaining treatments. The Hastings Center has addressed ethical problems in medicine, biology and life sciences, and the professions since its founding in 1969. The *Guidelines* may be purchased from The Hastings Center, Dept. T, 255 Elm Road, Briarcliff Manor, NY 10510.

THE MILBANK QUARTERLY'S *Medical Decision Making for the Demented and Dying* (Vol. 64, Supplement 2, 1986) contain several essays that range from a patient's autonomy to legal perceptions and medical decision making. It is published for The Milbank Memorial Fund (1 East 75th Street, New York, NY 10021) by Cambridge University Press (32 East 57th Street, New York, NY 10022.)

THE SOCIETY FOR THE RIGHT TO DIE, 250 West 57th Street, New York, NY 10107, works for the recognition of a patient's right to die with dignity. It offers information about laws in each state and court decisions; it distributes living will declarations with appropriate documents authorized in every state; it serves as a clearinghouse for attorneys, consults with physicians and health care providers on terminal care issues, and publishes newsletters and other materials.

THE STANFORD UNIVERSITY MEDICAL CENTER developed guidelines, "Initiating and Withdrawing Life Support," published in the *New England Journal of Medicine,* January 7, 1988. These offer practical, specific guidance and stress patient autonomy. The *New England Journal of Medicine* can be obtained through most major libraries, or a reprint of the guidelines can be obtained by writing to Dr. Thomas Alfred Raffin, Stanford University Medical Center, Room C-56, Stanford, CA 94305.

The wording of living wills and durable power of attorney forms vary from state to state. The following living will and durable power of attorney declaration are generic. While a generic version is acceptable in states that have passed living will legislation, you may want to consult an attorney in your state, or you can obtain your state's version of living will laws from the Society for the Right to Die, 250 East 57th Street, New York, NY 10107 (212-246-6973).

LIVING WILL DECLARATION

To My Family, Doctors, and All Those Concerned with My Care

I, _____, being of sound mind, make this statement as a directive to be followed if I become unable to participate in decisions regarding my medical care.

If I should be in an incurable or irreversible mental or physical condition with no reasonable expectation of recovery, I direct my attending physician to withhold or withdraw treatment that merely prolongs my dying. I further direct that treatment be limited to measures to keep me comfortable and to relieve pain.

These directions express my legal right to refuse treatment. Therefore, I expect my family, doctors, and everyone concerned with my care to regard themselves as legally and morally bound to act in accord with my wishes, and in so doing to be free of any legal liability for having followed my directions.

I especially do not want: _____

_____

_____

Other instructions/comments: _____

_____

_____

Proxy Designation Clause: Should I become unable to communicate my instructions as stated above, I designate the following person to act in my behalf:

Name _____

Address _____

If the person I have named above is unable to act in my behalf, I authorize the following person to do so:

Name _____

Address _____

Signed: _____ Date: _____

Witness: _____ Witness: _____

Keep the signed original with your personal papers at home. Give signed copies to doctors, family, and proxy. Review your Declaration from time to time; initial and date it to show it still expresses your intent.

DURABLE POWER OF ATTORNEY

I hereby designate _____ to serve as my attorney-in-fact for the purpose of making medical decisions. This power of attorney shall remain effective in the event that I become incompetent or otherwise unable to make such decisions for myself.

Optional Notarization:

"Sworn and subscribed to before me this _____ day of _____, 19____.

Signed _____

Date _____

Witness _____

_____
Notary Public
(seal)

_____
Address

Witness _____

_____
Address

Copies of this request have been given to

_____

_____